POLISH

D0889512

is a perceptive artistic and cultural g‌u‌ide to Cracow, Gdańsk, and Warsaw, with excursions to the mountains around Zakopane, the salt-mines of Wieliczka, the concentration-camp complex of Auschwitz-Birkenau, the Teutonic Order's castle at Malbork, and the Baltic towns of Sopot and Gdynia.

The largest of the Soviet Union's allies in Eastern Europe, Poland has a population of 35 million, but ten million Poles live overseas, most of them in North America and Western Europe.

Cracow, the mediaeval capital, remains one of the most romantic cities of Central Europe, with Wawel Castle and Cathedral, the Renaissance Cloth Hall and Market Square, great churches and monasteries, museums and theatres.

A vibrant hub of Hanseatic trade in former times and Solidarity more recently, Gdańsk is a bustling seaport with long maritime traditions and a totally different atmosphere from other Polish cities.

Warsaw, devastated in World War II, has become a lively centre of commerce, industry and government. Explore the whole Royal Way from the newly-restored Castle to Wilanów Palace, with shops, great palaces, and the picturesque Old Market Square.

PHILIP WARD, FRGS, FRSA, ALA, has travelled throughout fifty countries during three decades, providing standard travel guides such as *Albania*, *Bangkok*, *Come with me to Ireland*, *Japanese Capitals*, *Sabratha* (Libya), and *Travels in Oman*. *Library Journal* wrote that Philip Ward's *Finnish Cities* 'is packed with information, particularly on art, architecture, culture, and history, and will prove invaluable both to first visitors and to many who claim a fair prior knowledge of the country'. *The Times* described his novel on the conquest of Mexico, *Forgotten Games*, as 'brilliant in concept, written in prose as spare, lush and pointed as a cactus garden, as powerful and evocative as a rational nightmare, a logical daydream.' His interpretation of the face and heart of Poland, past and present, will strike the reader as compelling, provoking, and above all individual.

Polish Cities

Travels in Cracow and the South, Gdańsk, Malbork and Warsaw

Philip Ward

THE OLEANDER PRESS LTD

The Oleander Press
17 Stansgate Avenue
Cambridge CB2 2QZ
England

The Oleander Press
210 Fifth Avenue
New York, N.Y. 10010
USA

© 1988 Philip Ward
and The Oleander Press

British Library Cataloguing in Publication Data

Ward, Philip, 1938-
Polish cities: travels in Cracow and the South,
  Gdańsk, Malbork, and Warsaw.–
(Oleander travel books, v. 14).
1. Poland - Visitors' guides
I. Title
914.38′0456

ISBN 0–906672–73–2

Printed and bound in Great Britain

Contents

  High-season charter flights on LOT are available from Gatwick
and Manchester to Warsaw once a week, at weekends, and from
Gatwick to Cracow. Connecting flights in the U.K. are arranged by
your agent, who can also offer onward connections in Poland to
Gdańsk, Katowice, Koszalin, Poznań, Rzeszów, Szczecin, Wrocław
and Zielona Góra.

Acknowledgements

I owe particular thanks to Polish friends who accommodated me and talked to me at length about their experiences, and those of their circles, during my period of travel. I hope they will think that my attempted frankness and objectivity shows sympathy and understanding towards their lives and aspirations, because that was my intention while writing.

Dr Frank Carter of University College London, an expert on Poland in general and Cracow in particular, has passed favourable judgement on the Cracow and Warsaw chapters, and thanks are also due to his Polish-born wife Krystyna for her encouragement and help, though neither can of course be held responsible for my opinions or any errors of fact.

Co-operation following my travels has been courteously provided by Pan A. Rakowski of Polorbis Travel, the staff of the Polish Cultural Institute in London, and Pan A. Doliński of the Polish Tourist Information Centre in Warsaw. Pani Bogdana Carpenter, Department of Slavic Languages and Literatures, University of Michigan at Ann Arbor, has generously discussed her translations (with her husband John) of the poems of Zbigniew Herbert, and made available lines from their *Report from the Besieged City* (Oxford University Press, 1987). Pani Jadwiga Bingham, friend and neighbour, taught me the Polish I needed for everyday use, and for this gift I shall always be grateful. My wife, Audrey, and my daughters, Carolyn and Angela, afforded me that time and emotional security which authors appreciate more than any tangible possession. To all who made it possible: dziękuję!

PHILIP WARD

Introduction

A straightforward narrative must present a false picture of travels on Poland. Think of the adventure instead as a game of snakes and ladders that you are trying to win. A 'snake' could be visually similar: a queue that would take up forty minutes of your time; or an unexpected 'Nieczynny' sign on a door indicating that a museum is closed when you thought it would be open; or the absence of a bus leaving from Wieliczka to Cracow in the next three hours. A 'ladder' will scheme round these problems: leaving the queue and doing something else nearby; an alternative sequence of visits based on the assumption that some museums will always be unexpectedly closed; and the discovery that trains leave Wieliczka for Cracow much more frequently than buses.

Some delays in Poland could be revealing, as when a stranger tweaks your elbow at an outdoor *kawiarnia* in Długi Targ at Gdańsk and invites you for coffee and cake. All will add up to that picture of frustration leading to ingenuities great and infinitesimal so characteristic of life in Eastern Europe. If you prefer the expensive organised tour, you will spend most of your time in Poland with people like yourself instead of with the Poles, and much of the Polish experience will be lost; so will some, but not all, of the delays.

I have consequently interspersed the narrative with anecdotes and quotations which are intended to improve understanding of the complex texture of Polish life today, inviting a three-dimensional view.

The sequence of the book can be explained thus: Cracow was the capital of Poland from the end of the thirteenth century until the end of the sixteenth; it alone shows the full, virtually undisturbed flow of Poland's history from the Old Stone Age to the present day. Capital status was transferred to Warsaw in 1609, with the departure from King Sigismund III Vasa from Cracow.

The rise of Gdańsk as a commercial city can be traced to the decision by the Order of Teutonic Knights to move their headquarters in 1309 from Venice to Marienburg, now a backwater known as Malbork. From Malbork, with its maritime outlet then known as Danzig, the Grand Masters of the Order treated with the Hanseatic League for the development of Baltic trade. The Order developed Elbląg (the former

Elbing), Toruń (Thorn) and Braniewo (Braunsberg), as well as Königsberg, now in the U.S.S.R., where it has been renamed Kaliningrad. Gdańsk reached a peak of prosperity in 1600, with some fifty thousand inhabitants, when the Golden Gate and Great Armoury were built, and the Town Hall rebuilt.

Warsaw by contrast has seen its greatest days in the half-century since the end of World War II, after the reconstruction of the capital. Virtually everything on the left bank of the Vistula had been demolished, and the 1¼ million inhabitants had been reduced to a scant 20,000. Of Warsaw's 957 classified historic monuments, as many as 781 were razed during the War, so the city we see today is virtually new.

I do not mean to diminish the importance of Poznań, Wrocław, Katowice, Szczecin, Bydgoszcz, Łódź, or the pilgrimage town of Częstochowa. But anyone with only two or three weeks in Poland would do very well to learn the pleasures of mediaeval Cracow, Hanseatic Gdańsk, and modern Warsaw. This plan enables you to see the far south, the far north, and the centre of the country.

Illustrations

Photographs are by the Author unless otherwise credited. Colour photographs on the covers were kindly supplied by the Polish Tourist Information Centre in Warsaw: they show Cracow's Cloth Hall (Sukiennice) on Market Square; Ulica Mariacka in Gdańsk; and Łazienki Palace in Warsaw.

1 CRACOW

Once upon a time, if you listen to the old legend, there lived a ruler of the land we now call Poland, whose name was Krak, and in Jan of Wiślica's epic poem *Belli Pruthencini libri III* (1516) we enter that realm of historical fiction mingling with a possible core of fact with which modern students of Polish historiography have become so familiar.

Krak built his royal castle on the high hill called Wawel, above the banks of the Vistula, and around the castle he established a town called 'Kraków', named after himself. Now in a cave beneath Wawel dwelt a fearsome dragon, who ravaged the fields and the town, devouring cattle, sheep and even human beings. The people of Krak's town pleaded with their ruler to destroy the dragon and he did so, not like S. George in single combat, but in this wise, by stratagem. He caused his servants to fill the carcase of a cow with tar, wax and sulphur, unobtrusively set fire to the whole, then hurl it into the dragon's cave. The poor monster succumbed to the bait, and duly blew itself into smithereens. Would that all such fantasies were as easy to explode! But even today you can see 'the very den' where the dragon lived and died, overlooking the Vistula, near a bronze of the dragon sculpted by Bronisław Chromy.

'Krak' survives in modern versions of the city's name: Kraków (Polish), Krakau (German), Cracovie (French) and the mellifluous Cracovia (Italian) which is also the name of a high-class hotel opposite Nowy Gmach on the junction between Aleja 3 Maja and Aleja Krasińskiego, on the ring road round the Old City.

Exploration of Cracow should begin on the Wawel Hill, where archaeologists have discovered traces of mammoth and rhinoceros bones fashioned into tools by palaeolithic man fifty thousand years ago. They also found continuous settlement through the Mesolithic (which in this region can be dated 9000-4000 B.C.) and the subsequent Neolithic, when the first sedentary tribes arrived. These are known as the 'Band' people after the decoration on their pottery; they farmed, domesticated animals, and practised weaving. A second wave of tribesmen have been identified by string ornamentation on their pottery and conical goblets. Bronze Age weapons and ceramics surviving from the castle-town on Wawel – and from the present-day Old Town – include bowls, cups and

Southern Poland, showing Krakow (top centre), Oświęcim (top right), and Zakopane (bottom centre), with the Czech border

twin-coned vases. Iron Age contacts with Rome are proved by coins, but it is not until the 6th century A.D. that Slavs are certainly recorded in Cracow. Despite the contemporary 'Autochthonous School' of Polish prehistory, working with censorship and their academic tenure in mind, 'it is not entirely improbable that the 'proto-Poles' had already begun to settle somewhere in the lands between the Baltic shore and ridge of the Carpathians.' But the historian Norman Davies adds that their arrival 'would in no sense discount the presence of the Goths on the lower Vistula, of Balts to the East of the Vistula delta, or of the Celts in Silesia and in the environs of modern Cracow'. After all, the very name of Poland, *'Polska'*, does not appear until the tenth century, and then it is merely the tiny habitat of one small Slavonic tribe, the *Polanie*, who settled on the Warta's banks near modern Poznań. The semi-legendary Piast, founder (if he existed) of a dynasty that was to unite a number of disparate Slavonic tribes into a single Polish kingdom, would possibly have been chief of these *Polanie*, and could conceivably have lived in the ninth century. But we do not know, and it is most unlikely that we ever shall. Pagan Vislanian Slavs spread around a region usually called 'Little Poland' or Małopolska to differentiate it from the Wielkopolska ('Great Poland') inhabited by Polanians, around modern Poznań.

We know a little of tenth-century Cracow from the traveller Ibrahim ibn Yaqub, from Cordova, who saw the city in 965, when Cracow belonged to Boleslaus I, King of Bohemia, ruling from Prague since 929. As a major hub of Central European trade, Cracow was beginning to replace its wooden buildings, those fire hazards, with permanent stone churches, patrician houses, and commercial offices. One such was a rectangular ducal palace, and another the pre-Romanesque Rotunda of SS. Felix and Adauctus. Gniezno, now only a small town near Poznań, was the first secular and ecclesiastical capital of Poland, but Cracow's bishopric was established in 969, only a year after that of Poznań. King Boleslaus I Chrobry ('the Brave') erected a first cathedral on Wawel in 1020, but after the fall of his son Mieszko's state in 1034 the Vislanes abandoned the Christianity that had been forced upon them until King Casimir I Odnowiciel ('the Restorer') suppressed pagan customs again in 1038, when Cracow became recognised as the capital of the Piast kingdom. Boleslaus II Śmiały ('the Bold') started a second cathedral on Wawel in about 1070, but it was not completed for a century and a half: the catalogue of the library exists but not a single book or manuscript; some of the treasures remain, but of the structures only S. Leonard's crypt and the Silver Bell Tower can now be seen. Of other Romanesque buildings in Cracow, you can still find the original walls of S. Andrew's Church (Ulica Grodzka), and much of S. Adalbert (Św. Wojciech in Polish) in the Market Square (Rynek) and the Church of Our Saviour (Salwator or Zbawiciela), farther west along the Vistula, on Ulica Św. Bronisławy. Under the floor, much of the Romanesque foundations, including that of the apse, were discovered recently, and you can imagine Salwator, a thousand years ago, as one segment of the fortified castle-settlement surrounded by defensive earthworks.

A major invasion by the Muslim Tatars in 1241 devastated much of Cracow, though their raiding tactics did not involve long-term settlement or colonisation, and paradoxically it was due to them that Christian Europe resolved to continue fortifying Cracow and cities like Cracow, constantly modernising them, and garrisoning them to afford permanent strength and stability. This is the age of Gothic architecture, characterised by flying buttresses, tall brick buildings, ampler windows, graceful arches. The age of the new town charter (1257) modelled on that of Magdeburg, a second devastation by the Tatars (1259), gradual colonisation by Germans, the Cloth Hall, the fortification walls, and the founding of Wawel's third Cathedral begun about 1320 and consecrated in 1364. Gothic is the time and the spirit of such marvellous churches as S. Mary's, the townspeople's church, built between the 13th and the 16th centuries on the site of two earlier Romanesque edifices. Gothic is the time of the walls of the Cloth Hall, near S. Mary's, but the restoration of the building itself, the so-called Sukiennice, is an Italianate Renaissance achievement by il Mosca, or Gianmaria Padovano as he is known in Poland.

We halt our review of Cracow's urban development with the Gothic, for we have started our visit on Wawel Hill (pronounced 'VAR-vel', stressing as usual on the penultimate syllable), with the Cathedral. Hours of opening are currently 9-5.30 every day except Sundays (12.15-5.50) but do check these times before going. Its irregular plan is due to the fact that the builders, financially supported by King Casimir the Great, incorporated the burnt remains of the second Romanesque Cathedral.

Look for the highly variable opening hours of Wawel's monuments and museums on a notice-board. The Royal Tombs (below the Cathedral), and the Sigismund Tower, with the great Sigismund Bell cast from forty captured Turkish cannon (beside the Cathedral), may be visited at the same time and with the same ticket as the Cathedral.

The Cathedral Museum nearby has a separate ticket and may be open from 10-3 daily (except 12-5 on Tuesdays).

You may have to queue for up to an hour for a ticket to the Royal Castle, open from 11 to 3.15 (except 12-6 on Wednesdays and Fridays). Avoid weekends if you can, for that is when Poles generally prefer to visit. The Treasury, Armoury and exhibition of the Orient in the Wawel Collections will generally be open during Royal Castle opening hours, but as elsewhere in Poland galleries may be closed without any warning or explanation, so visit the Royal Castle early in your stay at Cracow,

Cracow. Wawel Hill. (Courtesy PTIC)

especially since you may wish to enjoy the site slowly, in two separate visits: one for the Cathedral, Tombs, Sigismund Tower and Cathedral Museum; the other for the Castle and its collections.

Just as Wawel Cathedral represents the focal point of religious and monarchical nationalism, so Wawel Castle stands for the secular power and traditions of the Polish people. Standing in the courtyard, facing elegantly arcaded Renaissance galleries, you are transported to sixteenth-century Italy, for the architecture is by Francesco Fiorentino (to his death in 1516) and Bartolommeo Berrecci (until his death in 1537). Conceding to the northern clime, however, a heavy sloping roof could destroy the visual effect, so stand close enough to one of the two staircases to remove the overpowering chimneyed roof from view. This is the Wawel not of Casimir the Great (only two of whose Gothic rooms of the 14th century survive), but of Sigismund I (1506-48). As a young prince, Sigismund first fell in love with Italian art in Hungary, while visiting his brother Ladislaus, and he determined to extend the new humanism throughout the Kingdom of Poland and the Grand Duchy of Lithuania then under his control. In this period, Italian (and in the north also Dutch) architects transformed the face not only of Cracow and Gdańsk, but also those of much humbler towns. Town halls of the Renaissance arose in Cracow, Tarnów, Poznań, Sandomierz, Przemyśl, Gdańsk and Łowicz, and wealthy burghers built opulent new stone houses around the main market squares. Artistic unities could be fulfilled in the creation of fortified trading centres such as Zamość (south-east of Lublin on the road to Lwów), completed between 1580 and 1600 for the entrepreneurial Chancellor Jan Zamoyski by the Italian architect Bernardo Morando.

The northern part of Renaissance Wawel, however, was demolished by two fires in 1595, and a less distinguished baroque replacement was effected by Giovanni Trevano for Sigismund III Vasa, a king whose passion for the arts extended to the practice of goldsmithing, painting and music. Possibly he might have chosen a more brilliant court painter than Tommaso Dolabella (1570-1650), a Bellunese best known for his court portraits of Sigismund and his courtiers, but the royal taste was eclectic, catholic, and tolerant: he even employed a resident English theatre company for several years! Cracovians will never forgive him, however, because in 1609 he abandoned Wawel and its city in favour of Warsaw, whose only virtue was that it lay strategically central. Wawel predictably declined throughout the seventeenth and eighteenth centuries, and soldiers of the occupying Austrian army turned it into a mere barracks in 1795, just as the Nazis did from September 1939 to 1945, but many of the most significant treasures had been removed secretly to Canada before World War II. They were returned in 1961 and the restoration of Wawel was finally completed in 1964.

Visiting Wawel, you experience more than a building and its contents; Poles argue that you breathe the atmosphere of Polish secular history in the castle and Polish religious fervour in the Cathedral. Together, the nationalism and Catholicism so potent on Wawel Hill represent heartfelt resistance to the internationalist Marxism-Leninism imposed on Poland for more than forty years: an arid ideology of 19th-century utopianism which finds little echo in the folk-memory or present-day aspirations of the average Pole.

Having bought your ticket at the little cubby-hole, after queueing so long that you feel determined to exact every moment of enjoyment from the Castle, you try to find a pair of comfortable overshoes, and slop along the floors and up stairs, making sounds like a masseur slapping naked flesh. In the first three rooms on the ground floor, note the original 16th-century larchwood ceilings and the once polychrome door-frames designed by Benedykt of Sandomierz. The 17th-century tapestries in Room 1 show Hercules and Cacus and Scipio with Hannibal before the Battle of Zama. The first tapestries were acquired by Sigismund I, but many disappeared after he died, and the collection was not built up to its greatest point until 1632, the year of his death. Of the 356 works, up to 9 x 5 metres in dimension, only 136 survive the vagaries of time, plunder, warfare, and downright theft. The greatest of these are eighteen representing the stories of Eden, Noah's Ark, and the Tower of Babel. Another 45 depict animals and landscapes, while a third series of 48 portray coats-of-arms, grotesque, initials and other such miscellanea relevant once but now of only minimal interest. The finest tapestries are to designs by the so-called 'Flemish Raphael', Michiel Coxcie (1499-1592) of Mechelen, in his youth a partner with Barent van Orley running the Vatican tapestry works.

Room 2 has a Brussels tapestry of the mid-16th century showing David's victory over Goliath (though in another part of the Bible one recalls that Goliath was defeated by Elhanan...) and a slightly later Francesco Bassano painting, the 'Annunciation to the Shepherds', painfully in need of conservation, like hundreds of other canvasses throughout Poland, neglected and dark with layers of unwanted varnish. In Room 3, the last of the servants' quarters in this part of Wawel, a Brussels tapestry portrays Venus as she prognosticates for Aeneas from a flight of swans.

Imagine the Envoys' Stairs and balustrades in original sandstone, wishing away the marble facings unaccountably added in 1927. The first floor belonged to the royal family and their immediate entourage, while the ground floor comprised waiting-rooms, chancery, treasury and law courts. The great rooms of the second floor were used for ceremonial occasions: the Audience Room for the formal business of the Court, and the Senatorial Room for sessions of the Senate, balls and banquets, operas and plays. The first-floor vestibule, with baroque portraits of Spanish ladies, is agreeably dominated by a mid-17th century Brussels tapestry from the van der Hecke workshop after a Rubens cartoon depicting the death of the Roman Consul Decius Mus. Take another staircase and you reach the second-floor vestibule, with a Flemish early 17th-century landscape tapestry.

The Tournament Room is named for a frieze painted by Hans Dürer (brother to the great Albrecht) and Antoni of Wrocław, naive work of great charm, with subdued colours and fascinating details of caparisoned horses, knights with plumed helmets, and raised swords; but a much lovelier work is the first of the 'Flood' tapestries showing Noah being instructed by God. Regrettably, the best of the paintings disappeared during one or other of Cracow's foreign occupations, and all we have left are the second- and third-best: workshop pieces such as the 'Madonna adoring the Child' associated with Lorenzo di Credi, or 'The Holy Family' ascribed to the circle of Andrea del Sarto.

The Military Review Hall has another interesting frieze (1535), by Antoni of Wrocław (German Breslau), showing troops parading before the bearded Sigismund I, who sits on a simple, surprisingly modern-looking throne, serene and dignified. As well as tapestries bearing coats of arms, you can enjoy fine royal portraits, the best being Martin Kober's 'Anna Jagiellońka' and 'King Stefan Batory' also attributed by some to Kober, like Antoni a Wrocław painter.

Formerly the Throne Room, the Audience Hall is also known as the Room of Heads, because of the marvellous polychrome carved heads, one to a panel, that gaze down for all eternity at the ebb and flow of visitors. Most of the heads are now missing, but I tried to imagine which one might have been credited with the legendary exhortation to Sigismund Augustus, after he had pronounced sentence, 'Rex Auguste, iudica iuste' ('King Augustus, judge fairly!'). The heads were carved by Sebastian Tauerbach of Wrocław and Jan Snycerz (1531-5) and represent a *tour de force* of characterisation, mainly through faithful portrayal of contemporary headgear. Then there is the frieze portraying 'The Life of Man' based on a Greek dialogue, *Pinax* (Picture), once attributed to the fourth-century B.C. Theban writer Cebes, but now known to date from the 1st century A.D. In the place of the throne stands an Italian 16th-century chair with a tapestry bearing the royal initials. But, just as the Long Saloon at Longleat House in Wiltshire glories in its Flemish 16th-century hangings depicting scenes from the life of Cyrus, Shah of Persia, so the Audience Hall in Wawel Castle revels in its Garden of Eden tapestries, from the same place and time. Even the verdures (tapestries portraying landscapes, trees, or plants, often with bird life) are sumptuous, but as always we anthropocentric individuals look for the expression of man's relationships to God and man: the banishing of Adam and Eve from Eden, the murder of Abel by Cain. There is no comfort here: we are all tainted with sin, which must be expiated with humility and grace.

After returning to the vestibule, you next come to the Zodiac Room, with a 1929 reconstruction of a 16th-century fresco showing the zodiac dwarfed by a supreme set of tapestries on the Babel legend: Building the Tower; the Wrath of God; the Confusion of Tongues; and the Dispersal of the Peoples. A 'Madonna and Child' canvas is attributed to the Florentine Raffaellino del Garbo, and certainly seems to possess that gentle refinement associated with del Garbo and his kindred spirit Perugino.

The spirit quickens as one enters the Planets Room, with hangings to show God blessing Noah and Noah's drunkenness. A portrait of Gian Jacopo Caraglio, the royal goldsmith, has been credited to Paris Bordone and dated 1552. Next is the vestibule of the Battle of Orsza, named for the reconstructed frieze depicting a 1514 battle between Poland and Muscovy. Tommaso Dolabella painted the 1571 Battle of Lepanto in about 1630. Now in Giovanni Trevano's baroque north wing, we come to the Bird Room, called after the ceiling carvings made in the 17th century; the walls are covered with cordovan leather both embossed and painted. Paintings on the vault in the adjacent chapel are recent, but the stucco is original, from about 1600. Next we come to Sigismund III's dining-room, with some excellent portraits, the best being Dolabella's impression of Stanislaus Tęczynski, son of the Voivod of Cracow. The Eagle Room, named for the national emblem, once acted as the Court of Justice on Wawel. As a document, I enjoyed the oldest painted view of Wawel: Ladislaus IV seen against a military camp at the foot of Wawel Hill from the Dolabella workshop, a pedestrian enough concept weakly executed about 1650.

In Warsaw's Wilanów Palace one floor acts as an unofficial Polish National Portrait Gallery, but Wawel too presents a fascinating series of canvases, modest in dimensions against the outsize Lenin-Stalin-Khrushchev hoardings of the U.S.S.R. and the Marx-Lenin-Mao banners of mainland China, and created for a totally different purpose. These portraits of kings and aristocrats were painted as a reminder of present glories as a hostage for oblivion. The totalitarian, gigantic oversimplified images of 'Our Great Leader' present a view intended to overcome freedom of choice, of thought, of action. There is almost literally 'no room' for anyone else. The vestibule near Wawel's Senatorial Hall, by contrast, displays familiar homely portraits of modest size which could be lived with: from left to right Daniel Schultz's 'King Michael I Wisniowiecki' (1668-72) and 'King Jan Casimir' (1648-60); then a Flemish painting of Jan Casimir's mother Constance of Austria and Charles Beaubrun's portrait of Jan Casimir's wife, Marie-Louise Gonzaga. Don't miss Chancellor Jerzy Ossoliński's entry into Rome in 1633, an Italian work.

The Senatorial Hall, impressive with its Minstrels' Gallery, resounds to the Building of the Ark, the noisy Embarkation of the Animals, the roar of the Flood, the pandemonium of Disembarkation from the Ark, and the sobbing relief of Noah's Thanksgiving, a fitting climax albeit on two-dimensional tapestry to the restoration of a monument symbolising the indestructibility of the Polish soul, no matter how secretly and how deeply it has to burrow beneath superficial compliance. Or one aspect of the Polish soul. Or an image of the Polish soul that governments favour.

Anyone familiar with the Crown Jewels in the Tower of London will head for the Crown Treasury in Wawel Castle's Gothic north-east corner on the ground floor. But disappointment will be inevitable, for Poland's treasures have been sadly depleted by plunder, melting down in time of war, and theft.

The Treasury's first room, named for Casimir the Great, takes us back to the Gothic age in Poland, in the mid-14th century, with its fireplace and cross-ribbed vaulting. On the west wall, look for a small polychrome fragment: the monogram MM relating to the Anjou family and thus to Queen Jadwiga of Anjou, Queen of Poland (1384-99) and wife of Ladislaus II Jagiello, King of Poland from 1386 to 1434. In Case 1 is the earliest relic: a 5th-century ring inscribed MARTINVS, with an 11th-century ring and 12th-century Romanesque rock crystal and gold pendant, both recovered in excavations of 1964-6 near the Wawel Hill's Rotunda of SS. Felix and Adauctus. If you find time to visit the Church and Benedictine Monastery at Tyniec, 9 km from Cracow's city centre, you will be able to associate the *genius loci* with a contemporary golden chalice, paten, and fragments of two abbot's croziers, one contemporary and one a century later, excavated at Tyniec in 1961. Other objects of note are a silver-gilt chalice of Casimir the Great's time (1351) and another chalice of 1500. Case 2 includes the burial crown of Sigismund I, and a beautiful fragment from an Italian enamelled gold chain from Sigismund III's coffin. In Case 3 look out for an 18th-century miniature of Augustus III attributed to the Venetian painter Rosalba Carriera (1675-1757), and another of Sigismund III (1591) by Martin Kober. Augsburg and Nuremberg silver of the 16th and early 17th centuries merited international celebrity, and in Case 4 one fine gilded *tazza* is attributed to Tobias Kramer of Augsburg, while another belonged to Sigismund III, and bears the date 1600.

Enter the Jadwiga and Jagiello Room, for three dramatic highlights. The jagged sword, *Szczerbiec*, (pronounced 'shchairbyets') with which Ladislaus the Short was crowned in Cracow in 1320 has miraculously survived despite being stolen by the Prussians in 1795, finding its way to the Hermitage Museum in S. Petersburg in 1884, and returning to

Wawel in 1928. It is shown on two French Romanesque columns, below a Gothic cross-ribbed vault with keystones bearing the arms of Ladislaus and Queen Jadwiga.

In the corner is the slender early 16th-century sword made in Cracow for King Sigismund I (1506-48) decorated with the king in his coronation robes. Lastly, the oldest extant Royal banner: made in 1553 for the coronation of his third wife, Catherine, and so bears the arms not only of Poland and Lithuania, but also of the Hapsburgs. Back in Room 1, a further dazzling selection of royal tableware hints at the magnitude of what has been lost over the centuries: silver-gilt cups from Nuremberg, Gdańsk silver, *tazze* from Augsburg, and an 18th-century Augsburg portable shrine once in Jan III Sobieski's family.

Room 3 is Baroque, of the early 17th century, with objects connected with Jan III Sobieski (1674-96): his Mantle of the Knights of the Order of the Holy Ghost, sword and hat. The barrel-vaulted Room 4 dates from the early 16th century; it is devoted to banners, parade weapons, and horse-trappings. Look for batons of command, called *bulava*, which signified the status of a Polish or Cossack military commander or *hetman*; arms and armour from the Vasa epoch; South German decorated helmets of the 16th century.

The adjacent Armoury will appeal to all those fascinated by weapons and the paraphernalia of warfare: débris of bloody struggles that have threatened to annihilate every Pole several times each century. Here are German, Italian, Austrian, Polish and Russian guns, swords, shields and rapiers from the 12th century to the 17th. Look for copies of Teutonic banners captured in the historic Battle of Grunwald (1410) and a hussar's half-armour complete with original wings.

Subterranean Wawel is a separate exhibition in three parts: Renaissance and Baroque stove-tiles of great variety: both in colour and decoration, many made by Bartosz of Kazimierz, tiler to King Sigismund the Old; architectural details by masons working for the same king; and the chapel called the Rotunda of SS. Felix and Adauctus, formerly of S. Mary, the oldest stone building on Wawel, dating back to the 10th century. It became a defensive tower in the 13th century, consecrated afresh in the 14th, returned to domestic use in the 16th, and suffered severe damage by the Austrians in the 19th.

'The Orient in the Wawel' forms a fine display in the west of the castle, near the entry gatehouse. The cultures represented are mainly Armenia, Turkey (whence Armenians fled at certain times), and Iran, contacts dating mainly from the Middle Ages; China and Japan. In the early 16th century, Sigismund the Old corresponded with Sulaiman the Magnificent with a view to reducing taxes on Polish merchants. Trade concerned above all furs and amber from the north in exchange for silks, carpets and metalwork.

The second floor features tents, carpets, and weapons from Turkey and Iran. On the first floor, Room 1 displays historical paintings: 'The Battle of Chocim' (1673) between the Poles, led by Jan Sobieski, and the Ottoman Turks, painted by Jan van Hughtenburgh (1647-1733); and 'The Battle of Vienna' (1683) painted by Romeyn de Hooghe. Naturally, the painters have selected moments glorifying Polish triumphs, particularly that epic charge of winged hussars at the siege of Vienna. One has to be aware, however, of the collapse following these 17th-century campaigns. In the Great Northern War (1700-21), Charles XII and Peter the Great proved more than capable of overcoming Polish forces, who fell almost as silent as the Sejm (Parliament) of 1717 during the War of the Polish Succession (1733-5), the War of the Austrian Succession (1740-8), and the Seven Years' War of 1756-63. Room 2 exhibits captured Turkish banners, sabres and prayer-mats; Room 3 Persian carpets and ceramics; Room 4 Chinese ceramics; Room 5 Japanese ceramics and lacquer.

Wawel Cathedral and the separate Cathedral Museum should be approached from Ulica Kanoniczna, named for the canons whose early 16th-century homes give the street such atmospheric resonance, with Renaissance or Baroque portals, courtyards and cloisters. I especially enjoyed the Deanery (14th-15th centuries) at no. 21 and the home of the patriotic historian Jan Długosz (1415-80) at no. 25. Climbing the hill, we can see the Cathedral Museum, or Treasury, and two towers: the Clock Tower, and the Sigismund Tower. Having reached the Cathedral courtyard, there is a third tower, of the Silver Bell, whose lower segments date from the 12th century, making it contemporary with the original Clock Tower, redesigned in the 14th and provided with a decorated baroque spire in the 18th. The 14th-century Sigismund Tower houses the Sigismund Bell, the largest in Poland, cast from the metal of forty captured cannon in 1520, by Johann Beham of Nuremberg. It is heard only at major church festivals and significant national occasions. You pay to enter the Tower and the Royal Tombs as well as the Cathedral, an exploration greatly to be recommended. Writing as Archbishop of the Metropolis of Cracow, and Cardinal Karol Wojtyła, Pope John Paul II referred to Wawel Cathedral as 'the sanctuary of the Polish nation' which 'cannot be entered without an inner trembling, without awe, for here – as in few cathedrals of the world – is contained a vast greatness which speaks to us of all the history of Poland, of all our past; together the monuments, tombs, altars, sculptures and above all the host of names of those long dead, remind us of what has gone by'. His implication is that each tyranny, whether imposed internally or from abroad, will inevitably pass, and only the thousand-year-old weight of Catholic Polish tradition will remain.

Take the analogy with Canterbury Cathedral. Thomas à Becket was murdered for disobedience to temporal authority in 1170. But long before that, in 1079, Bishop Stanislaus, Bishop of Cracow, had also been canonised by the Church for opposition to the tyranny of Boleslaus II and his knights. Nothing changes: agents of the secret police murdered Father Jerzy Popiełuszko in 1984. The saint's remains are buried in a shrine in the heart of the Cathedral of SS Vaclav and Stanislaus, where nave meets transept.

Like Canterbury, Wawel's Cathedral is a national shrine, Cracow's Pantheon, a meeting-place where the struggle for freedom, or even to survive daily frustrations, can be subsumed in a steady flame of glory: mute testimony to the persistence of Poland despite all persecution. A stubborn belief, a gleam of redemption, the focus of various resurrections. Boleslaus I started it in about 1020, and parts of that beginning remain under the western wing of the Castle, but little survived invasions from the south and a second cathedral was built from 1090 to 1142. From this we possess only the crypt of S. Leonard and the Silver Bell Tower, the rest having vanished in the fire of 1305. Imagine the scene in 1320, when the Archbishop of Gniezno crowned Ladislaus I (called Łokietek, or 'Elbow-high') and his Queen Jadwiga in the ruins of the burnt-out cathedrál. Immediately thereafter, the Bishop of Cracow started a third edifice, completing it in 44 years, when it was consecrated by Archbishop Jarosław of Gniezno in the presence of King Casimir III the Great, honoured in Jewish annals for his extension of Jewish liberties (guaranteed in a charter of 1265) and his welcome to Jewish refugees from other lands. The height was increased between 1679 and 1715, and radical restoration carried out 1891-1910.

Among the ravages that the Cathedral has seen are two lootings by Swedish Protestants, the first in 1655-7 and the second in 1702, and one by the Germans during World War II. Before entering the main portal, look up to see the rosette, then the eagle emblematic of the Piast dynasty, and below the small cross the standing figure of S. Stanislaus from the 14th century, the same age as the bas-reliefs of S. Michael and S. Margaret fighting the dragons at the sides of the portal, which dates from 1640, a work of the so-called 'black baroque'. The dizzy mix of styles continues with the baroque choir gallery of 1758 (by Francesco Placidi) with an organ of 1785, and four wood sculptures of church fathers on corbels of the pillars between the aisles: S. Jerome and his lion and S. Ambrose with his church from the workshop of Wit Stwosz (or Veit Stoss as the Germans know the master), S. Gregory as Pope and S. Augustine as bishop. Possibly the most radiantly effective Renaissance sculpture in Poland is the realistic red Hungarian marble figure of King Ladislaus Jagiełło, created in a Florentine spirit shortly after the king's death in 1434. Sigismund the Old commissioned the baldacchino in 1519-24 from Giovanni Cini to replace the original

Cracow. Wawel Cathedral. Chapel of S. Sigismund

Gothic canopy. To set the Ladislaus masterpiece in historical perspective, it was achieved roughly when Alberti was writing his *Treatise on the Art of Painting*, when Rogier van der Weyden was appointed city painter to Brussels, when Brunelleschi was working on the Florentine S. Maria degli Angeli, when Pisanello was creating his fresco S. George and the Princess in Verona, and when Donatello was beginning his Cantoria for the Florentine Duomo. It is of Donatello, and his slightly later bronze Gattamelata statue ordered by the Venetian Senate, that I think when gazing at the imperious Ladislaus II, his lower lip curling in eternal scorn at the effrontery of death.

Other wonderful Gothic and Renaissance pieces include the sarcophagi of Ladislaus Łokietek and his son Casimir the Great, respectively towards the end of the north and south aisles. These last two Piast monarchs were the first to be laid to rest in Wawel Cathedral. The Ladislaus grave sculpture was carved in the 1340s, with mourners in bas-relief around the sides. Casimir, who commissioned this work, can be found commemorated symmetrically opposite. A brilliant evocation of Casimir, commissioned by King Louis of Hungary, his nephew and successor, the Hungarian red marble sarcophagus dates from the 1370s; courtiers in mourning flank the king. If Austrian influence can be detected here, then the unmistakable greatness of Wit Stwosz irradiates the Chapel of the Holy Cross, built on to the West Front. He is responsible (as his signature shows beside the date, 1492) for the sarcophagus of Casimir Jagiello, in which the father of the future kings Jan Olbracht, Alexander, and Sigismund the Old stares quizzically up at the heavens, all his features as clear as the sun seen from the upper atmosphere. Sculpture is the most enduring of the arts, as these Polish kings and their consorts acutely perceived. Wit Stwosz subtly reminds us across five centuries that it is the skill of the sculptor which restores individuality to the historical name when all archives are charred in flames, and all memories distorted. Scenes from the Gospels were painted on the walls and Gothic vaulting by painters of the Pskov school about 1470. A little later is the Gothic triptych of Our Lady of Sorrows. Its wings are painted and show when open Christ in the Temple, Christ among the Doctors, the Crucifixion and the Descent from the Cross; when closed, the Annunciation to Mary, the Birth of Christ, Circumcision, and the Adoration of the Magi. The east wall has a triptych of the Holy Trinity of 1467, with a carved central panel and painted wings. The saints surrounding the Trinity are Dorothy, Margaret, Catherine and Barbara. The figures above represent the Risen Christ with two angels, accompanied by the Holy Wisdom (later personified as S. Sophia) and S. Anne. Polish masters have painted the open wings with choirs praising God, and the closed wings with four scenes from the lives of saints: Paul, Eustace, George, and Secundus.

Now it is time for the central Shrine of S. Stanislaus, a sanctified place since his martyrdom in 1079, though the relics of S. Florian were not laid here until 1184, and those of S. Stanislaus not until 1254. The first silver coffin of Stanislaus provided by Kinga was melted down and the metal reused for the present coffin, decorated in 1669-71 by scenes from the saint's life and miracles, the silversmiths being Jacob Jaeger of Augsburg and Pieter van der Rennen, a Dutchman living in Gdańsk. The second coffin, donated by Sigismund III Vasa in 1633, was looted by the Swedish army in 1657. The mausoleum we see today was designed by Giovanni Trevano (1626-9) with images of Polish saints by Antonio Lagostini.

Baroque stalls by Jan Szabura of 1620 give the presbytery an extra dimension, as if the ineluctable passage of time had fluttered downward, from the mid-14th stone bosses, on the presbytery ceiling, representing Christ the Saviour, S. Vaclav (whom we know as 'Good King Wenceslas' of Bohemia), S. Stanislaus, and the crest of Bishop Jan Grot (a maiden riding a bear). Poland's churches are almost suffocated with baroque high altars, and Wawel Cathedral is no exception. Such gilded decoration of the mid-17th century, when monarchies were absolute, and due magnificence the rule, could be interchanged with hundreds more, as could the Christ Crucified attributed to Tommaso Dolabella. Concentrate instead on Vischer of Nuremberg's bronze relief on the tomb of Cardinal Fryderyk Jagiellończyk, Bishop of Cracow and Archbishop of Gniezno, who died in 1503. This is found on the steps up to the altar. The good Cardinal, son of Casimir IV and brother to three kings, is shown being commended into the care of the Blessed Virgin Mary by S. Stanislaus and (behind him) the newly resurrected Piotrowin, miraculously brought back to life by the saint.

Since near-religious veneration is accorded to classical writers in Poland, it is rewarding to visit Wawel's equivalent of Westminster Abbey's Poets' Corner: the crypt of Juliusz Słowacki (1809-1849) and Adam Mickiewicz (1798-1855).

The Lady Chapel (where the apse would be) dates from the late 14th century, but Queen Anna Jagiellońka transformed it in 1594-5 into a chantry for her consort King Stefan Batory of Hungary, commissioning Santi Gucci, and it was reconstructed in the mid-17th century by Canon Serebryski.

It will be clear by now that every chapel is remarkable for one feature or another: Francesco Fiorentino's red marble sarcophagus of King Jan Olbracht (d. 1501) in the Chapel of Corpus Christi and S. Andrew; Bartolommeo Berrecci's penthouse tomb of Bishop Jan Konarski (1521) in the Chapel of S. Joachim; Antoni Madejski's Carrara marble sarcophagus of Queen Jadwiga of 1902. But the most splendid Renaissance work on Wawel is Bartolommeo Berrecci's Sigismund

Chapel (1519-33), commissioned by Sigismund to commemorate the death of his first wife Barbara, with a cupola gilded in 1591-2. Berrecci's, too, is the Renaissance throne with angels bearing the royal crown, but he brought with him from Siena Gianmaria Padovano, Niccolò da Castiglione, Giovanni Cini, from Fiesole Antonio and Filippo, and all these sculptors and decorators, unsung in their native land, created an atmosphere of lightness, brilliance, and southern invention hitherto alien to Polish lands. Later on, Santi Gucci maintained the tradition of Mediterranean elegance with the flowing robes of Queen Anna Jagiellonka (d. 1596) and the half-turned figure, vigorous even in repose, of Sigismund Augustus. By contrast, the silversmiths of Nuremberg were responsible for the masterpiece in silver: the altar of the Virgin Mary (1531-8) commissioned by Sigismund I and carried out by Melchior Baier. When the altar is closed, paintings of the Passion of Our Lord by Georg Pencz can be seen. A pupil of Dürer, Pencz was associated with the Behams, and banned from Nuremberg with them in 1524, though his several sojourns in Italy made no less an impact on his style. (Incidentally, I have seen his portraits of Erasmus in Donaueschingen, Nuremberg and Vienna, and those of S. Jerome in Würzburg, Stuttgart, Nuremberg, and the Louvre). Pencz is even better known as an engraver, chiefly of classical and allegorical themes.

I felt cold, unwelcome, in the neighbouring Chapel of the Immaculate Conception, possibly because of the effect of black marble, from Kielce and Dębnik, which covers the interior. The chapel replaced a 13th-century chapel, and was consecrated in 1676, being the mausoleum of the Vasa dynasty which governed Poland from 1587 to 1668.

Viewing Wawel Cathedral simply as a sculpture gallery, the price of admission would be well spent on a glimpse of the bronze low-relief of Piotr Kmita the Elder (Voivod of Cracow), made in the early years of the 16th century by Peter Vischer the Elder (1460-1529). Kmita could be a raffish, curly-haired, loose-limbed condottiere of Parma or Ferrara, a sword in his left hand and a flying standard laconically held in his right. Encased from shoulder to foot in armour, he presents an arrogantly militaristic stance in a House theoretically held in fief for the Prince of Peace. His son, Kmita the Younger, also a Voivod of Cracow (from 1529), can be seen immortalised in marble near the Chapel of the Holy Cross, by the western end of the north aisle. Similarly fitted out in armour, young Piotr is shown later in life, when recklessness has given way to sagacity. As a patron of art and learning, he typifies the Polish Renaissance humanist. It was Kmita who paid for Klemens Janicius to study in Padua (1538-40): Janicius, of peasant origins, became one of the greatest Latin poets of the age.

The Royal Tombs, or perhaps catacombs might be a more appropriate name, can be visited through the Czartoryski Chapel, which is also the ground floor of the Clock Tower. The best is first: S. Leonard's Romanesque crypt of 1090-1118 with stellate vaulting on eight columns. The stone altar by the distinguished French architect Eugène Viollet-le-Duc (1814-79) must be commended for its tact; in the centre is the tomb of Bishop Maurus (d.1118) near the jarring neo-classical note of King Jan III Sobieski's sarcophagus of 1783. The great Polish hero Tadeusz Kościuszko (d.1817) is laid to rest in a grey marble sarcophagus made in 1832 to a design by Francesco Maria Lanci.

Other crypts deserve less attention, as taste becomes more flamboyant, and magnificence unduly ostentatious. One after another they pass before our eyes, like the ghostly successors of doomed Banquo in *Macbeth*: King Stefan Batory in pewter; Jan Christian Bierpfaff's ornate coffins for Ladislaus IV and his consort; Sigismund Augustus and his sister Anna Jagiellonka; in the Vasa crypt Sigismund III, Jan Casimir and his son Jan Sigismund; and finally the crypt under the Silver Bell Tower, with the remains of the revered Marshal Józef Piłsudski, who died in 1935. A place beside Piłsudski has been prepared for the remains of General Ladislaus Sikorski, who is buried in Britain. Negotiations between Britain and Poland are difficult. Sikorski himself said that he wanted to be buried among his soldiers.

Take the stairs up to the highest level of the Sigismund Tower, with the eponymous great bell. The tower itself dates from the later 14th century. To raise this huge bell, a great stone-filled chest was placed on a pulley at the top of the tower and, as it began to sink, the bell was hoisted up.

The Cathedral Museum has a separate entrance, near the Cathedral itself. Its building dates from 1481-1500, but a first inventory was made in 1101, and some objects of great value survive nearly nine centuries of pillage. Here is the spear of S. Maurice, for example, given to Boleslaus the Brave by Emperor Otto III at the Congress of Gniezno in 1000; a silver reliquary from the Crusades, a 13th-century cross, made from the diadems of Kinga and Boleslaus the Shy in Venice. Croziers and monstrances, chalices and ecclesiastical regalia, all testify to the tenacity of the Church despite the fury and longevity of its varied enemies.

After Wawel, the visitor to Cracow should spend as much time as possible in the Main Market Square, in Polish Rynek Główny ('rünek gwoovni'), heart of the district called City Centre, in Polish Srodmieście. In the early 19th century, the fortification walls of Cracow were demolished to the Haberdashers' Tower, or Pasamoników) and the city council encircled the city centre with an emerald necklace of gardens called Planty. If we mentally wish away Planty, we can visualise the

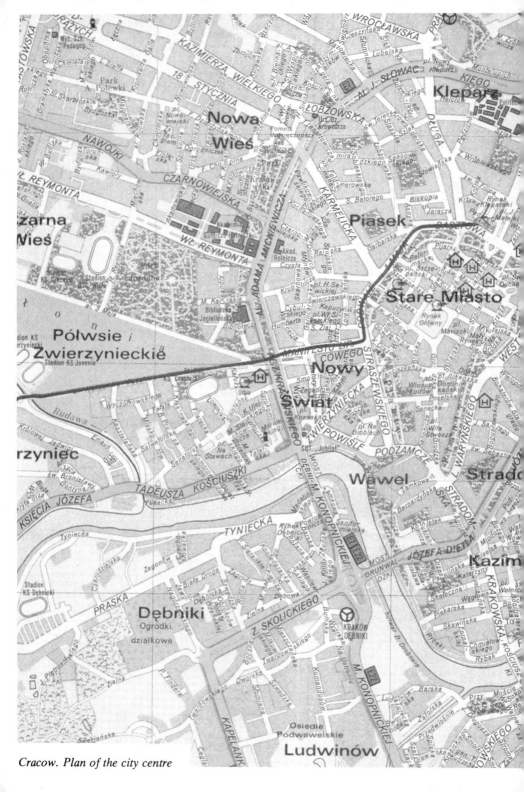

Cracow. Plan of the city centre

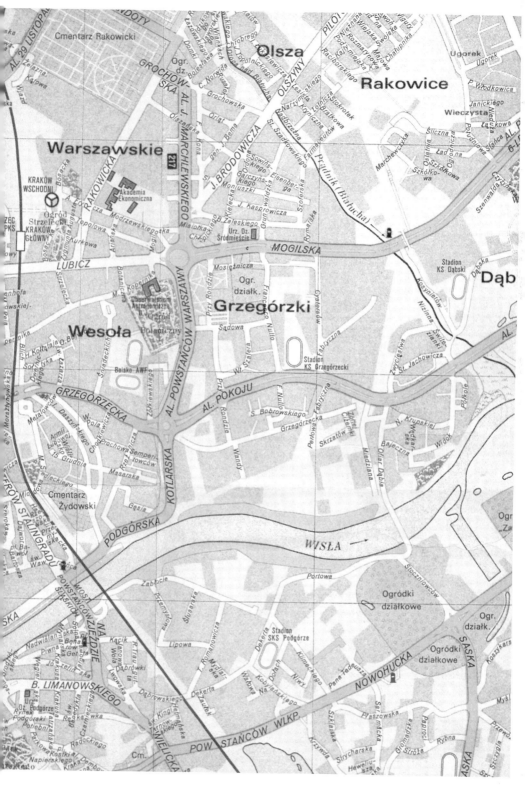

Royal Road from Warsaw which to all intents and purposes ended at the Market Square of Kleparz, now a suburb just north of the walled city. From Kleparz, crossroads radiated west, east and north. The royal progress, for a coronation or a funeral at Wawel, proceeded along Ulica Floriańska, alongside the great parish church of S. Mary and the eastern flank of Rynek Główny, and down Ulica Grodzka to the foot of Wawel. We reverse this route and, on the right hand side of Grodzka, come to the Romanesque Church of S. Andrew with a Baroque interior. According to local tradition, the citizens of Cracow defended themselves within S. Andrew's from the Tatar invasion of Cracow in 1241. It was then the parish church of a district called Okół ('Environs') between Wawel and the city centre around Rynek Główny, but the modern visitor is likely to be disappointed by the clash between its plain 12th-century structure and lavish Baroque additions.

Next to it, facing Plac Wita Stwosza, stands the Church of SS. Peter and Paul, set back from Grodzka, which was modelled by Giovanni Trevano on the Church of Jesus in Rome and dates from 1605-19, with stucco work of 1619-33 by Falconi. Late Baroque free-standing figures of the Apostles greet the somewhat daunted visitor before entering. The Jesuits came to Cracow to staunch the flow of converts to the Reformation: this church served as the hub of their operations, and its activist Piotr Skarga (1536-1612) became its leading zealot: he lies buried in the chancel.

Just north of Plac Wita Stwosza in Grodzka is the Collegium Iuridicum, since 1403 a faculty of the University, with original Gothic portals and late Renaissance arcades in a memorable courtyard. Wit Stwosz lived at No. 32 for some years. The Dominican Church, on the right-hand-side of Grodzka, is of 13th-14th century date, and hence Gothic, but Renaissance and Baroque chapels restore that sense of a palimpsest common to all the oldest Central European cities. It is as though a unity in architecture or decoration would represent a falsified oversimplification of the past; a repudiation of certain rungs on the ladder of history which must not be missed if one is to reach the top for a bird's eye view of understanding. The Franciscan Church, near the 17th-century Wielopolski Palace, seat of the Cracow City People's Council, was founded in 1269, but its present appearance dates from the 14th century. Whereas the Dominicans enjoyed the patronage of the nobles and wealthier townspeople, the Franciscans had fewer material advantages, even though Ladislaus the Short must have shown his gratitude for events before his Coronation. Pursued by enemies, he hid with the Franciscans and, disguised in their habit, was lowered by friendly monks in a basket outside the city walls. Do not miss the 15th-century frescoes of scenes from the life of S. Francis, unluckily in a poor state of preservation.

I recommend at least a brief visit to the Archaeological Museum at Ulica Poselska 3, off Ulica Grodzka, in a 17th-century monastery, now secularised. Permanent exhibitions are devoted to Ancient and Mediaeval 'Little Poland', as the area around Cracow is known; the Early History of Nowa Huta, following rescue excavations since 1949; and Mediterranean Archaeology. There is a plain yet subtle pleasure to be derived from a clay vase dating to the radial-decorated culture of about 2,000 B.C. From about the same age, found in Bilcze Złote, Soviet Ukraine, are coloured-band clay bowls and vases, again delightful in shape but now decorated with characteristic bands. Dramatic gold and silver ornaments (650-480 B.C.) from Scythian tombs are familiar to anyone who has roamed museums in the Soviet Union, but this barrow from Ryżanówka (Ukraine) is the only one to yield its secrets in a Polish setting.

Egyptian mummies are displayed, but are seen to better advantage in Cairo, the Louvre, the British Museum or the Metropolitan. Here in Poland the revelation is a slender but arrogant pre-Christian stele put up by the pagan Slavs to Światowid in the 9th or 10th century and found in 1848 in the river Zbrucz near Liczkowce, Husiatyn district (Ukraine). Once bright red, the pillar reminded me of an Egyptian obelisk in hieratic solemnity, though it has the height (256 cm) of a minor Irish cross. The horn, sabre and horse figuring on the column denote attributes of the god Światowid. While in Cracow, some batteries ran down, and I entered a hardware shop to buy replacements. A counter salesman looked at my spent Duracell batteries incredulously. 'Where did you get these?' 'Cambridge'. 'Ah, that accounts for it. You'll not find any like this for złoty in Poland. If you want good batteries, you can go to this address, and pay 2 dollars if they have them. But I'm sure they won't have any.' The salesman was right: they didn't.

Rynek, forty thousand square metres in area, feels something like an inland, more northerly Piazza San Marco, dizzy with raucous pigeons and oddly distanced, as though the great parish church of S. Mary's, seen from the Tower, could fit between your thumb and index finger. We owe Rynek to the town planners of 1257, yet they deferred to existing buildings, as can be shown by the divergence from straight axis of the Clothiers' Hall, and the bend in Ulica Bracka. Further, S. Mary's is not where you might have predicted, and S. Adalbert's seems askew.

Imagine the whole mediaeval square cluttered with a thousand cries of stallholders and itinerant vendors, the more sedate shopkeepers gazing superciliously at the teeming mob. The square possessed a Town Hall, a huge granary, a whipping-post for thieves and vagabonds, and a cage in which gossips and scolds cooled their heels and sharpened their tongues. Oh, and yes, the inevitable crop of pigeons. The 13th-century Town Hall was demolished in the officious 19th century, like most of the buildings in the square, leaving only the Tower: not the first destroyed by fire in 1680, but its early replacement.

S. Adalbert of Prague, known in Polish as S. Wojciech, is alleged to have preached on the spot where 'his' church is located today, but the fact is that traces of a much earlier wooden pagan temple have been identified, as have pre-Romanesque, Romanesque, Gothic, Renaissance, and Baroque phases. Its interior is much less interesting than an exposition of its history in a display below the tiny church.

I climbed the Leaning Tower of Cracow (only 55 cms out of the vertical, but worth mentioning), where rooms have been laid out with objects and documents charting the history of Cracow. The view from the roof must be seen: it corresponds to the Palace of Culture view in Warsaw or that from the Town Hall tower in Gdańsk.

The Clothiers' Hall (Sukiennice) elegantly centred in Rynek and designed in its present form (1556-60) by Gianmaria Padovano replaces a simple mediaeval street of two rows of stalls, locked at night to protect travelling merchants and their gods. The original 13th-14th century Gothic walls survive, but of course the Renaissance upper floor and staircase provide the charm combined with imposing size that dazzle one at the same distance from the Palazzo Ducale in Venice. The Hall was restored in the 19th century by Tomasz Pryliński, and the first floor remodelled to provide a stunning setting for the first National Museum in Poland, founded in 1879.

Within Sukiennice, on the ground floor, one can buy a range of souvenirs from the DESA and CEPELIA shops. One might contemplate ceramics or woodcarving, costume dolls, engravings and modern drawings or oils, amber and other jewellery, lace and embroidery. Cheapest of all are books, and many are available in English, standards of book production having improved dramatically in the last few years. Outside Sukiennice, coffee houses and travel agencies proliferate, and stalls of fruit and flowers in season under gaily-coloured parasols bestow an air of festival well outside the famous 'Days of Cracow' held in June. Diminutive horse-drawn buses should not be missed: they clop along to Barbican, for example.

The National Museum (Muzeum Narodowe) consists of seven parts in seven buildings, and the separate Historical Museum of the City of Cracow yet another seven, also scattered, but some will be closed during your visit, and times of opening are erratic (often varying from those shown outside the building at the time), so it is a matter of taking your chances as you can, and relating itineraries to Rynek Główny as the nexus. The main part of the National Museum is the Gallery of Classical Polish Painting (1764-1900), which can be reached by an unobtrusive door facing the Mickiewicz Monument. Room 1 is dominated by the portraits and personality of Marcello Bacciarelli (1731-1818), court

Cracow. Rynek. Flower-sellers, with the Renaissance Cloth Hall in the background

painter to King Stanislaus Augustus Poniatowski (1764-95). Compare his self-portrait with splendid portraits of his royal and noble sitters; also noteworthy are Wojciech Gerson's 'Road beside a Stream' and Kazimierz Wojniakowski's portrait of General Józef Kossakowski. Room 2 is devoted to Piotr Michałowski (1800-55), a Cracovian less interested in mankind than in horses and their importance during battle: his 'Krakus Unit' is outstanding. Room 3 offers the celebrated 'Prussian Tribute' (1882) by Jan Matejko (1838-93), depicting the moment in 1525, in Cracow's Rynek, when the Grand Master of the Teutonic Order, Albrecht Hohenzollern, Duke of Prussia, presented his oath of loyalty to Sigismund I of Poland. Vigour in handling, an expressive palette, and a deft choice of theme mark the works of Matejko, who was painting in the sullen years of Partition which we shall see exemplified in his Warsaw 'Stanczyk'. For a short while a pupil of Matejko, Maurycy Gottlieb (1856-1879) was mainly noted for exotic Biblical and historical oils, such as 'Ahasuerus' here in Cracow, but I prefer his affecting 'Portrait of a Jewess' and a most serene 'Portrait of his Sister', both in Warsaw. Henryk Siemiradzki's gift of his 'Torches of Nero' in 1879 stimulated the foundation of the National Museum. On the upper level, Christian martyrs are burnt at the order of a sullen Nero, placed lower down for compositional and symbolic reasons. 'Et lux in tenebris lucet', affirms the motto, 'et tenebrae eam non comprehenderunt'. 'Light shall shine in the darkness, and the darkness shall not devour it'. Jacek Malczewski (1854-1929), in his Warsaw self-portrait a comic mixture of Lenin and Mephistopheles, could be considered the Polish Akseli Gallen-Kallela. See for instance his 'Little Painter' (1890), and his moving 'Christmas Eve in Siberia'.

Józef Chełmoński (1849-1914) is perhaps best known for his 'Quadriga', hurtling headlong at you with speed, noise and colour, but I preferred the nearby 'Storm' and his loving delineation of the Polish countryside. Polish Impressionism, beginning with Aleksander Gierymski (1850-1901) and Julian Fałat (1853-1929), adds another dimension to the heroic style of Matejko and the tendencies of Malczewski, Siemiradzki, and Chełmoński. Those impressionists who took their cue from Paris, and from Poles influenced by the French, include Leon Wyczółkowski ('A Game of Croquet'), Józef Pankiewicz ('Hay Wain'), and Władysław Podkowiński ('The Wolverine' and the symbolist 'Fury').

The temptation of a Western visitor is to note only the derivative, the crude, and the rhetorical. Fame and international fortune evaded these artists, but they inhabited the same lands as Chopin, composing in his manor-house at Żelazowa Wola near Warsaw, and the same mental world as Mickiewicz, whose 'poem of the gentry' paradoxically became the national poem of all classes, including the numerically dominant peasantry. Staff, in a Franciscan moment, wrote of 'sister pine' and Kasprowicz listened to 'humming trees', just as Chełmoński painted the Sukiennice 'Forest Road'. His 'Estate' may evoke vivid memories of Maria Dąbrowska's classic novel *Nights and Days* so eloquently filmed in the Polish countryside. Poland's socialist masters might well consider Stanisław Przybyszewski's *Confiteor*: 'Art is a replica of what is everlasting, independent of all change or incidental circumstances, free of both time and space, and thus reflecting essence, or soul. An artist', he added, 'is anchored in the nation, but not in its politics nor in its external changes, only in what is everlasting.' This accounts for the almost religious urgency with which Poles approach music, painting, and poetry: the arts of essence, or soul.

I never rush around Rynek, for its atmosphere remains mediaeval in its tranquillity. Take a coffee; watch the children feeding pigeons; accept the chance of a conversation with a young student of English; take pleasure in the chivalry of a man kissing a lady acquaintance's hand. But leave plenty of time for S. Mary's, the celebrated Gothic church, and try to be there by noon, when the trumpeter plays to all four corners of the world, a message broadcast to celebrate the endurance of Cracow and Poland. A predecessor, blowing his trumpet from the tower to warn the citizens of the Tatar advance, was killed by an arrow in the throat and, ever since, all subsequent trumpeters have cut short their call.

The effect of S. Mary's is diminished by its corner position: one could hardly imagine Milan's Sant' Ambrogio being thus treated! Romanesque churches of the 11th and 13th centuries gave way to a Gothic church started in the 13th century and constantly remodelled until the 16th. The Trumpeter Tower is 81 metres high, with a 15th-century cupola; the lower bell-tower, with the bell cast in 1438 and called 'Half Sigismund' in reference to the greater bell on Wawel, supports a later 16th-century Renaissance spire.

S. Mary's was the church of Cracow's burghers and patricians, just as Wawel was the church of King and Court, so great men of the city vied for its richest chapels. The first Renaissance chapel on the left was dedicated to S. John the Baptist, by Seweryn Boner (financial adviser to the king), the standing tombstones for Boner and his wife dating from 1538.

The chancel is illuminated by light filtering through mediaeval stained glass on to early Baroque stalls, and murals by Jan Matejko and his pupils Wyspiański (1869-1907) and Mehoffer (1869-1946). The choir of 1365 is the oldest part of the church, but the monuments of the Cellari and Montelupi families date from the Renaissance.

Born in Horb on the Neckar, Swabia, in 1438, Wit Stwosz came to Cracow in 1477, and worked on the altar of S. Mary's that was to become the pride of Cracow, and one of the masterpieces of its age, carved, in limewood, gilded and polychromed. At eleven metres by thirteen, it is possibly the largest Gothic altar in Europe and it cost 2,808 florins, then roughly the entire budget of the city for one year. I recommend the exceptionally well-documented illustrated monograph by Tadeusz Chrzanowski, *The Marian Altar of Wit Stwosz* (Interpress, Warsaw, 1985). Gothic polychrome religious sculpture is hardly the most fashionable art-form today, yet it takes barely a moment for the mastery of Wit to take our breath away. When closed, the altar shows twelve panels in mezzo-rilievo. On the far left, the top scene compresses into one panel the Meeting of St. Joachim and S. Anne and the Annunciation to Joachim of the birth of a daughter; the middle scene

Cracow. S. Mary's Church

depicts the birth of the Virgin; the lower scene, the Presentation of the Virgin in the Temple. The left folding wing portrays from the lower panel upwards: Christ's Presentation in the Temple, the Dispute with the Doctors, and the Arrest. The right folding wing shows from the upper panel downwards the Crucifixion, Deposition and Entombment. On the far right, from the upper panel downwards one can identify Christ in Limbo, the Three Marys at the Tomb, and the 'Noli me tangere'. A uniform blue background adds a tranquil pictorial unit to the sculptural diversity, while the dense gilded canopy above each scene completes the eloquent grandeur. The predella and coping of the whole, are always visible whether the great altar is open or closed. While the predella is comparatively small and insignificant, demonstrating the theological view of the world before the Virgin through her antecedents in the Tree of Jesse, the coping reconstructed in the 19th century reverberates with spiritual power and glory: the heavenly Coronation of Mary, with her relationship to Poland emphasised by the country's patron saints Stanislaus and Adalbert.

When the altar is opened, the left wing can be seen to comprise three panels: the Annunciation to the Virgin, the Adoration of the Shepherds, and the Adoration of the Magi. The right wing presents the Resurrection, Ascension, and Descent of the Holy Spirit.

Nobody can fail to be moved by the boldness and originality of the huge central panel, in which massive lime trunks five centuries old were carved and coloured into light, delicate human figures lifesize and almost supernaturally lifelike.

At the lower level, saints are shown almost literally on a floor, surrounding the Dormition of the Virgin here shown bodily and not spiritually as in the 1475 'Assumption' by Franciszek of Sieradz in Wrocław Cathedral. On a higher physical and spiritual plane, though within the same arch and religious context, we see the Virgin reborn at the moment of her death as personifying *Ekklesia*, the universal church, in a golden canopy of heavenly blue. The crowd of apostles represents the whole of humanity, and five of them stand fully alert at this cardinal moment in the story of Catholic mankind. Their faces are quite individual, their fluttering shapely hands uncontrolled at this transcendent instant, but above all their robes billowing in sudden swirls reveal the tempestuous nature of what is occurring. The drapery, brilliantly gilded, glittering in shrewdly placed spotlights, arcs and droops, folds and flourishes in a mischief of cataracts whirling and dipping in a manner both abstract and decorative, as though the slightly elongated Gothic bodies beneath have only contingent reality.

While working in Cracow, Wit Stwosz created a stone bas-relief of Christ at Gethsemane for S. Mary's cemetery. Now in the National Museum in Cracow, the work can be seen not far from his miniature

Cracow. S. Mary's Church. The Marian Altar of Wit Stwosz

wooden Crucifix. Stwosz may be the sculptor of the great stone Crucifix on the Baroque altar at the end of the south aisle at S. Mary's (scholars disagree), but he is certainly not responsible for the much later Crucifix on the rood screen, once attributed to him but actually dated to 1520,' long after his departure for Nuremberg.

The former cemetery has been replaced by a charming square, with a fountain bearing a bronze boy copied from a figure on the Marian Altar. The adjacent late 15th-century Gothic church of S. Barbara is worth a visit, and my suggestion is to savour Rynek's houses, dating mainly to the 14th-16th centuries, and their portals, usually somewhat later in their present form. Number 6, partly occupied by the Family Planning Society, is popularly known as Szara Kamienica (Grey House), the magnificent residence of the Zebrzydowski and Zborowski patrician families. The national hero Kościuszko made his HQ here in 1794, and the Provisional Government theirs in 1848. Number 7 belonged to the Montelupis, whose emblem appears on the portal: the first regular coach for Venice started from this 'Italian House' in 1558. Number 8, At the Salamanders (Pod Jaszczurami), is occupied by the Salamanders Student Club and Theatre 38. If you can obtain entry, you can see Gothic ribbed vaults and parts of mediaeval walls on the ground floor. Number 9 is the original Boner Mansion, with a neo-classical attic surmounting Gothic and Renaissance window frames. Number 11, the Venetian House, housed envoys from la Serenissima to the King at Wawel. Number 12 was occupied for some time by the stuccoist Baldassare Fontana from Chiasso (Ticino, 1658-1738) who worked at S. Anne, S. Andrew, the Dominican Basilica, and sculpted the Archangel Michael for S. Mark's. The Pipan family lived at number 13, and apothecaries lived 'At the Sign of the Golden Head' almost continuously thereafter. Number 15, site of the Wierzynek Restaurant, is named for its original patrician household. Taken aback when first asked by a waiter if I wanted my main course to be accompanied 'with misery', I gamely acquiesced, and found to my amazement that the phrase 'z mizerią' actually defined finely-chopped cucumber with delicious sour cream. Nearby is a DESA showroom, and you can see a picture of the Virgin of 1718 on the residence of the Cellaris. On the corner of Ulica Bracka (Friars' Street), number 20 was the home of Spytek Jordan, a late 16th-century castellan of Wawel Castle: the Renaissance palace later belonged to the Potocki family, among others. Such palaces, enlarged by patricians from earlier and tinier town houses, were sacked by the Swedish invaders in the late 17th century, when the conquerors removed anything and everything, to the marble portals themselves, which is why we see later neo-classical portals today on much earlier houses. Try to see the Jordan Palace's hallway and courtyard, the first-floor ceilings on the Bolepinowski House, the first-floor polychromes in the Straszewski House, and the Gothic cellars of the Kromerowski House. Look for the image of S. John of Capistrano high up on the corner wall of number 26, the so-called House of the Prince. 'At the Rams' (Pod Baranami) has a famous weekend cabaret in the Gothic cellars here at number 27, and you should not miss the arcaded courtyard and neo-classical finish of the upper floors. 'At the Lamb' (Pod Jagnięciem) once belonged to the Florentine sculptor Santi Gucci (1550-c.1600). Number 34 is the Spisz Palace of the princely Lubomirski family, and number 35 the even more beautiful four-storey Krzysztofory Palace on the corner of Ulica Szczepańska. We shall visit the interior later, for here is a department of the Historical Museum of Cracow. For many years the innovative Cricot amateur theatre performed in the cellars, closing down in 1939; then in 1956 the painter and producer Tadeusz Kantor started up Cricot 2 (elsewhere), moving back here in 1960 when it ran not only avant-garde theatre and subversive cabaret, but also displays of photography, art, film shows and music recitals which could not be shown for whatever reason in 'official' theatres or galleries. The patron writer of Cricot 2 is Stanisław Ignacy Witkiewicz ('Witkacy'), the group's first production being his *The Cuttlefish*, but those of us who attended *The Dead Class* at the 1976 Edinburgh Festival will never forget this obsessive amalgam of Schulz, Gombrowicz and Witkacy, with Kantor's own powerful, weird and original theories about live marionettes and the 'theatre of death'. Needless to say, geniuses like Kantor run counter to the received prejudices of socialist art, and Kantor no longer runs Cricot 2.

'At the Pear' (Pod Gruszką), at Ulica Szczepańska 1, has Gothic ribbed vaulting, Renaissance polychrome, and Baroque stucco by Baldassare Fontana. During the 19th century these rooms buzzed to the conversation of the Sauer Coffeehouse, but today they are occupied by the Journalists' Club.

The remaining side of Rynek is less interesting perhaps, though number 47 is worth a look for the early 18th-century Baroque façade. If you turn down Sławkowska and cross over Ludwika Solskiego, you will come to Ulica Św. Marka, with S. Mark's Church, remodelled in the 15th century. S. John's St. houses at no. 12 a Museum devoted to the History and Culture of Cracow. The Gothic cellars, ground floor and first floor were extended in 1611 by Giovanni Petrini and Giovanni Trevano. The objects displayed nowadays are clocks, watches, and militaria such as pistols, rifles, cannon, armour, heavy swords of the 16th and 17th centuries, and on the lower floor a model showing the Floriańska Gate and Barbican in earlier times, when surrounded by a moat. On the upper floor, I was claustrophobically besieged by the throttling of time by innumerable ticks, tocks, chimes: the barely tolerable burden of wasting away, helpless to prevent a hundred clocks rubbing at the edges of my life, like perpetual sandpaper.

Number 14 is the studio-salesroom of the satirical cartoonist Andrzej Mleczko (b. 1949), who studied architecture in Cracow, but has since become nationally celebrated for his political caricatures in such magazines as *Polityka, Szpilki* and *Student*. Booklets of his cartoons hanging from strings were being eagerly studied by young men and women, who were crowding to buy posters, handbills, and booklets. His targets are platitudinous politicians, callous bureaucrats, and social and economic evils; in a one-party state his very existence is something extraordinary, to be cherished. For if you criticise a party member, you criticise the party that put him there, and because the party takes itself to be the only legitimate source of power and opinion you are criticising the legitimacy of the state itself. One cartoon by Mleczko shows several operators in a telephone exchange endlessly repeating their own phrases: 'There is no such number', 'Try again in twenty minutes', 'Put in a coin, put in a coin', 'Prrr, prrr, prrr, prrr'. Another depicts a familiar Minister cheerfully teaching his surly parrot: 'And now repeat after me. "I am free", "I am happy".'

At Number 11 in Ulica Św. Jana is the neo-classical façade of the Wodzicki Palace, erected in 1787 when the palace was rebuilt after fire.

The Lubomirski Palace dates from the 17th century but was acquired by the Czartoryski family in the 18th and Prince Lubomirski in the mid-19th. The Czartoryski Palace nearby is immediately comparable for its magnificence, and should be seen as an extension of the collecting genius of Isabella Fleming, who became Princess Izabela Czartoryska and wrote a popular history of Poland published in 1818. King Stanislaus Augustus devoted more time to the arts and education than to governing, importing Enlightenment ideas from France, artists from Italy, and musicians from Germany. Prince Adam Czartoryski and his family preferred to emphasise national traditions, which became crucial after the fall of the monarchy.

Poland in the later 18th century was fossilised into a class system with the Court at the apex, the landed gentry dominating the hereditary state administration, a small merchant class, and a huge peasantry. As in England or France at the same period, the aristocracy provided the spectacle (like the Rococo Czartoryski Gardens at Powązki, 1774-83) and the pageantry, creating town palaces, country villas, and even virtual states outnumbering in serfs some contemporary English counties or German princedoms. The Ogiński family developed musical excellence at Słonim, while the Czartoryskis among others collected national treasures. The Radziwiłł and Sapieha families of Lithuanian descent; the Ostrogskis and Zasławskis of Ukrainian descent; the Potockis, Branickis and Lubomirskis: all continued to strengthen their wealth and power, sometimes with Jewish aid, sometimes with foreign alliances of marriage or business. In *The Temple of Sybil*, Jan Paweł Woronicz (1757-1829) could quote Izabela Czartoryska's prophecy on the tragic homeland after the fall of the state, describing her collection of treasures apocalyptically. Paintings, textiles, sculptures, arms and armour, silverware and gold objects found their way to Puławy (their estate between Radom and Lublin) from Wawel, private mansions, palaces, and castles, being thus protected from the depredations of the Austrian, Prussian and Russian invaders. The Czartoryski treasures were confiscated with their estates when the 1831 revolution failed, but gradually the family recovered many of the items for their Paris home. The collections returned to Poland after the Franco-Prussian War of 1870, and are housed in the former Piarist convent, opposite the Baroque Piarist Church (1702-27) and in three other buildings on Ulica Pijarska. One must add the sad rider that the Nazis stole many of the most valuable items, and not all have found their way back. Every gallery is an enchanted meadow, with untold and uncounted surprises of flowers, plants and weeds; or a night sky spangled with a myriad stars, each of which vibrates with its own light and histories. In the Czartoryski the centre-piece is Leonardo da Vinci's 'Cecilia Gallerani', also known as 'A Lady with an Ermine', painted about 1483, shortly after Leonardo arrived at the court of Lodovico Moro. Gallerani became mistress to Lodovico in 1481, and the identification is proved by the typical pun on her name, *galé* being the Greek for marten or polecat, and by Lodovico's nickname 'Ermelino', or ermine. We recall the juniper *(ginevra)* in his portrait of Ginevra de' Benci (1474-8?) in Vaduz, and the knots *(vinci)* he used to symbolise his own name. It is Cecilia's vicious little animal which survives best from the master's hand, the dark background being recent, and repainting obvious in the lower hand, the left shoulder, and the dress below the creature's right claw. Despite all, la Gallerani remains the most attractive canvas in Poland and should not be missed by anyone even slightly affected by inexplicable genius.

Despite the dispersal of some fine works, many are still on show, such as Rembrandt's 'Stormy Landscape, with the Good Samaritan', of 1638, in which the Good Samaritan plays no more of a part than in the 'Stormy Landscape' in Brunswick. You might enjoy the fantastic mannerism of Alessandro Magnasco's 'Washerwomen' (his 'Barrel Organ Player' is in Warsaw), or the serene 'Holy Family' by Jacopo Palma il Vecchio (1480-1528).

An 'Adoration of Christ' here attributed to Lotto is not so ascribed by Bernard Berenson, but there seems no such difficulty about the deeply spiritual 'Master Dolorosa' of Aelbrecht Bouts (c.1460-1549). Enthusiasts for early Sienese paintings will appreciate the 'Crucifixion' (third quarter of the 14th century) which would have crowned a polyptych.

From the Czartoryski Gallery it is but a few steps to the Floriańska Gate and the Barbican, between the Haberdashers' Tower and the Joiners' Tower, both of the later 15th century. The first defences of Cracow were mediaeval wooden palisades, but in the 13th century stone walls and towers replaced the ineffective wooden barriers, and eight gates were closed at night to protect the citizens from sudden attack. To resist an expected attack by Turks or any other possible enemy, the Barbican was constructed in 1498-9 on the model of Arab fortifications which the Crusaders had seen and admired, and of Carcassonne, in southern France. The Barbican is now a museum, with some craft stalls and shops, including amber, silver, and superstitious ornaments such as amulets and pendants showing signs of the zodiac. Below the Barbican, the Rudawa river which encircled the town also filled this moat to a width of more than twenty metres: a daunting enigma for besiegers. The Floriańska tower, a responsibility of the furriers' guild, dates from 1300, though the Piast eagle above the gate is a recent work by Zygmunt Landman. Nearly 35 metres high, the tower withstands the centuries at once an object of aesthetic value and of defensive security.

If you follow Ulica Pijarska eastward you enter the vast Holy Spirit Square, dominated by the great Juliusz Słowacki Theatre, completed in 1891 in neo-classical style to a design by Jan Zawiejski based on the Paris Opera. It seats 922, and it remains the leading theatre outside Warsaw, enjoying especial respect for its conscientious attempt to present a rounded repertoire of Polish and foreign theatre, opera and ballet, all at prices which seem ridiculously low by Anglo-American standards. Performances are given not only on the 'Large Stage', but also in a 'Miniature Theatre' unobtrusively set at the back of the theatre. One evening I saw the opera company in Verdi's *La Traviata*, conducted by Ewa Michnik, with Krystyna Tyburowska in the title rôle. On another evening, I revelled in Słowacki's own Romantic tragedy, *Balladyna* (1834), with Beata Wojciechowska in the title rôle. The poet never saw his plays acted, having left Poland in 1831, but his mystical, fantastic evocation of antecedents to the national character recognised as 'Polish' today has been utilised on Solidarność posters. From his *Brother Marek*, the independent trade unionists proclaimed 'We'll never agree to be allies of kings, nor to yield in the face of the tyrants. Only from Christ do we take our commands, serving only the Mother of God!' Heady stuff, and in this case solidly historical, for Marek Jandołowicz (1713-99) *did* yell defiance at the Russians who were storming Bar (now in Soviet Ukraine) in 1768, prophesying the death of Poland, and her rebirth like a phoenix. Słowacki's thought, like that of his contemporary, the master-poet Mickiewicz, was impregnated by the Messianic teachings of Andrzej Towiański. Arriving in Paris from Lithuania in 1841, Towiański taught his fellow-exiles that they should purify themselves of all sin, for they were to return to Poland as saviours, undergoing persecution like the Israelites of old. Towiański's 'spiritual evolutionism' taught that spirits existing independently of God begged God to give them material form, but the form was so imperfect that the spirits within are obliged to carry out unceasing desperate attempts to reach a higher form of life, eventually grow weary, and must be strengthened by inner (and sometimes outer) revolution. Strands of these doctrines dangle in the theories of Teilhard de Chardin, Hegel and Marx, and have found their way as surely into Polish thought as Descartes or Existentialism infiltrate modern French thought.

Of course you can enjoy many other theatres in Cracow, concert-halls, and cabarets offering satirical fare. Ask for the cheaply-priced current 'Informator Kulturalny' at a 'Ruch' kiosk: the anwer 'nie ma' will mean that they have sold out or the new issue has not yet been delivered. I enjoyed a version of Rabelais' *Gargantua* at the Maszkaron Satirical Theatre, at Stalingrad Heroes Street 21, performed with a sly exuberance not exempt from a whiff of danger. Were there plain-clothes secret police totting up veiled references to the state and memorising the faces of those present? The Operetta plays to those nostalgic for old Vienna at Ul. Lubicz 28. The Old Theatre named for the actress Modrzejewska welcomes playgoers at Ul. Jagiellońska 1, and the Szymanowski State Philharmonic Hall caters for music-lovers at Ul. Zwierzyniecka 1. Others come and go, but I was curious to see a theatre built as recently as 1902, on the way to Nowa Huta, the Stalinist steelworks and proletarian city just east of Cracow. Nowa Huta, a stronghold of Solidarność, became famous outside Poland with Andrzej Wajda's film *Man of Iron,* publicly screened in Poland from July 1981. It caught the mood of a nation made conscious of its manipulation by the Party personally, politically, industrially. I cannot walk the spiritless streets of Nowa Huta without frustration at the dehumanization of man predicted by Ortega y Gasset. This is the time of enforced collectivisation so abhorred by the peasantry. Of introducing the Russian-style second-person plural 'Wy' instead of the third-person singular Polish 'Pan' (feminine 'Pani'). Of propagandistic art subsumed under the general title 'socialist realism' as if it were an autonomous artistic style instead of a political instrument of indoctrination. Nowa Huta was officially built without a church, to 'prove' the people had no need of religion. It took them twenty years to create a church after the foundation of Nowa Huta (1949) and its steelworks (1950). You can get there by tram no. 4 or bus, and the ten-kilometre excursion is instructive, if ugly: a cautionary tale for anyone momentarily enticed by the concept of a proletarian society.

Two thin-faced men in black leather jackets gave me directions to a plebeian 'Restauracja Teatralna' situated anonymous behind a block of shops and flats from which the paint was peeling in a forlorn attempt to get away. A smoke-filled hall was packed with beer-drinkers too polite to stare at me as I sauntered stiffly through, towards a darkened room with tables set with white covers. 'Sala Bezalkoholowa', proclaimed a nicotine-stained sign: 'Non-Alcoholic Room'. Defiantly, four middle-aged men came through into it, occupying one of the empty tables; they ordered beer and were served by a waitress, stout and pasty-faced, walking as though cursed with varicose veins. What did she recommend to eat? Hungarian goulash. Cheap, tasty, filling, and nourishing after a day's hard walking.

With a quarter of an hour to spare before the evening performance, I managed to find a War Museum, with a tank outside. A lad was clambering all over it as it glistened in the rain, and peering into the driver's cabin.

I attended a Polish-language performance of Gogol's *The Inspector-General* (1836) at the Teatr Ludowy ('People's Theatre') but was the only paying spectator. At the last minute a blank-faced unit of the military filed in, and only when the lights dimmed did they begin sniggering, with ribald comments at the satire on provincial Russian bureaucrats.

Nowa Huta. People's Theatre

The bus will take you back into Cracow to the main bus station (PKS) northeast of the Old City, very close to the main rail station (PKP), across the Planty from the Słowacki Theatre. Three parallel roads run south.

The first is Ulica Św. Krzyża (Holy Cross Street), now named after a Romanesque church replaced by the present 14th-century building, which is nearly all that remains after a demolition plan in Holy Spirit Square carried out in the 19th century. The whole square was once covered by mediaeval hospital buildings as ancient as the 13th century, but the only remnant of these at Ulica Szpitalna 21, is a building of the mid-15th century serving formerly as the hospital for the university students, now a Theatre Museum but worth visiting in its own right, with its own chapel, cellars, portals, and barrel-vaulting. At the corner of Szpitalna and the Little Market Square (Mały Rynek), look for the early 17th-century Renaissance house designed by Jan Zatorczyk and called Prałatówka, with a Latin inscription: 'Let it be open to friends and the poor'. The Little Market was formerly the province of the butchers' guild, which is why Holy Cross Street once bore the rather less spiritual name Pig Street.

The third of the parallel streets is the finest: Floriańska. It is also very fashionable, even perhaps chic, with fashion shops, jewellery, and elegant cafés. At No. 45, for instance, Jama Michalikowa became a haunt of writers such as Stanisław Przybyszewski, the playwright and novelist considered the leading light in Polish symbolism at the turn of the century. No. 34 is a Gallery of Contemporary Art, which comprises paintings, pottery, engravings, fabrics, woodwork and jewellery. No. 41 can be seen during museum opening-hours, for it is the former home of the major artist Jan Matejko (1838-1893). I was particularly keen to see this studio-home because Matejko appeals to me as a man, and because when you have finished Chapter 50 (about a visit to this very house), you have completed the Polish reader *Uczymy się polskiego* by Barbara Bartnicka and others (Wiedza Powszechna, Warsaw, 1984). The lower two floors date from the 16th century, the second from the 18th, and the third from the 19th. Jan's mother, née Rossberg, came from a family of saddlers who owned this house from 1794, but died when Jan was seven. Her husband Franciszek struck a new low in avarice by providing only one candle among seven sons and a daughter. Jan was appointed Director of the Fine Arts School in Cracow after studies in Cracow, Munich and Vienna. Matejko's major paintings are too large to be shown here, and should be explored in the galleries of Cracow, Lublin, Poznań, Wrocław, and especially Warsaw. But you can see here a study for 'Sobieski at Vienna', for example, and the jester Stanczyk pretending to have toothache. See Matejko's studio on the third floor, his sitting-room and bedroom on the first floor, and a fascinating array of historical costume, weapons, and drawings.

From the Matejko House, return through Floriańska Gate, cross Planty and Ulica Basztowa to Plac Matejki and the Academy of Fine Arts, as Matejko's school was renamed in 1910, though its establishment dates back to 1745, when painters – previously members of a guild – were first trained in the University.

Nearby S. Florian's Church may look Baroque to you now, but this is its sixth incarnation, following many catastrophes by fire. Whether a 'Florian' ever lived is doubtful, but Pope Lucius III sent the then Bishop of Cracow the purported remains of a Roman knight believed to have suffered martyrdom during the reign of Diocletian nine hundred years earlier, and at that distance there is no saying what are saintly relics... Jan Triciusz was responsible for the 'portrait' of S. Florian on the main altar (1686), but I suggest a glance instead at the mediaeval sculptures outside the chancel, with all the hallmarks of Wit Stwosz's studio.

The western side of the Old City is the old University Quarter, with the Church of S. Anne, and the Szolayski House on Szczepański Square.

S. Anne was modelled by Tylman van Gameren on Sant'Andrea della Valle in Rome and dates from 1689-1705. Baldassare Fontana created the elaborate stucco-work for which the university church became rightly celebrated. Opposite at No. 12 stands the Collegium named for its founder Bartłomiej Nowodworski, its charming Baroque arcaded courtyard built from 1639 to 1643. Next door at No. 8 is Collegium Maius, its graceful courtyard to Cracow what Christ Church's imposing Tom Quad is to Oxford: an eloquent symbol. The 'Greatest College' is the oldest seat of the 'Jagiellonian' University named for the second dynasty, but there was a *studium* somewhere in Cracow (we cannot be sure exactly where) during the Piast era.

The founding of Cracow University in 1364 took as its model the organization of Bologna (1088) and Padua (1222) in a charter by King Casimir, but the *studium* probably died with its founder six years later. King Ladislaus Jagiello reopened the *studium* in 1400, but adopted the organization of the more recent, closer universities of greater Germany: Prague, Vienna, Heidelberg, Cologne, Erfurt. Cracow University subsequently enjoyed almost uninterrupted prestige, drawing students not only from all parts of Poland, but also from Hungary, and from Germany itself.

Throughout the 15th century, church dignitaries, noblemen, merchants, poets and historians travelled to the Vatican and other strongholds of the Church, princely courts, business houses and vibrant centres of cultural life such as Rome, Bologna, Ferrara, Florence, Mantua, Milan, Padua and Venice. In 1569 Cardinal Stanislaus Hosius created a permanent hostel in Rome, enabling even young Poles without independent means to study, travel and live in Italy: in the 16th century, records show that more Poles were studying at times in Padua than in Cracow.

Cracow. Collegium Maius. Courtyard

Collegium Maius can be appreciated both for itself and for what it contains. The edifice enjoyed sensitive restoration in 1949-64, and you can see the arcaded courtyard of 1492-7 even when the museum is closed; here are fragments of architectural decoration and sculpture. The ground floor *lectoria* have murals and objects connected with the study of science: Copernicus studied here under the astronomer and mathematician Wojciech of Brudzew, but was only one star in a constellation including Conrad Celtis (1459-1508), a wandering humanist whose exuberant Latin poetry caused him to be crowned laureate in 1487 by Frederick III. Celtis founded the literary society known as Sodalitas Litteraria Vistulana, and his contemporary Filippo Buonaccorsi (also known as Callimachus) founded another society of humanists in Cracow, including university men and courtiers.

The Professors' Staircase leads to the spacious upper rooms, the largest being the Aula, with a wooden ceiling, a Renaissance portal declaring the motto *Plus ratio quam vis*, 'Reason rather than Force'. The treasury includes a gilded copper and brass globe of 1510 inscribed in Latin 'America, newly discovered land'. Next to the treasury rooms is the Common-Room, used as a refectory for teaching staff; then comes the original Library, or Corner Room.

Collegium Minus is to be found in Ulica Gołębia, parallel with S.

Anne's St., at No. 11, Collegium Physicum at No. 13, Collegium Slavisticum at No. 20. The present headquarters of the University at No. 24, called Collegium Novum, were rebuilt after a fire in 1883-7. Copernicus can be seen in a sculpture by Cyprian Godebski (1900) outside Collegium Novum, and in a painting by Jan Matejko within. The valuable University Library at Ul. Mickiewicza 23 contains more than a million and a half volumes, including numerous incunabula and manuscripts, such as the Balthasar Behem *Codex* of 1505 with miniatures of everyday life such as a goldsmith's and bellfounder's, and a manuscript (mainly in the author's own hand) of Copernicus' *De revolutionibus orbium coelestium* published in the year of his death: 1543.

Retracing our steps northward to Plac Szczepański, we find at No. 9 the Szolayski House, with its exhibition of Polish art from the Middle Ages to the 18th century. Throughout the centuries Polish art and artists have suffered from a crisis of confidence, and insecurity due to a feeling of being provincial: distant from the artistic centres of Western Europe, mainly Italy, Germany, latterly Moscow in terms of ideological orthodoxy and Paris and New York in terms of free expression. So the mediaeval art here owes much to German masters and Germanic influences such as Saxon madonnas. The so-called Beautiful Madonna of Krużlowa (c. 1410) in limewood is one of these; another is a slightly earlier Madonna and Child. I preferred a delicate tomb-painting for Wierzbięta of Branice (c. 1425), the fully-armoured knight diminutive and humble against the green satin drapery of the Madonna's cloak. The local artist Mikołaj Haberschrack painted panels for the Church of S. Catherine's in Cracow after 1468. Side panels from a Lusina polyptych (c. 1500) have been attributed to the school of Wit Stwosz, but no attribution is possible to a polyptych of S. John the Mendicant (c. 1504) from the Augustinian Monastery in Cracow. Hans Dürer's 'S. Jerome' dates from 1526, eight years before the artist's death in Cracow.

Sequentially, the latest epoch of official Polish art is to be sought in the New Building ('Nowy Gmach'), facing the Old City across the inner ring road to the east and Hotel Cracovia (with its good bookshop) to the south. Here are approved artists, more adventurous than Soviet official art of the 20th century but too often followers rather than leaders such as the abstract painter Henryk Stażewski or the Francophile Józef Pankiewicz. The best Polish artists transmuted Western movements into Polish styles: Lebenstejn, Rudowicz, Jonasz Stern, but the aggressive 'Young Poland' visionary Stanisław Wyspiański stands almost alone in his magnificent portraits, his plays, his poems and his book illustrations, utilising techniques of intimist realism, melancholy symbolism, and powerful expressionism. His travels reflect his restlessly eclectic art: France, Italy, Switzerland, Germany, Czechoslavakia, and above all Poland.

The Jewish community has been of crucial importance in the history of Poland since 1335, when the last Piast ruler, Casimir the Great, gave the Jews sanctuary after their persecution and expulsion from Bohemia, Germany and Spain. But a community is recorded in Cracow in the 13th century, living in the region of S. Anne's St. As the *studium* needed new buildings, Jewish properties were bought up and the Jews moved to Plac Szczepański, but soon the competition of Jewish money-lenders, merchants and artisans proved intolerable to the Cracow citizens who, after the pretext of a fire in 1494, urged King Jan Olbracht to expel the Jews from the city. They decided to settle in the suburb of Kazimierz (just north of the Vistula bend), concentrating in the district bounded by Józefa, Bożego Ciała, Miodowa and Dajwór.

Fires repeatedly devastated Kazimierz, one in 1504 destroying the southern part completely. Floods of the Vistula and plagues, especially that of 1651, endangered Kazimierz, but the Swedish occupation of 1655 posed the severest threat, 173 houses being damaged out of the total of 430. Kazimierz was permanently joined to Cracow in 1791 by the Great Sejm. In 1812, Jews were permitted to settle in the Christian sector of Kazimierz, so that towards the second half of the 19th century they comprised about 75) of the town's population, as opposed to 30) of the whole population of Cracow city. In 1939, the city's Jewish population totalled 68,400, but only a few hundred survived the Nazi invasion.

Kazimierz's Christian sector centres on Plac Wolnica, with a 16th-century Renaissance Town Hall later used by the Jewish community as an elementary school and rebuilt (1875-6) with a new pseudo-Renaissance southern wing. It was transformed into an Ethnographic Museum in 1947.

The Nazis destroyed Warsaw Ethnographic Museum's collections in World War II, but they kept the Cracow collections in the Institut für Deutsche Ostarbeit (Sektion Rassenkunde) as objects of anthropological interest concerning a race that they had determined should become extinct. Many private collectors (Seweryn Udziela, Józef Świstek, for instance) doggedly built up their own collections to represent Polish folk culture, and some fifty thousand items have been collected over the years, in an attempt to compensate for racist depredations. More than 300 complete folk costumes, mainly from Southern Poland, offer a lavish overview of mainly rural clothes, with for instance a bridal party, the veiled bride in a myrtle wreath. A peasant cottage reconstructed from east of Cracow shows naive religious paintings, and paintings on the wooden ceiling, walls and doors. Here are glass paintings from Lower Silesia, papercuts from Łowicz, and a wayside oaken shrine from Anielów (Siedlce) made in 1858, showing a 'Sorrowing Christ' in limewood inscribed 'Holy Jesus, Holy and Strong,

Holy and Eternal, Have Pity on Us'. Other European cultures represented include Byelorussia and Ukraine, Germany, Austria and Czechoslovakia, while Asia is pre-eminently represented by objects from Indonesia, Tibet, Mongolia, and northern U.S.S.R. Pieces have come from Peru, Colombia, and Brazil. African items typify work from Tanzania, Ethiopia, Sudan and Nigeria, the Bushmen, Cameroon, and the Arab North.

The present Church of Corpus Christi (1405) possesses stained glass windows of 1420 and Baroque choir-stalls of 1624-32. Casimir, who established the original Corpus Christi in 1340, two years later founded S. Catherine's, which was completed about 1400 and likewise represents the Cracow Gothic school in its five-span presbytery and pillar-buttress design. A third Gothic church, of the later 15th century, was owned by Paulines brought to Kazimierz by Jan Długosz, but this was replaced in 1733-51 by a Baroque church dedicated to SS. Michael and Stanislaus, and designed by Antoni Mützer and Antoni Solari. It too is named for its position the Church on the Rock, twin towers on the west front rising into the sky high above the Vistula.

But we have come here to mourn the passing of all but a few shattered fragments of Jewish Cracow, virtually confined now to Ulica Szeroka, 'Broad Street'. At one end rises the Old Synagogue, converted into a Judaic Museum, with broken walls of the ancient Jewish quarter protruding through overgrown land like stumps of teeth through an old man's gums. The first synagogue on this site dated from about 1500 in a style familiar from Worms and Prague, suggesting a Bohemian or Rhenish origin, with two naves and a late Gothic vault on two columns. This synagogue fell victim to fire in 1557, and for thirteen years thereafter the Florentine architect Matteo Gucci laboured intermittently on a new Renaissance façade and interior. The original synagogue consisted of only three rooms: the Prayer Hall exclusively for men, a room adjacent to the Prayer Hall, and a women's gallery above it. Subsequently, a Cantor's Room and Women's Room were added, at the south, and other changes were made before the large-scale neo-Renaissance reconstruction by Zygmunt Hendel (1913-23). The Nazis desecrated the building, using it as a warehouse, and plundered everything of value. Postwar restoration (1957-9) has brought back pride, if not wealth, and echoes of the centuries resound again, if feebly. The Hebrew inscription above the arch on the Renaissance portal signifies, 'This is the gate of the Lord; only the righteous may enter'.

In the Prayer Hall, reading and explication of the Scriptures took place on the Sabbath and festivals, and part of the Torah was recited from the *bimah* or raised platform in the centre. A cantor sang from his prayer-book on a lectern to the right of the stairs leading to the platform in front of the altar shrine. Parchment scrolls of the Torah were kept in a niche on the east wall. Showcases present prayer-books and scriptural commentaries. Paintings in the adjoining Cantors' Hall include a series by the notable 'ghetto-painter' Artur Markowicz (1872-1934). Sombre portraits of Cracovian and Galician Jews seem to foresee a destiny as black as the haunted past, as in the pastel 'Jews in a Synagogue' (1923). By contrast the radiance of Heaven permeates the upper half of I.K. Hruzik's 'Jews Praying in the Old Synagogue' (1879). Showcases have scrolls of the Torah, and breastplates: one Torah has a complete set of ornaments, and one silver breastplate from Wrocław is dated 1796-1800, showing Moses and Aaron with an opened Torah. Among other objects on display are *atarahs* (embroidered strips sewn on to prayer shawls) and *tephillin* (leather prayer-cases with extracts from the Pentateuch, or first five books of the Old Testament), strapped as a pair to the left forearm during prayers.

The Women's Hall offers an insight into Jewish festivals. Sabbath is exemplified by candlesticks for Sabbath candles, spice-boxes, *kiddush* or sanctification cups, and special tablecloths embroidered with references to Sabbath. Passover is represented by *seder* plates and matzah bags. The Festival of Lights or Hanukkah is recalled by candelabra: brass for the poorer Jews in the *shtetl*s or Jewish communities of the countryside, and silver for the richer urban Jews; most examples date from the 19th century. The Festival of Lots or Purim is commemorated by a display of special cases for scrolls of the Book of Esther. Other objects are connected with birth, circumcision, marriage, divorce and death. The upper floor has two rooms with photographs and paintings of the Jews in Cracow, and events during World War II. Nazi persecution in Kazimierz began officially in September 1939 with the requirement that every Jew over 12 years of age should wear a white distinguishing armband, and every Jewish shop or company should be similarly marked. On 13 March 1943 a thousand Jews were massacred where they lived, six thousand were taken to the nearby death camp at Płaszów, and the rest transported towards Auschwitz, but half of these were murdered in forests at Skawina on the way.

A synagogue at the other end of Ulica Szeroka, No. 40, still functions, and its disused cemetery founded by Israel Isserles in 1552 exists as yet another *memento mori* in a city where images of the past seem to follow in your footsteps, and leap out at you from every corner. A scattering of silent, ancient Jews sat around or stood. An old woman offered me a skull-cap so that I should not enter the active synagogue building bareheaded. Within the small synagogue, I closed my eyes for silent minutes before examining the Renaissance ark of the covenant. Outside again, a black and white cat recognised my companionable felinity, rubbing against my leg and raising her head for a stroke. On an outer wall a myriad of smashed tomb-stones had been lovingly collected and

Cracow. Jewish Cemetery in Kazimierz

patched up in piety. 'To the Memory of Max Judd who loved children, died May 7 1906, donated by his fond wife Jennie'. Many such gifts are mutilated beyond recognition, but even more have been destroyed by the lunatic, evil rage of Jew-haters and their henchmen. So it is with an indrawn breath of wonder that one steps through into the 'secret garden'. During conservation work after World War II, workers discovered tombstones that had been buried to avoid desecration by Swedish troops during the city's occupation in 1704, and among seven hundred rescued graves, some dating back more than four centuries, archaeologists identified remarkable Renaissance sarcophagi carved under Italian influence.

The cemetery is called Rema, after the abbreviation for 'Rabbi Moses', son of Israel Isserles. His tomb bears an inscription testifying *Mi Moshe ad Moshe lo kam ke Moshe.* (From Moses (Maimonides) to Moses (Isserles) there was no greater Moses). The present burial-place for Jews in Cracow can be found off Ulica Miodowa, to the right of the railway line. Let us remember here the great rabbis of Old Poland, among them Elimelech of Leżajsk, Yehaskel Shraga of Sieniawa, and Hayyim and Aaron Halberstam in Nowy Sącz.

At Ulica Szeroka 16 you can find the former Poper Prayer-House of 1620, and at nearby Ulica Józefa 38, a Renaissance Prayer-House known as Wysoka, meaning 'high' or 'tall'. The so-called Isaac

Prayer-House in Ulica Jakuba 25 has a hall stuccoed by Giovanni Falconi. Wandering around Kazimierz, you may come across the Spytek Jordan Palace at Miodowa 41, housing the Monument Restoration Enterprise. Ulica Krakowska possesses numerous architectonic details of interest, as well as the late Baroque Trinitarian Church of the Order of S. John of God, designed by Francesco Placidi (1752-8), and at no. 13 the neo-classical Raczyński Palace. In a historical atmosphere as thick as honey, I scrutinised Krakowska 9, 20, 22, 26, 29, 36, 47 and 50; Józefa 11, 12, 25, 28 and 41, and 19th-century attics and balustrades, typified by Bożego Ciała 21 and Augustiańska 17. At Skawińska 8 is the Jewish Hospital.

Here in Cracow, of a population in 1900 totalling 91,310, 65,310 were Poles, 5,000 Germans, and more than 21,000 Jews. These last, their children, and their grandchildren were massacred amid scenes equalled only by the Soviet 'great terror' under Lenin, Stalin and their successors, in a process of totalitarian dictatorship still, if to a much lesser extent, persisting, and documented by Robert Conquest in *The Great Terror*. In satellite Poland, nothing is officially known or said about the latter, but the Hitlerite atrocities are exhibited at the sites known in Polish as Oświęcim and Brzezinka, and to the rest of us in German forms: Auschwitz and Birkenau.

Auschwitz

It was with a coward's beating heart that, early one morning, the sky stained yellow with dawn, I caught a train from Cracow to Oświęcim. About sixty kilometres of flat land and polluted streams and rivers separate mediaeval Cracow from the concentration camps. A sign in the sky above a building made me shiver: 'Koncentraty, Skawina'. Hayfields and trees near Jaśkowice, by contrast, could have been photographed in Suffolk. I gazed around the railway compartment for consolation: a civil servant, formally dressed in suit and tie and polished shoes, correctly scrutinised every word of *Dziennik Polski*. A young married couple, at the stage where silence is no longer interpretable as callous or rude, held hands, he with a Lech Wałęsa beard and moustache, both with pullovers, open-necked shirts, jeans and sneakers, she with a golden cross on a gold chain round her neck. Near Brzeźnica some horses pulled ploughs, others carts. Men looked into the broken-up earth as if for an answer to a question too obvious to state. Past Zator, tractors in flat fields made modern progress, emulating our little local train for speed. I engaged conversation with a student from Poznań, the only one in the compartment with enough English to allow me to speak at a level above the conventional. He described the *nomenklatura* system of elitism by which Poland is actually run, ensuring that all key positions in the State are held by 'safe' hands. As the economy collapses, and the black economy ascends in power and profitability, the privileges attainable by 'safe' bureaucrats become ever more desirable and consequently more eagerly sought. It is common knowledge that hidden benefits accrue to those in power: holidays at resorts closed to the public; hospitals with private rooms and resources in a country agonisingly short of medical supplies; special apartments, shops, cars... And yet the young may not rebel, at least openly, on the streets. His father had protested in 1968 about the closing of Mickiewicz's classic play *Dziady* at Warsaw's National Theatre, because the audience had seen fit to applaud in the wrong places: 'We Poles have sold our souls for a few roubles'. And so on. Students had congregated around the Mickiewicz monument to convey their anger at the closing of the classic Polish play on 30 January 1968, and the police had moved in on them, arresting thirty-five people. This was during Gomułka's Poland.

I was sorry to say goodbye to the young man from Poznań, even if his attitude towards his father's outrage seemed ambivalent, but the train was slowing into Oświęcim, and my short walk to the concentration camp began. Try to read the autobiography of Rudolf Hoess, *Commandant of Auschwitz* (1959), and hope that you cannot begin to comprehend the vicious racist hatred implied in it throughout. Himmler sent Hoess to see how extermination should be carried out, at Treblinka, but Hoess thought arrangements there 'rather primitive' and decided on a more 'efficient' plan, to be based on a settlement near Auschwitz, the hub of four railway lines. From April 1940 he quickly cleared the thinly-populated vicinity of Poles who could have borne witness, and on 14 June the first transport of Poles arrived: 728 political prisoners, from Tarnów. As a rule, prisoners fit for work would be sent to Auschwitz, and those unfit direct to the gas chambers at Birkenau: some four million in all probability, though of course the exact figures could never be known: first Poles, then Jews from Poland, Russians, Czechs, Yugoslavs, Greeks, Dutchmen, Belgians, Germans... wherever there was a Jew to be hunted out in the so-called 'Final Solution'. The most moving story of a victim is probably *Se questo è un uomo* (1947) by Primo Levi, translated as *If this is a Man*, with its companion volume *La tregua* (The Truce) and meditative sequel, *I sommersi e i salvati* (1986). Levi does not seek to denounce, to avenge himself or his murdered companions, but to understand. On his left forearm he bore, to the day of his suicide in 1987, the tattooed number 174517. I cannot relate to 'four million' or suchlike gigantic numbers. And there is no souvenir of Primo Levi. So I sought one lost soul with whom to communicate among the hundreds of melancholy portrait photographs lining the blockhouses in Auschwitz. There he is: Płoszyński, Edward, born 5 October 1913, a government official, shaven of course, arrived in Auschwitz 5 April 1941, died 18 October 1941. A man who managed to last out more than six months. I can hardly bear to remember more than this, but we must all make the effort. If travel elsewhere broadens the mind, struggling around the emotional minefield of Auschwitz must deepen it.

As you enter the barbed-wire encampment, the horrendous jibe 'Arbeit Macht Frei' stands in Mephistophelean immortality above the entrance where 'Abandon hope, all ye who enter here' would be more apposite. The first major arrival of Soviet prisoners-of-war occurred on 7 October 1941, and more than thirteen thousand are known, but on liberation in 1945 only 92 remained alive. Over twenty thousand gipsies arrived in Birkenau, of whom virtually none survived. After 'selection' for death at the ramp at Birkenau, following long train journeys in closed carriages from all over occupied Europe, Jews and other victims

Auschwitz. Barbed-wire fence and corner watch-tower, from Block 25

were told they were going to the bathhouse. They would be shaved, women would have their hair cut off, and they would be bludgeoned and crowded, two thousand at once, into a chamber. The door would be closed, and the poison gas Cyclon B discharged into the room. In Block 4, Room 4, tins and samples of Cyclon B capsules can be seen today, having caused 'death due to suffocation, accompanied by sensations of fear, dizziness, and vomiting.'

Time and again the heartrending words of Marina Tsvetaeva knocked at memory's door: 'Za chuzhie ya grekhi terpela', 'For the sins of someone else I suffered', words just distant enough from the New Testament to enact their own drama beyond the door.

A few days before Auschwitz was liberated, Nazi troops set fire to all warehouses, but not everything was consumed in the flames. The Soviet Army found 348,820 men's suits, 836,525 women's dresses, 13,694 carpets, about 43,000 pairs of shoes, and mountains of suitcases ('M. Frank, 12.4.45 HOLLAND' was scrawled on one I saw), toothbrushes, shaving-brushes, spectacles, artificial limbs and crutches. If you have the courage, you can enter cellars used for punishment cells, and exhibitions of executions and punishments (Block 11, rooms 11-12), or of the extermination of national groups: Hungary, U.S.S.R., Czechoslovakia, Germany... Two and half million Jews, as well as criminals and political offenders. 'No poetry after Auschwitz', cried Adorno, but what is a poet if not someone who can understand the deepest tragedy and convey his grief with the compassion of art? Yet after all, in the last hour we spend within the confines of the barbed wire, mercifully no longer liable to electrocute us, we should be completely silent. There is no better eloquence in a dirty world.

Auschwitz

A few fields in Poland commandeered:
no, I cannot understand 'six million dead'
but I can remember six:

remember the shorn head of Bogdan Tkaczyk
farmer, Wadowice,
who thought he never made any trouble
but the Jew he helped to escape
was caught, and though nobody
squealed to the Nazis,
somehow they knew
by the shadows in his forehead,
the darkness in his step,
the cut of his old jacket,
the mud on his boots,
the knot in the wood on his door,
that he was the one
the one to blame.

remember Andrzej, son of lame Leszek,
surnamed Kuźma, from Trzebinia,
government clerk, cunning, a winner.
    To become Blockmeister you must know what they want,
sprechen deutsch aber *sehr* gut, you must say
'jawohl' instead of 'ja', remove glasses from
those who wear them, pass the roll-call numbers
to the Blockführer, keep alert (smiling
is for *Untermenschen*) and never ask for favours,
except to serve the Reich.

remember Grymaszowska, Alicja, factory-worker,
Katowice, daughter of Pan Marek and Pani Anna,
deep-voiced, hoarse from shouting
fairy-tales
to myself
amid the terrible machines
that in my dreams waved levers,
pulleys, wheels, towards me,
swallowing my fairy-tales. 'Alicja
will never marry', said a girl in
the lavatory, hoping I could hear.
'She sings like a frog'. I hoped
for a blue-eyed man who would ask me
to undress, once. Here, I am to undress
tomorrow.

remember Regina Matraszek, housewife,
Częstochowa, who stared at the wall,
transferring her memories to the bricks,
turning her back at the sun as it slunk up
on the morning, for 'just another day'
as in her childhood, as though nothing
could change. She goes back to dozing,
sitting in the cracks of other people's lives,
dreading to be left alone. 'Before the War,'
was all she ever said, 'you could set the
clock by the trains coming through'.

remember Ryszard Okoń, actor from Kraków,
playing the part of Shylock too often,
mistaken for the real man. 'I came first
in the drama school, first to the watchtower
above the forbidden fence, about ten thousand
four hundred and twenty-ninth to the chamber,
where I was to take a shower'. My name
was Ryszard Okoń.

remember Bogumil Żyżuń, last in his
class at school, his mouth opening
like a cod's on failing to grasp
the right idea, the right word, the right globe
on which his simplicity could fit
like a glove in relief. This is the

suitcase
which he bought with the last
of his money,
to bring his clothes
to Auschwitz.

As I shook the dust of Auschwitz from my dull shoes, birds made me blush with indignation at their untroubled song. Their innocence, my innocence (I was a babe-in-arms at the start of World War II), but a landscape still heavy with guilt, shadowy with shameful secrets. At the end of the long, winding flat country road, empty except for two or three cars, a cyclist, an old woman in black trudging with a sack (of fodder?) on her back, loomed the main gate of Birkenau, with the Nazi guardhouse atop. Prisoners from Auschwitz began to construct Birkenau from October 1941. Höss records: 'According to the orders of SS Reichsführer, only the strongest of the Russian prisoners-of-war were to be chosen... They were dying off because of general exhaustion, succumbing to even the slightest illness because they were too weak to resist. I saw them dying even as they chewed beet or potatoes.' The barracks and crematoria then built have been left just as the fleeing Nazis abandoned them. Doors creak. Leaves rustle in corners like nesting mice. In Block 21, my fingers traced the curve of long wash-basins, with uniform places for pieces of soap: a manic Prussian tidiness in the face of unutterable horror. Flies buzzed in the warmth. Peasants were scything grass between the long lines of low barracks. I realised that the majority of people who ever came to Birkenau had been slaughtered here. Today, very few of the visitors who flock to Auschwitz ever continue to these isolated barracks, each seemingly identical to the next, until you notice the graffiti, fragrant of written pain prolonging those screams. Women lived in Auschwitz until 16 August 1942, when they were transferred to Birkenau, in three-tiered bunks, as many as six or eight to a bunk. Humiliation led to mental breakdown, then to physical breakdown. Separated from the sight of male prisoners, their horizon was limited to barbed wire, barracks, and watchtowers permanently manned by guards with machine-guns. I walked along the railway track, standing motionless beside the ramp where closed railway-carriages were at last thrown open, allowing inmates a hideously cruel illusion of fresh air before they were gassed to death. Not far from the ruinous crematoria is the monument to 'Four million killed here, 1940-5'. As you explore the mysterious fields where murder was inscribed as the first item on the human agenda, you will come across the sardonic hoardings 'Chodzenie po ruinach jest niebezpieczne': 'Walking among the ruins is dangerous'.

What you will not find – either at Auschwitz or in any other public museum, library or monument – is a tribute to the 14,500 Polish officers and intellectuals who were 'made to disappear' from Soviet prisoner-of-war camps in 1940. The remains of 4,143 of them were uncovered by the German Army in the Katyn forest near Smolensk, and an investigating tribunal discovered evidence that the massacre of Katyn took place not after the Germans invaded that area but before: the massacre of Poles at Katyn is therefore a war crime of the Soviet Government, but is unpublicised in Poland because of its client status towards the U.S.S.R.

The humming of millions of cicadas reminded me of that other dead city, Pompeii, annihilated by the intelligible natural disaster of a volcanic eruption. I remembered the dead of Sobibor, too, of Treblinka, Chełmno, Bełzec. More than a million Polish Christians died in the camps altogether, but in Birkenau the Nazis boasted that they could gas and burn sixty thousand victims *in one day*.

Tyniec and Wolski Forest

If you have time, try to see the Ojców National Park 22 km northwest from Cracow on the road E22 in the direction of Częstochowa. The Ojców Valley, with ruined castles on its peaks giving it the name 'Eagle-Nests' Trail', was created by the river Prądnik. Permeable limestone has been worn into gorges and caverns; in caves at Ojców it is related that Ladislaus the Short found refuge at the end of the 13th century, against the might of Wenceslaus of Bohemia. The castle of Pieskowa Skała, restored during the Renaissance, houses fine art and furniture of that period and may be visited.

Much closer to Cracow, on opposite banks of the Vistula west of the city, are Tyniec, a village dominated by a Benedictine Monastery, and the Zoological Gardens of Wolski Forest, a pleasant weekend resort for Cracovians of all ages.

From the main railway station of Cracow take the bus 119 to Grunwald Bridge ('Most Grunwaldski'), then change to a 112, departing roughly every half-hour. The bus drops you in the village centre, and a gentle ten-minute stroll uphill brings you through pleasant lanes flanked by private homes with gardens full of sunflowers and fuchsias, dahlias and chrysanthemums. At last, you reach an 11th-century Romanesque church, raised by King Boleslaus the Bold, which suffered many vicissitudes, becoming in turn Gothic and Baroque: it is in the latter, 17th-century, reincarnation that we find it today. The original 11th-century monastery too has gone, though recent excavations brought to light graves in a crypt below the chancel with a leaden cross, a golden crozier, and a 12th-century golden chalice and paten, all now in the Treasury at Wawel.

The fortified monastery we see today dates from the 15th century, with later additions and restoration. I chatted with one of the Benedictine brothers, who is accustomed to visitors all the year round, and particularly in the Summer, when organ concerts are held here. He indicated the range of monastic orders still active in Poland: Cistercians in four locations, Samaritans, Missionaries, Loretanians, Camaldolenses, Oblates, Sacramentalists, and many Benedictines. A 15th-century polychrome can be seen in the chapter-house, and a very deep well in the courtyard, making the brothers self-sufficient in water at least. The view northward across the Vistula in the warm dusk sunlight could have been copied from Constable's *Hay Wain*, yapping dogs, wooden carts, lazy clouds and all.

In good weather, you could take a bus or one of the taxis at a rank (there are no cruising taxis in Poland) from Cracow to the zoo at Wolski Forest (ask for 'Las Wolski') and to the 16th-century palace of Ludwig Dietz, follower of Erasmus, and secretary-eulogist to King Sigismund the Old. We have a Latin letter of 1523 from Erasmus to the banker and humanist Dietz, or Decius, in which he compliments Poland 'which in the past was mocked for its barbarity, on the fact that it has left barbarism behind it in science and law, customs, religions and all else, so that it blooms, and can bear comparison with the leading nations of the world'.

Wieliczka
Ever since exploring salt-mines at Hallein, near the aptly-named Salzburg, I have longed to see the fabulous mines below Wieliczka, a town of 16,000 inhabitants thirteen kilometres southwest of Cracow, and best reached by train from Cracow main railway station. The salt-bearing strata were formed 18-20 million years ago, during the Miocene, and prehistoric men produced salt from the strata as early as the Neolithic, that's about 3,500 B.C. Intensive mining began shortly before 1290, and within a few decades the revenues from salt underpinned a third of Casimir's expenditures, thus necessitating a protective town wall with eleven towers and a royal castle. Three hundred kilometres of galleries and shafts have been excavated on nine main strata or 'flats' and other subsidiaries, from 64 metres down to 342 metres down. The oldest preserved shaft, the 'Royal', dates from the early 14th century; with the passage of time, more shafts and galleries were needed, so that the present extent is six km long and 1 km wide. The upper three flats contain big, detached rocks occurring in loam, slate and sand; the lower six flats contain salt-bearing layers interleaving strata of slate, sand, gypsum and loam.

The mines were opened to tourism in 1935, but only the upper third is shown in part. You descend in a lift (not for claustrophobes) down the Daniłowicz shaft sunk in 1638, then walk down 394 steps (not for the infirm) and you should be warmly dressed, and braced for a three-hour adventure through halls and shafts, galleries and rooms reminiscent of Wagner's Nibelheim. Next to the 17th-century Copernicus stall is the coeval, breathtaking Chapel of S. Anthony, in which the miner-sculptor Antoni Kuczkowski provided us with a practical ecstasy, hewing in rock-salt not only the figures of a dozen saints, but also three altars, portal, and pulpit. Since the miner leading you may know no English, you will want to be prepared for the Great Legend stall, also of 17th-century age, with its modern life-size salt statue of Princess Kinga, daughter of Bela IV, and five others: knights from Hungary and Poland, and three miners. According to legend, the 13th-century princess on her way to marry Boleslaus the Shy threw a ring into a well in Hungary and, stopping at Wieliczka, ordered miners to dig a well to recover her ring, subsequently miraculously found. Hungary was then rich in salt, runs the legend, but Poland was poor, so the discovery of her ring in a deep shaft full of salt induced the local people to mine salt, forever solving the salt famine. Needless to say, there is no truth in this story, for salt had already long been mined here, but it may reflect folk-memory about the sinking of new shafts when old galleries had been mined clear. Nearby is a stall so frequently 'gutted by fire' that it has kept this title; the worst, in 1644, lasted for several months, killing men and horses. Methane gas, constantly threatening the lives of miners, had to be burned away by experts. They crawled on all fours to avoid disturbing the upper air too violently and wore a hooded cloak to protect their head and body, so they were respectfully known as 'penitents'. A miner-sculptor carved three such 'penitents' in rock-salt in 1972; another recently produced a huge figure of Casimir the Great, after whom this next hall is named. Casimir's Statutes of 1368 codified laws and customs in salt-mining, and regulated the production and marketing of the salt. Still overwhelmed by the unremitting industry of men, I zigzagged down the wooden steps of the excavated cave named for the village of Pieskowa Skała, enjoying the variety of salty stalactites like crystallised seaweed. Folklore about friendly underground 'salt-lovers' is personified by eight frolicking gnomes; the *solilubki* governed by the White Mistress of the mines, Salt White and the Eight Dwarfs, made in 1962-4. After the Holy Cross Chapel, we come to the magnificent Hall of Princess Kinga, excavated in the 17th century and transformed into a shrine by the Markowski brothers from 1896 to 1912. A ballroom effect is achieved by the grandiose dimensions, from which ten thousand cubic metres of salt have been removed; by five glorious chandeliers of salt; and by an ornate altar. Yet this is incredibly only half the volume of the 18th-century Michałowice Hall, reinforced with wooden supports in

Wieliczka. Chapel of S. Kinga, hewn from the rock

1905 and by concrete in 1962-3. Impressive cantilever and supports strengthen the Drozdowice cave. I felt a quickening of the pulse, entering the Weimar Lake and much larger Świerczewski Lake caverns. As a boy I had read Jules Verne's *Journey to the Centre of the Earth*, but never thought I should be able to take part in such adventures. The Staszic stall is named for the statesman who pioneered modern mining methods in the late 18th century. The Treasurer's cavern has a modern figure representing a folkloric elder whose appearance to a miner heralded disaster, whether fire, flood, gas explosion or rockfall.

Here we come to a café and souvenir-stand where you can rest and buy mineralogical specimens. The 'Warsaw' cave is an auditorium hewn from the solid rock, and available for carnivals or concerts, with a court marked out for volleyball and basketball. One might imagine the atmosphere to be dank or close: in fact Wieliczka mines have long been famous for their beneficial effects on chest conditions such as asthma, with full sanatorium facilities.

At this point you can return to the surface by lift, or pursue fascinating galleries into twelve museum rooms, showing the history of the mines, and techniques of salt-extraction as they have evolved over the centuries, using first men, then horses and men, (from 1620) and finally labour-saving machines such as water-pumps, Hungarian, Polish and German whims. The famous Crystal Grottoes on the second flat are currently closed to visitors because they are situated in a zone over-exploited and thus considered dangerous.

Zakopane

Why should a town of thirty thousand inhabitants see three million visitors a year? In the case of Zakopane, the answers range from hiking to landscapes, skiing to healthy air, quiet country ways to wild mountain animals. The annual festival invites folkdancing groups from all over Europe, art galleries are crowded with paintings and sculpture from all over Poland, and the little town buzzes with carefree backpacking youngsters, honeymooners gazing into each other's eyes, retiring couples taking a leisurely coffee, and schoolchildren queuing for ice-cream.

The train from Cracow takes four hours, and the express bus only two, but as they follow different routes I determined to try both, leaving on the 5.10 a.m. train which cost 168 złoty (about 40 pence or 75 US cents). For one thing, demand for the few seats on buses normally exceeds supply, so that you are certain to be able to reach Zakopane only by train, and if the buses back are also full, you have the alternative of returning by train. A stay of three or four days to relax would be ideal. Daylight slyly encroached on misty dawn at Leńcze station around six, revealing darkened woods and dewy fields. A charming lady inspector approved my choice of ticket at 6.10, but I was somewhat concerned to find that we were travelling *very slowly* westward instead of the southerly route prescribed on my road map. Skawce at 6.35, Sucha Beskidzka at 6.45, Maków Podkalański at 7.10, the large rail juction of Chabówka from 7.50-8.00. A fat frightened man with a loosened tie and collar assured me that the train contained a theoretical buffet car, but the kettles visible I found to be untended. By 8.20 conifers began to outnumber the deciduous trees as our train climbed painfully into the Tatra foothills. Stooks in hayfields leaned together for protection. At 8.45 we all got out at Szaflary: the train would go no further. We headed for the queue of coaches, and rolled into Zakopane at 9.10. Across the road, at the bus station, I reserved a ticket on a convenient bus back to Cracow, and sought a popular restaurant, for scrambled eggs, bread roll, and tea (30 pence or about 55 US cents), ordering from a written menu at the cash desk, and paying there in exchange for a till receipt handed over at the serving-hatch. 'Ach,' a bald German in a beige overcoat said to his wife at the doorway, 'only *Poles* go in there!' Transportation is Poland's most impressive achievement. When all else fails, you can at least travel. And many

Poles travel to Zakopane and the Tatras for some or the whole of their four-week annual subsidized vacation, while sanatoria care for the ill, Zakopane having earned fame for the successful treatment of tuberculosis. In polluted cities of Silesia, workers dream of the crisp Tatra air of Giewont (1,909 m.)

Wandering around traditional villas and smaller wooden chalets of Zakopane is a pleasure at any season, as you admire finely-carved gables, steep roofs, picturesque porches. The Tatra Museum at Ulica Krupówki 10 (near the Orbis office at no. 22) has a wealth of ethnographical and mountaineering displays, and music-lovers should not miss Villa Atma at Ulica Kasprusie 19 for the Karol Szymanowski Museum. If you intend to explore the Tatra National Park, three transverse valleys with comfortable hostels in each, visit first the Tatra National Park Museum in Zakopane at Chałubińskiego 42a. In some ways I found the Villa Tea at Bulwary Słowackiego 39 even more charming, for this little ethnographic museum is shown in a typical regional interior.

The Tatras form the highest peaks of the Carpathian range. Up to 1,500 metres high, they offer varied landscapes of lakes, woodland, and valleys, sub-Alpine spruce forest giving way to dwarf pines, peaks and granite crags. I took a bus from the central bus station to Morskie Oko and my driver, awaiting departure, underlined the opinion of those who had travelled with him over the years, that the 33-kilometre run to Morskie Oko provided the greatest landscape views in all Poland. The bus slid into Ulica Chramcówski, named after Andrzej Chramiec (1859-1939), a doctor who developed Zakopane in many ways. At his own Institute of Hydropathy he treated such luminaries as the novelist Sienkiewicz, the painters Fałat and Matejko, and the actress Modrzejewska; he urged the building of the rail link from Chabówka to Zakopane which opened in 1899; and he became first to town councillor, then *wójt,* roughly equivalent to Mayor. Driving left of the railway line, you leave Zakopane by the Ulica Jana Kasprowicza, named for the playwright and poet whose home-museum can be seen between 10 and 4 daily except on Mondays at Harenda 12a. Kasprowicz (1860-1926) retired from Lwów (now in the Soviet Union) in 1924, but he had lived in Zakopane since World War I, and many of his poems refer to the Tatras. 'Choose me a refuge on the river, here above this stony frontier/under the shelter of eternal winds', he appealed in his *Book of the Poor* (1916), lyrics of Franciscan simplicity and beauty. And his mausoleum is indeed here in the shadow of the Tatras, near a three-room museum, and an 18th-century church brought here forty years ago from Zakrzów, Kalwaria Zbrzydowska, not far from Pope John Paul's birthplace, Wadowice.

Kasprowicz wrote some of his poems in the Mardula cottage in the village of Poronin: a plaque marks the spot. A more renowned figure visited Biały Dunajec, at the limits of Poronin, during the summer of 1913 and 1914: Lenin. On 8 August 1914 Lenin was arrested for espionage at the outbreak of World War I and imprisoned at Nowy Targ. Among those who intervened for his release were Dr Chramiec and Kasprowicz, and on 19 August he was set free and made for Switzerland. The small Lenin Museum at Poronin (open daily except Mondays) is housed in a private house of 1901 which functioned in Lenin's time as a small hotel, where revolutionaries met Lenin in private. Following the stream Poroniec, the road winds round to Bukowina, with glorious views cn both sides at any season, steeply-roofed houses evoking a mediaeval Transylvania of the fantasy – though they are as surprisingly comfortable inside as log cabins in Canada or Sweden. The mountain-dwellers (or *górale*) number about 150,000. This region, called Podhale, between the rivers Białka and Czarny Dunajec, suffered such grinding poverty around the turn of the century that by 1910 one in five *górale* had left, mostly for the U.S.A. Later on, waves of wealth raised the standard of living here: nowadays the horses, cattle, and the people themselves are fatter than anywhere else in Poland. Smuggling, remittances from relatives abroad, a thriving black market, a constant demand for folk art, woollen goods, tourism such as winter sports and summer hikes: the *górale* have eventually prospered.

The village of Bukowina is first recorded in the early 17th century, paying rents and tribute to the Crown's *starost* at Nowy Targ. After partition (1772), the Tatras fell to Austria, who sold the area off in sectors, that of Białka and Zakopane ending up under the control of the Homolacs family from 1824. Bukowina and the rest of the Homolacs properties passed in 1870 to the Berlin banker Baron Ludwig Eichhorn, and from 1881 to his son-in-law, Magnus Pelz. Subsequently Ladislaus Zamoyski acquired the region in 1889, but he assigned them to the Kórnik Foundation in 1924 as part of the Tatra National Park, and in 1933 the Polish State assumed responsibility.

Another time – you cannot see this by the Morskie Oko bus – I strolled down the tree-lined main street of Bukowina, Ulica Tadeusza Kościuszki, past long wooden carts on lorry tyres, being dragged by placid chestnut horses. Yes, the corrugated iron roofs are ugly. Yes, the telegraph wires detract from the village's appeal. But I found a buzz of pleasure in the place: could it have been the disreputable cafés and bars, the heady mountain air, the skelter of a little boy in a new blue suit, waving a plastic windmill from a village shop as if he owned the mountains? Only 3 km from Bukowina Tatrzańska you arrive at Głodówka (1,150 m a.s.l.), with a splendid panorama across to the Tatras and from there the bus continues to Łysa Polana, near the Czech border point; to the forested, snow-covered slopes above the Białka Valley; and to a car park from which a walk of 1½ km brings you to Morskie Oko ('Eye of the Sea'). Horse-carts ply this distance in Summer. The largest and most beautifully-situated lake in the Tatras, Morskie Oko is situated 1,393 m. above sea level. A Jesuit 'naturalist' called Gabriel Rzączynski wrote in his *Historia naturalis curiosa Regni Poloniae* (1721): 'In the highest part of the Carpathian mountains there are enormous lakes, the largest being called Oculus Maris, where one can find wrecks of ships. These wrecks possibly drifted here by a secret subterranean passageway'. This level of absurdity was maintained by Benedykt Chmielowski, in *Nowe Ateny*, which claims that chamois in the Tatras 'do not use their legs to move about, but jump between branches and rocks by using their horns'. A saunter around the lake's perimeter takes about half an hour, and is particularly memorable for the Dwoista Siklawa waterfall, and ever-changing avalanche couloirs. And don't be fooled by appearances: the peak called Rysy may seem unimportant from Morskie Oko but, at 2500 m. a.s.l. it is not only higher than the more impressive Mięguszowiecki Szczyt (2440 m. a.s.l.): it is actually the highest peak in all the Polska Rzeczpospolita Ludowa.

II GDAŃSK

Landscapes on the rail journey from Cracow to Warsaw and Gdańsk reminded me of Cambridge to Peterborough via Ely: flat plains dedicated almost entirely to agriculture, interspersed by woods and streams. But an East Anglia of a hundred years ago, with old red-tiled houses, ploughs drawn by slow horses, before grandfather clocks were replaced by clever-tick wristwatches. Everything has to be done more quickly, with a guilty conscience, if you take time with you everywhere you go. Back in the railway carriage, elders nodded over *Zycie Warszawy*, believing that sleep is the best reply and, next to sleep, pragmatism. How else could they have survived? I read again the clear, carefully-phrased statement of Hans Frank, Governor-General of the area including Bełzec, Cracow and Warsaw, an area known to the Nazis as the General Government.

'The General Government comprises all that is left of historic Poland. It is essential that Poles residing here understand the nature of the new state, which is governed not by law but by the demands and wishes of the Third Reich. The Pole has no rights whatsoever. His only obligation is to obey what we order him to do.' And later, to the same officials responsible for carrying out Himmler's horrific plans:

'Every vestige of Polish culture is to be eliminated. Those Poles who seem to have Nordic appearance will be taken to Germany to work in our factories. Children of Nordic appearance will be taken from their parents and raised as German labourers. As to the rest, they will work, eat very little, and eventually they will die. There will never again be a Poland.'

Martyrdoms are quickly covered with the snows of silence, before they become grey slush. A poet's task can be to help to show that there is more to life than a straight answer, especially since there will always be more than one question. What, for instance, should I have done as a Pole of Nordic appearance, taken to Germany to work as a labourer? How should I have reacted as a German civilian, supervising slave labour on the outskirts of Majdanek concentration camp? How, as a Jew, could I have survived the hours of roster, standing for hours in rags during the Winter months? How, as a Polish Christian, should I have responded to a Jew asking for asylum from the Nazis? What is courage, and what mere bravura? Does one hate the oppressor and seek to kill him in the knowledge that one is thereby signing one's own death warrant? Or does one try to undermine his influence by sabotage, and underground activities? Whom can you trust?

These are daily burning questions for those who remember – or youngsters who learn about – the betrayal of Poland in World War II. By the Nazi-Soviet Pact, the U.S.S.R. invaded undefended eastern Poland on 17 September 1939. Ten days earlier, Germany's Tenth Army, having advanced 140 miles in a week, rushed into Warsaw. President Moscicki, the Government, and the Commander-in-Chief crossed into Romania, allied with Poland, but found Romania too fearful of reprisals to honour the treaty: they interned Poland's last official representatives. Molotov, the Soviet Foreign Commissar, smoothly noted that Poland 'had ceased to exist', but to be on the safe side, a German-Soviet Friendship Treaty signed on 28 September provided for joint action against anticipated resistance by Poles.

At 6.55 a.m. I watched a woman milking a patient cow in a field. I slipped into my pocket the poems of Adam Zagajewski I had been reading, and made my way along the rattling train to carriage 7, for a breakfast of questionable sausage, roll and butter, gherkin, lettuce and mushrooms, finishing with a *napój jabłkowy*, a peculiar fizzy 'apple' drink. Very crowded it may be, but Poles are generous with private space, and avoid the affectionate touching of the arm or shoulders so common in Italy. Two tea-drinkers folded their newspapers and jolted away in unison, so I put my plate down on their stained table and ate on a hard chair instead of standing up. The 'Krakus' express continued to speed along, without stops, on its northward way through Kielce and Radom.

Returning to my reserved seat, I noted how the same flat fields and copses had followed me all the way. An old man, with eyebrows so bushy that they seemed to be on the verge of flying loose, was engaged in a Polish magazine corresponding to our *Reader's Digest*, never looking out of the window or at his fellow-passengers. Next to me sat an earnest young student, in appearance not unlike Trotsky, with pages of closely-written notes brought close up to his tired eyes. Opposite me, by the corridor window, a small businessman with a worn briefcase drummed his fingers nervously, darting anxious glances at each of us in turn, like a small starling not knowing where the next morsel will come from. Beside him, two athletic young brothers, about eighteen and sixteen, sniggered incoherently at their own jokes. Opposite the old man a worried little woman of an age and background familiar in Poland as 'gray youth' (anywhere between 30 and 45) quickly gave up all pretence of reading *Trybuna Ludu*, and sank her hibernatory head ever farther down into a formless mauve cardigan within her red anorak. Nobody says a word for minutes on end: we could be in deepest Lincolnshire, with flat fens extending as far as the mist, except that here the farms are uneconomically small, mostly below thirty acres or twelve hectares, and farm mechanization is a thing of the future.

Serried greenhouses indicate the national passion for tomatoes and cucumber. By now, the express has switched off its tape of Elvis Presley's 'You ain't nuthin' but a houn' dawg', followed by the would-be sultry 'Love me tender'. A ticket inspector of impeccable manners appeared at the door. 'Good morning, ladies and gentlemen. (His word was the untranslatable 'państwo'). May I please see your tickets. Thank you so much. Thank you. Have a pleasant trip. Till we meet again.'

Cracow. Railway Station, with passengers and ice-cream stall (Lody)

Two hours and ten minutes north of Cracow, hence only one hour south of Warsaw, we could still see horse-drawn ploughs in pre-industrial plains. By now I was standing in the corridor, hoping to launch into conversation. A retired professor at Cracow University eagerly, in good German, narrated his hardships during the Stalinist terror of the 1950s. He was forced to leave his post, becoming unemployed at first, then granted a menial job in a library, before being permitted to return to professorial duties. His wife said little. Typically intelligent, durable, caring, silent unless provoked, she bore on her face lines etched by fear and worry over five decades. One of the most extraordinary records of the time is the painstaking (often painful) series of interviews with party officials edited by Teresa Torańska and laconically entitled *Oni* ('They'), as bureaucrats are scathingly described in contradistinction to 'us'. The book, circulating clandestinely in Poland, first appeared in French in 1986, then in English a year later. I think of this anonymous wife when I read Torańska's fearless interviews, notably with Jakub Berman, Stalinist and torturer under Bierut. On the subject of the 'law', for example, Berman admits 'It's certainly true that our courts were not among the best and the problem, in my view, lay not in that trials took place in the prison grounds, but in that judges were, unfortunately, prepared for what to expect from the outset and therefore not always impartial.' To which the wondrous Teresa adds: 'Those were the only kind you appointed.' The reputation of party politicians can be judged from her response to one of Berman's statements. 'Yes, well, perhaps we'd better stick to the facts'.

The old professor hugged me on saying goodbye, and I kissed his wife's hand in the Polish way as we separated: they to Warsaw and I to another platform for the train to Gdynia departing at 11.07, a journey of five hours.

Again we entered the seemingly endless plain of Mazovia, stopping at towns almost interchangeable in their lack of character: Ciechanów at 1.15, Dzułdowo at 1.55, Iława at 2.40, Prabuty at 3.05. How strange, I pondered, to have come back from Auschwitz alive! And from Birkenau! Generations of sparrows, flies, crickets, lice, fleas, and even the occasional mocking lark. And then I.

In its way, the great Teutonic Castle of Marienburg ('Malbork' in Polish) creates a similar impact, for power rather than peace, the rule of the mailed fist instead of the velvet glove, dictated that a fortress as impregnable as this had to be built for the Christian Knights of the Teutonic Order.

The Warsaw-Gdańsk train stops at Malbork, so you can stay there (advance information from PTTK at Ulica Hibnera 4) or leave your case at the station's left luggage office while visiting the largest feudal castle in Europe. Who were these knights that struck fear into the Baltic

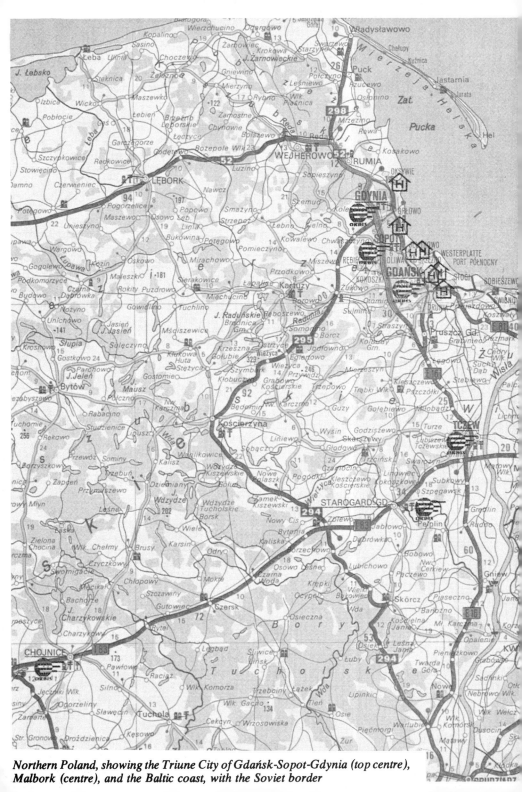

Northern Poland, showing the Triune City of Gdańsk-Sopot-Gdynia (top centre), Malbork (centre), and the Baltic coast, with the Soviet border

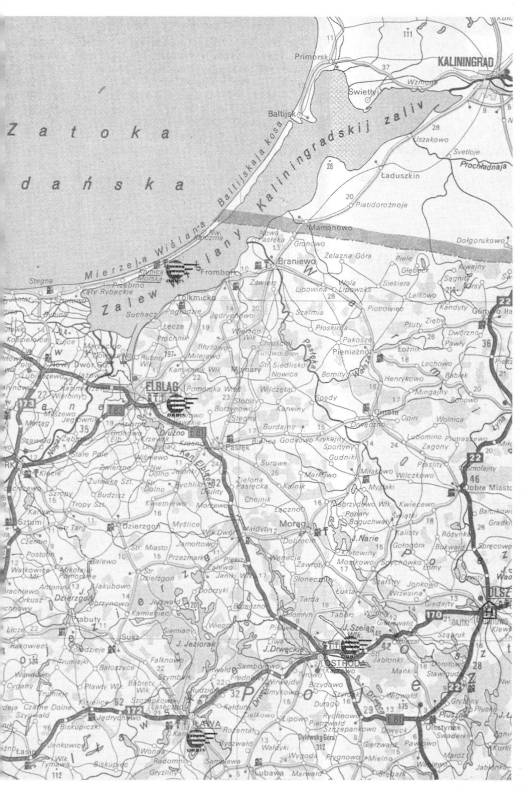

region in the Middle Ages? Founded in the Holy Land as the third great order of military chivalry, the Teutonic Order was authorized as a religious organization devoted to the Virgin Mary by a papal bull in 1191. The Order lost a struggle for power with the Knights Templar and Knights Hospitaller, and took up temporary quarters in Transylvania, in present-day Romania, before accepting an appeal in 1229 for support from Conrad of Mazovia. Conrad believed that the Pomeranians and Prussians threatened to overwhelm Mazovia, that is to say the central part of present-day Poland. The Teutonic Knights agreed to try to conquer Prussia, and indeed the 'Prussians' properly so-called were virtually wiped out, so that the people later called Prussians were in fact not their descendants, but successful enemies inhabiting their homeland. The Order's theocratic state, familiar in our own times in Khomeini's Iran, presumed total union of spiritual and temporal powers, and quickly became intolerable to townspeople who set fire to their towns in rebellion against their overlords. The Order's headquarters were transferred from Venice to Marienburg ('The Fortress of Mary') in 1309, thus removing the last pretence of crusading against the infidel in Palestine. A naked struggle for territory, for wealth, for the amber trade, for an even larger slice of the Hansa cities' trade: this became the obsession of the Order, which reached its zenith under Grand Master Winrich von Kniprode (1351-82). The Lithuanian armies conquered the Teutonic-held town of Kwidzyń in 1394: the Order's powers significantly diminished following defeat at the Battle of Grunwald in 1410 at the hands of King Ladislaus Jagiellon. By a shrewd Treaty of Toruń (1411) they retained all their possessions in Prussia, greatly to the dismay of towns oppressed by the Order. These towns offered their sovereignty to the Polish King in 1440, but it was not until 1454 that Casimir Jagiellon took up arms, and only in 1457 did he enter Malbork. The Grand Master fled to Königsberg, today Soviet Kaliningrad, and by the Peace of Toruń (1466), Malbork passed definitively to Poland and the Order's might came to a sudden end.

The present-day town of Malbork, with about 34,000 people, nestles on the right bank of the river Nogat. The rail station faces the bus station across Ulica Dworcowa; to reach the castle turn right out of the rail station and continue along Kościuszka, then right into Nowotki, over the canal bridge, and right into Hibnera. Then, instead of entering by the main gate, carry on to a ticket office a hundred metres farther on, past the castle. As a general guide, opening hours are 9-5 May-September and 8-3 October-April, closing day being Monday. The occasional concert is held in state rooms, or in the precincts during warm weather. *Son et Lumière* events occur during the Summer.

Malbork Castle is divided into three levels according to age, the latest being the lowest, near the main gate. By a grandiose, inspiring act of historical devotion, the Polish State has restored Malbork – long the seat of its sworn enemy – in every way as memorably as it has restored its own Warsaw Castle or Cracow's Wawel. In the Lower Castle, we can reconstruct in our mind's eye the splendour of the Order at its apogee, between the 14th century and the early 15th. An armoury was erected early in the 14th, followed by farm buildings and outhouses, and the S. Lawrence Chapel overlooking the Nogat.

The Middle Castle dates from the Order's capture of Gdańsk and its region in 1308-9, from which time Malbork became the Order's headquarters, and had to expand rapidly to satisfy the needs of increased personnel, both civilian and military. The Knights' Hall ('Sala Rycerska') appeared 1318-19 and beside it the magnificent Palace of the Grand Master slowly arose during this time of Gothic experimentation by German architects and builders: note especially the fine vaulting, crenellations, and turrets. The Knights' Hall possesses an evocative display of historical weapons in chronological order, and at Malbork other permanent and temporary exhibitions include amber ancient and modern, ceramics from Polish factories, regional archaeology, contemporary glass, paintings and sculpture.

Like the last act of a three-act play, the High Castle of Malbork ascends to a climax from which the impressionable visitor may never easily recover, like his first walk through the Moscow Kremlin, the Taj Mahal by moonlight, or dawn over Borobudur. For here, in 1274-80, the Order of Teutonic Knights established a Chapel of the Virgin Mary, their Patroness. Extensions concluded in 1344 turned the church into an upper church and a Chapel of S. Anne. Note the refectory with seven pillars, and the cloisters. The Gothic 'Golden Gate' dates from the end of the 13th century (shortly after the local commander of the Order moved here from Zantyr in 1276), and this has been copied by artists working on portals of S. Anne's, showing the discovery of the True Cross, and the Enthronement of the Virgin Mary.

I spent a couple of hours trying to get lost in the bastions, ramparts, spiral staircases, towers, and courtyards: a young squire seeking his Knight from Pomerania with news of an attack expected from the south. How could I persuade the castellan of my identity, and pass into the Middle Castle for the night above the moat and over a drawbridge into safety from vengeful peasant saboteurs roaming in bands armed with flint-edged cudgels? I never believed for one moment in the biased historical novels of Henryk Sienkiewicz (1846-1916), but who could ever forget his vision of Malbork, having read *Krzyżacy* (1900), translated by A. Tyszkiewicz as *The Teutonic Knights* (1943)?

And the romantic stronghold of the Knights by no means passed into meek oblivion, but served the Polish monarchs after the capitulation of the Order; the palace became a royal residence during visits to the

Malbork. Castle of the Teutonic Knights

north, the castle an administrative headquarters for governors, voivods and starosts. Strategically important once again during the Swedish invasion, it was taken and retaken by a remorseless tug-of-war between Poles, Swedes and Russians; during the Seven Years' War, for example, it was Russian. I saw it as the locale imagined by Alfred Jarry in his celebrated stage instruction: 'En Pologne, c'est à dire nulle part'. A blank stage, a tabula rasa, where everything can happen, as in Windsor Castle, or nothing, as in a fantasy-world created by Stanisław Lem.

I caught the 5.16 train to Gdańsk due in at 6.08, having paid 38 złoty (about 10 pence or 18 US cents) for my case in the left-luggage office. After crossing more flat fields, we negotiated a rickety rail bridge over the Vistula, next to an even more rickety road bridge, and pulled in to Tczew station at 5.40. A woman in her forties sitting opposite me, as passengers got on and off, patted her pink and white cardigan self-consciously, alternating glances at me through earnest steel-rimmed glasses with clenched-grip reading of *Maria i Magdalena*, a popular novel by Magdalena Samozwaniec. I alighted from the punctual train at Gdańsk Główny (the main railway station) and headed across Gorki Square to the Monopol Hotel, unexceptional nowadays but quite a landmark when constructed in 1949. Other first-class hotels in the city are the nearby Hewelius, the Novotel at Ulica Pszenna 1 very handy for the Main Town, and the Posejdon nearly all the way to Sopot, in the seaside suburb of Jelitkowo, at Ulica Kapliczna 33. I myself wanted to stay with a family, so I enquired at the Biuro Zakwaterowania near the rail station at Ulica Elżbietańska 10-11. This adds to the adventure, since you will probably be living in a residential district you would otherwise not see, and enter at least marginally into the life of real Poles; it reduces the price of accommodation significantly, especially since this would be your major expense; and the additional cost of taxis to your destinations will nowhere near add up to the savings on a hotel room. My own ticket in the lottery turned into a winner: I found a comfortable room in the leafy, quiet suburb of Oliwa, very close to the main thoroughfare linking Gdańsk with Sopot, Gdynia, and points north to Władysławowo (thence to – in the nicest possible way – Hel) and west to Wejherowo and Lębork. Since Gdańsk, Sopot and Gdynia constitute one administrative Triune City, with efficient buses and frequent suburban trains throughout their straggling length, you can quite easily stay in any one and visit the others, or stay three nights in Gdańsk and one night each in the others. Sopot offers a relaxed beach holiday, with Opera-in-the-Woods at Ulica Moniuszki 10 during the Summer. Gdynia is for 'messing about in boats', with stylish yacht clubs and historic vessels, and for festivals such as those devoted to films.

Gdańsk is mentioned as an important town as early as 997 (in Slavnikovic's *Vita Sancta Adalberti*), situated strategically on low-lying land on the Gulf of Gdańsk where the so-called 'Dead Vistula' river reaches the sea. Its population then is estimated at 1,200. The Main Town is almost completely surrounded by water: the Radunia canal, and the river Motława. The Old Town lies west of the Radunia, and the Triune City nudges the Baltic northward. Its position must always have seemed ideal to tribes from the south wanting to trade by sea with northern capitals and the Hanseatic League, in which Danzig, as it was known in German, swiftly rose to eminence, with Lübeck, Hamburg and Bremen. Linen was imported from England and the Low Countries. The Teutonic Knights whom we have heard shouting defiance from the battlements of Marienburg seized Gdańsk in 1308, and held it unchecked until the Battle of Grunwald (1410). In 1454 the Order's Castle in Gdańsk was razed. The Poles regained their city by the Peace of Toruń (1466) and offered it once more to King Casimir Jagielloń, though Polish kings enjoyed only nominal suzerainty for it was a free city with thirty-odd villages under its control. One royal privilege decreed that all goods imported or exported had to pass through merchants of Gdańsk, a measure producing immediate and long-term effects guaranteeing prosperity to the city at all levels of society.

By 1502 the Church of S. Mary had been virtually completed; the population had risen to more than 40,000. In 1518, the Reformation made itself felt in Poland, the 'State without Stakes', and the right to practise dissenting beliefs received royal confirmation from King Stefan Batory in 1584, ensuring liberty of conscience for the many Protestants who had fled Catholic persecution elsewhere, chiefly in the Netherlands. Around 1600 we enter the period of architectural and sculptural glories, when the port city echoed to a dozen languages, French being a language of taste and culture, German and Polish languages of commerce and administration. Master builders arrived from the Low Countries, creating works in the style of Antwerp, Ghent, and Mechelen throughout Ulica Długa and Długi Targ, familiar in German as Lange Gasse and Lange Markt.

Swedish armies besieged Gdańsk ineffectually from 1626 to 1629, but overran most of Poland 1654-6, withdrawing only after the Peace of Oliwa (1660). Huge destruction followed the Russian siege of Gdańsk (1734) and the Prussian attacks of 1772 and 1793; after the first disaster, Gdańsk became separated from Poland, and after the second it passed under Prussian sovereignty. A free city once more between 1807 and 1813 during a French victory in the Franco-Prussian War, Gdańsk was however ceded again to Prussia by the Congress of Vienna (1815), and this situation prevailed until 1919. The Treaty of Versailles then reintroduced 'free city' status, ruptured by a fusillade from the Battleship Schleswig-Holstein against Westerplatte. Gdańsk was devastated during World War II, which ended as far as the city was concerned on 30 March 1945. Modern shipyards arose from the ashes of war, and the port gradually revived. A new Gdańsk University opened in 1970 and a new international airport followed shortly thereafter at Rębiechowo.

Most recently Gdańsk has achieved world notoriety as the spark-point from which Solidarność set on fire the aspirations of a people too long inured to being ordered about. As the sixth *Gdańsk Strike Bulletin* told the Government: 'We are different now, above all because we are united, and therefore stronger. We are different, because in thirty years we have learnt that promises are illusions. We are different, because we understand that when we hear the phrase "financial re-organisation", it means merely "exploitation".'

Defeat was inevitable, because all the weapons remained in the hands of the Party: control of the means of production, food distribution, import and export, relations with the Soviet Union which would be wholly biased towards their own puppets in control and wholly opposed to free trade unions in theory and practice. Indeed, after early sparring, Solidarność seldom behaved like a true trade union, but much more like an ideological spearhead for political reforms, such as freedom of speech and democratisation: it behaved, in other words, like a mass political party without any official status as such. Military intervention to support the tottering regime had to occur, and occur it did in December 1981. The lifting of restrictions since then, according to Government spokesmen, has made life more free, but it is common knowledge that there is still no rule of law – no effective appeal against arbitrary detention, for instance.

Since we shall spend all the rest of our time in Gdańsk in exploring the past, I take you first to a monument unveiled in December 1980, to the Shipyard Workers. More than forty metres high, its three crosses and anchors symbolise the twenty-seven workers and police killed during protest riots against food-price increases in December 1970. The legs of the monument buckle, crumple, crack in defeat, to represent the rioting, and the murder of Poles by Poles. Think back to 16 December 1980, when Lech Wałęsa, a ginger-moustached orator in a brown anorak, stepped forward to light the eternal flame, in the presence of Henryk Jabłonski, the Head of State, and a dozen high-ranking party dignitaries and foreign diplomats (though not, I recall, the Soviet Ambassador).

Private, individual visits to the Lenin Shipyard in Gdańsk are not permitted, but group visits can be made through the Polish Tourist Association (PTTK) at Ulica Doki (tel. 37 26 20). Or you can see other parts of dockland on the 45-minute cruise to Westerplatte from Green Gate (Zielona Brama) beyond Long Market, returning either by later motor-launch or by bus 106 back to Plac 1 Maja via Siennica and Elbląska, giving you an insight to parts of Gdańsk beyond the traditional itinerary.

The ticket-office at Zielona Brama being closed, with full-up signs beside the launch *Joanna*, I explained what I wanted to a sailor collecting tickets and he kindly accepted the fare of 220 złoty in lieu. A slow, helpful and clear commentary in Polish changes every day, of course, with the changing circumstances of the busy port. Before setting off, look across the water to Granary Island (Spichlerze). Together with the wharves of Długie Pobrzeże on the near bank of the Motława, this area represents the earliest southern expansion of the original early mediaeval port, centred on the suburb of Zamczysko that we pass shortly on our left, before we reach the Hook of Poland (Polski Hak), which marks the flow of Motława into Vistula. The Vistula's main outlet into the sea is not here, however, but at Świbno. We now enter the bustling area of the Lenin Shipyard, teeming with vessels from – seemingly – all over the world. The shipyard opened in 1848 as the Royal Corvette Workshops, later the Imperial Shipyards, and quickly became the greatest shipyard in Poland. In 1923, it was taken over by a consortium in which Poland held only 20% of the shares. Destroyed in part during World War II, only 68% of landing quays survived, a mere 30% of loading installations, and less than 5% of warehouses. Among the 'shock workers' typical of totalitarian states which encourage emulation of hard work rather than Western financial incentives or company benefits and loyalty in the Japanese mode, was a certain Sołdek. He is credited with stupendous efforts as a loftsman (copying blueprints on to steel plates) during his working shifts and in his scant leisure qualifying as a ship-designer at Gdańsk Technical University. On 6 November 1948 the s.s. *Sołdek* was launched, honouring him and becoming the first ship wholly designed and built in Poland. In 1955, ships of 10,000 tonnes were being built in Gdańsk, and the tonnage gradually rose to 40,000 and upward. Gdańsk specialises in factory trawlers and base ships for fishing fleets, processing catches at sea.

We passed the *Finnsailor* from Naantali and the *Sovietskaya Konstitutsiya*, then Polish vessels: *H. Cegielski* (Gdynia), *Powiśle* and *Kujawy* (both from Szczecin), and the *Major Sucharski* (named after the commander of Westerplatte) of Gdynia. Little children who had been swarming excitedly all over the *Joanna*, like ants over an anthill, by now had settled down to sandwiches and bottled drinks. Mothers and teachers began to relax. The commentator managed to make his voice heard at a lower volume.

The *Joanna* chugged into the Kashubian Canal (1901-3), being the port's entrance from the west. Ostrów Island, to the west, lay concealed behind a procession of majestic ships at rest, like captured whales: the *Ellispontos* from Limassol, the *Viktor Strel'tsov* from Murmansk, the *Sanag Harmony* of Japan's Sanko Line, registered in Panama, the *Kharkov* from Leningrad, the *Asma'a* from Alexandria, and the

Gdańsk. The harbour cruise-launch 'Joanna' departing from Zielona Brama.

Universytet Śląski from Szczecin. To the left of us, reaching the Dead Vistula from the Kashubian Canal, was the Vistula Station, for transloading cargo such as fruit and vegetables; on the opposite bank the Timber Station offloaded low-grade timber for paper-mills and for mine-beams and -struts, while a boat at the Ores Landing Station (Nabrzeże Rudowe) discharged ore by a bridge crane before crossing the basin to pick up coal. Also on the right you can see the village of Wisłoujście; its small mediaeval moated fortress protected the entrance to the harbour when the sea lay much closer to it. Earth fortifications were supplemented in 1562 with a stone circle and batteries, and subsequently – forty years later – with a huge defensive barricade of brick and earth, designed by Antoon van Opberghen, Flemish architect of the mannerist Arsenal (1602-5). The Italian Gerolamo Ferrero planned external bastions (1624-6) which made Wisłoujście apparently impregnable from seaward: it is just ten minutes walk from the Westerplatte Monument, where our cruise ends.

Strategically, the Germans attacking Gdańsk in September 1939 needed to capture the transport and munitions depôt on this spit of land converted from island to peninsula in 1845. Orders were given for the Polish garrison of some 170 men to withstand the onslaught for twelve hours, but they resisted heroically for a week, before capitulating to far superior numbers, after they had killed three hundred of the enemy for only fifteen losses to themselves. The ruined barracks and guardhouses are preserved, giving some idea of the heroism of those involved, attacked by a battleship with four guns, 3,200 Germans with 65 heavy guns, three companies of heavy machine-guns, a company of heavy mortars, and dozens of aircraft. The Monument itself is in appalling taste, mistaking mere bulk and height for majesty. I shivered against blustery winds from the north-east: heroism is a bitter business.

Returning to the Green Gate, constructed in 1568 by Johann Kramer, I found the shields of Poland, Gdańsk City, and Prussia, cut in stone above the porches of the doors, and then strolled along the quays.

The Green Gate is a masterpiece by Regnier, the architect from Amsterdam, who used small Dutch bricks that arrived as ballast in cargo ships from the Netherlands. A mannerist work of 1564-8, it was designed as a royal residence, with superb views one way down Long Market, and in the other direction over the water to Spichlerze. It now houses the Organization for the Conservation of Historical Monuments.

Strolling along the quays, I turned left before the old Chlebnicka Brama into Ulica Chlebnicka. At no. 16 the English House designed by Johann Kramer of Dresden in 1569-70 was at that time the tallest building in the city, with eight storeys, but due to the Polish monopoly in Gdańsk the English failed to keep a fingergrip in the city and moved to Elbląg. Marygate (Brama Mariacka) closes Ulica Mariacka: it dates

Gdańsk. Plan of the city centre.

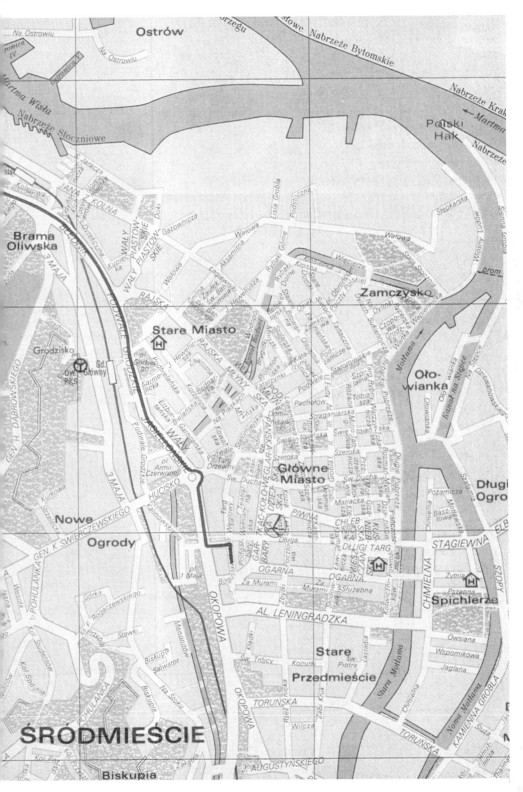

from the end of the 15th century: the gate and the Late Renaissance Naturalists' House (1597-9), and an annex, are all occupied by the Archaeological Museum, open daily except Mondays, with erratic hours to be checked beforehand. I saw a temporary exhibition on ancient Egypt, but permanent displays evoke Gdańsk and its Pomeranian hinterland, with a tragic photograph of blitzed Ulica Mariacka in 1945, and the heartening awareness of what has been achieved since in sensitive reconstruction. Pomerania has been inhabited by proto-Slavonic and Slavonic peoples from the tenth millennium B.C., as well as by Germanic races. Here are artefacts from Lusatian, Wendish and East Pomeranian cultures up to the 6th century A.D.: the ages of Stone, Bronze and Iron. The rest of the exhibition deals with Pomerania and Gdańsk between the 7th and early 14th centuries: before Hansa.

Back to the quays, I circled round the great crane of 1442-4, formerly a fortified gate; the 15th-century Stągiewne Towers to defend the approach to Spichlerze, and the granaries, opposite the crane on Olowianka Island. These range in date from the 15th century (Olive Oil) to the 19th (Copper). Grain and other produce from royal estates were stored in the Royal Granary (1606-21) designed by Abraham van den Block and Jerzy Strakowski.

At Broad St (Ulica Szeroka) 67-8, the Central Maritime Museum defines the situation of Gdańsk in the Baltic and within the Hanseatic network, linking with Riga, Visby and the powerful German ports. Amber, recurring in most periods, enriched merchants on the coast, but timber, grain and general cargo kept Gdańsk port busy, and shipyards sprang up not only in Gdańsk but, since 1923, also in Gdynia. A prehistoric Slav longboat merits a room to itself in the Archaeological Museum, but here a 15th-century boat called 'copper' from its cargo takes pride of place. A room devoted to the 15th-18th centuries displays a map to prove the centrality of the Vistula in Polish mercantile life: smaller boats could pass from Cracow through Warsaw to Gdańsk, trading all the way. Today's agricultural gloom in Poland must be seen in the historical light of the 16th century, when Poland was termed 'the granary of Europe'. Rafts brought timber and agricultural produce of many kinds to the mouth of the Vistula: as many as two thousand vessels are believed to have travelled to Gdańsk each year. Such scenes are vividly exemplified in such paintings as a 'Polish Riverscape' by Franciszek Ruśkiewicz (1819-83) and 'Rafters' Rest' by Wilhelm August Stryowski (1834-1917). A fine view of the blockade of Gdańsk (1627) by Stefan Plużański celebrates a Polish victory over the Swedish fleet at the so-called 'Battle of Oliwa'. A model of the frigate *Estrada* of 1788 exemplifies a fascinating room devoted to the age of discoveries, while anglophones will deplore particularly in the 'Conrad and the Sea' display the absence of any English-language captions. Everything is solely in Polish.

On a seat near the water's edge a gaunt figure in his late sixties looked at his hands, turning them over suddenly, stiffening his palms and searching the fingers, stretching them. He seemed to be hunting for a blemish, or a scar that had once disfigured him, but remained perpetually dissatisfied with himself, like an ageing movie star in front of a pitiless mirror.

I wandered farther along Długie Pobrzeże to S. John's Gate, part of which dates back to the 14th century, and to Straganiarska Gate (15th century). S. John's St. leads to the incredibly ornate S. Nicholas' Church (Św. Mikołaj), in its present incarnation dating to 1340-80, with vaulting of 1487. The superb organ (1755) accompanied my visit with a Bach prelude and fugue. Dominicans have preached here from 1227 (when they arrived in an earlier church on the site, from Cracow), with an interval from 1840 (when their Order was dissolved) until 1945. A notable *Christ Crucified* by a Gdańsk sculptor known as Paul governs irrepressibly the area behind the rosary chandelier with full-length Virgin Mary, at the entrance to the rococo pews. The Virgin takes our attention as we head towards the parish church of Main Town in that node where Chlebnicka debouches into Piwna, and Ulica Mariacka (rebuilt from 1956 to 1960) opens out into S. Mary's Square. The largest Gothic church in Poland (1343-61) ascends into Baltic skies on the site of an early church, but the basilica we see today has little in common with its predecessor. At the end of the 14th century a transept and presbytery were added to the nave; the east front was built between 1425-7 and the domes went up in 1487-1502. Here if anywhere you can smell like incense the money that Gdańsk merchants converted into sacred paintings, altars, tombstones and chapels to the greater glory of God and themselves. Twenty-five thousand worshippers can be accommodated with ease. The ensemble overwhelms any intention to concentrate on detail, which is a pity, because several outstanding works have been rescued from bombs and looting. The fourth chapel in the northern nave, from the west front, showers us with glory: a Gothic stone 'Beautiful Madonna' in the Gdańsk style of about 1410. In the transept Abraham van den Block created tomb monuments (1620) to Herr and Frau Bahr, nobles of the city, adjacent to the Von Werden tombstone, decorated with bronze and datable to the later 16th century. An Antwerp Gothic altar to SS. Simon and Jude (1510) can be found nearby.

Near a pillar, see a beautifully-decorated wooden sacrarium (1478-82), then high in the Church, full of late Gothic solemnity, looms the massive Crucifixion by Paul, the local sculptor we know already from S. Nicholas, his figures more than lifesize, as befits the great basilica. The main altar (1515-17) by Michael of Augsburg, depicts the Coronation of the Virgin. To the left of the main altar a mannerist monument commemorates Ann Loys (1563) and chapels are protected

Gdańsk. Panorama of the Old Town.

by splendidly-carved wooden partitions. To the right of the main altar you can enjoy a monument to Michael Loys (c.1560), and a Crucifixion of c.1435 celebrated for its moving realism. Continuing towards the west, we reach the Edward Blemke monument by the Fleming Willem van den Block, who also made the Brandes monument in the second chapel of the southern nave. Once outside the church, lyrical in its almost infinite space and time, the human scale is revived in the Royal Chapel, commissioned by King Jan III from the great Tylman van Gameren, the architect being Bartholomäus Ranisch and the sculpted façade by Andreas Schlüter the Younger.

Virtually every house in S. Mary's Street (Ulica Mariacka) is worthy of loving attention, except that throngs of people attending the

Gdańsk. Royal Chapel

Dominican Fair will make it difficult to see anything in tranquillity during the first fortnight in August, a tradition traceable to 1260. No. 1, with a brick façade, goes back to 1451, with its reconstructed stone staircase, railings, and 15th-century stone slabs. The mannerist façade on no. 6 dates to 1600, Tuscan pillars framing a delightful porch. No. 42 (mid-17th century) and no. 44 (c.1600) have been reconstructed from Dutch bricks recovered from post-war rubble.

Brewery Street (Ulica Piwna) sparkles with architectural effervescence as it meets the Armoury (also called the Arsenal, in Polish 'Zbrojownia'). At no. 1, the Restaurant Pod Wieżą: the Tower prepares matchless polędwica (beef ragout with eggs) in an original house of 1638-40 with baroque sculpture by Andreas Schlüter the Elder, though the rococo porch cannot date from before 1750. Rococo façades decorate no. 51 and 64. Antoon van Opberghen of Malines, architect to Gdańsk Town Council, designed the Old Armoury, now recognised as a masterpiece of Flemish mannerism, and it was constructed 1602-5, with the help of the sculptors Willem van der Meer and Abraham van den Block. The interior, totally devastated in the War, has been replaced as a combination of shops (on the lower floor) and educational premises for students of art and design. Across the Coal Market (Targ Węglowy) you can find the Straw Tower (Baszta Słomiana) of the 15th century and the Coast Theatre (Teatr Wybrzeże), a modern auditorium seating 700 on the site of an old theatre dating from 1797. Theatre life is very active in Gdańsk.

Gdańsk gave a home from 1923 until 1935 to the dramatist Stanisława Przybyszewska, who wrote *Thermidor* (1925), *93* (1927) and *The Case of Danton* (1928), a trilogy on the French Revolution. The sixth child of the Satanist and leader of Young Poland Stanisław Przybyszewski and his mistress, the painter Aniela Pająk, Stanisława died alone of malnutrition and exhaustion due to morphine addiction. Perhaps her most enduring monument is the collection of letters, most of them never posted, addressed to such luminaries as Thomas Mann, Bernanos and Cocteau. Her plays are now regularly performed in Poland, being published in 1975, *Sprawa Dantona* being filmed by Andrzej Wajda (released in 1983), and reaching England as *The Danton Affair* (Royal Shakespeare Company, 1986).

During Przybyszewska's lifetime, the Polish population of Gdańsk did not exceed 15%. She wrote equally fluently in Polish and German. She hardly ever went out, refusing to get a job and living solely for her painting and writing. 'My room is a corner one', she noted in a letter to her aunt Helena Barlińska (23 June – 2 July 1929), 'and on two sides faces the courtyard, where innumerable teams play football and shriek all day long from 8 a.m., without any break for lunch (since by some miracle one class or another always has a free hour)'. Her room was at

Gdańsk. Ulica Piwna.

the White Tower 1, Barrack 12. 'Apparently the idea is to ensure that the external flame of screaming (may God preserve us!) is not extinguished for a single second till ten at night. But more than that. Our barracks now house excursion groups from Poland, so that I have intolerably boorish neighbours on the other sides: ten to a side. The south wall has a door with a two-centimetre gap at the top so they might just as well be yelling here in my room. Their yelling never stops before 2 in the morning.' Stanisława's heartfelt cries for silence and intellectual companionship can be read in Jadwiga Kosicka and Daniel Gerould's *A Life of Solitude* (1986).

We are going to cross the busy thoroughfare Aleja Leningradzka by the underpass, noting on the way the one-time Town Stables designed by Jerzy Strakowski in 1620, on Ulica Bogusławskiego, and nearby, on Ulica Ogarna, the Corner Tower (1343), connected with defensive city walls.

This sector of the city is the Old Suburb, with the Church of the Holy Trinity and the National Museum in the former Franciscan Monastery. The Franciscans came to Gdańsk in 1419 and their church rose between 1481 and 1514, though the adjacent S. Anne's Chapel was not finished until 1484. During Reformation times it was converted to Protestant use, but the Franciscans returned in 1945, having left in 1555. In the form of a basilica with three naves, Holy Trinity has a late Gothic pulpit of 1541. At the east end an early 16th-century crucifix is flanked by altars from polyptychs painted in the workshop of the local master Michael. Don't miss the little burgher's house of c.1610 near the west front.

If you turn the corner from Rzeźnicka into Toruńska you will come to the imposing National Museum, imaginatively utilising the former monastery so that, for example, the former Chapter House, glittering with midday light, houses appropriate works of mediaeval Pomeranian art, especially sculpture, paintings, textiles and gold plate. My particular joy here is S. George from the Artusz Mansion (by Hans Brandt, c.1485), in which a diminutive princess seems in imminent danger of being trampled underfoot by her saviour's horse. A Spanish silk chasuble of the 15th century, Angelo Bronzino's 'Caterina de' Medici' (urgently in need of cleaning), and Dutch Renaissance furniture give the visitor some inkling of the wealth and taste of the cultured, intellectual and artistic middle classes of Hanseatic Danzig from the 16th century to the 18th. The patricians and merchants could afford to acquire the best, and to support local craftsmen such as cabinetmakers and sculptors. Teschke, von Klose, Transchke, Stryowski and Giełdziński count among donors, while S. Mary's Church presented 450 of its liturgical vestments, including fabrics from Gdańsk and abroad: Spain, Italy, Germany.

The Low Countries provide the Museum with its choicest items, ranging from 'Cottages by the Canal' of Jan van Goyen to 'The Organ-Grinder' by Adriaen van Ostade. Pieter de Hooch is represented by 'A Woman Plucking a Fowl' and 'At the Fortune-Teller's'. Nobody could go away unmoved by a 'Landscape with Ruins' attributed to Jacob van Ruisdael or a boy's portrait by Jordaens.

The most wonderful works stand at opposite ends of the spiritual spectrum: Jan Steen's 'The Science of Reading', in which a boy sets a black and white cat in front of a book held by his sister; and Hans Memling's 'Last Judgment' (1473), dazzling with exact painterly definitions of Heaven and Hell presaged in the expressions and limbs of the saved or damned. The early history of the altarpiece can be seen on the reverse of the wings (visible in the Museum because the polyptych is displayed in the centre of the gallery). On the left Angelo Tani kneels in black before the Madonna and Child; on the right his wife Caterina kneels in red before the Archangel Michael in *grisaille*.

Tani managed the Medici banking interests in Bruges and intended to offer the altarpiece to a Florentine church; but *S. Thomas*, an English ship carrying it from Sluys towards London, was attacked by the *Peter* of Gdańsk and surrendered its cargo, including the painting. It remained in S. Mary's until Napoleon seized it in 1807; then the Prussians removed it to Berlin in 1815, returning it to Gdańsk the following year. The Nazis stole it, but the Soviets found it in a mine near Halle and, after restoring it at the Hermitage, returned it to Gdańsk in 1956. Such is the turmoil that may surround great, coveted, works of art. Many other masterpieces have never been recovered, but the National Museum has to some extent compensated by acquiring other works, such as a 'Portrait of a Young Woman in Profile' by Wojciech Gerson and fine portraits by Jacek Malczewski and Jan Matejko. A marvellous display of contemporary graphics concerned with the sea proved the vitality of current Polish artists, among them Małgorzata Hołowka, Eugeniusz Delekta, and Władysław Koscielniak.

Continuing to the end of Ulica Rzeźnicka and crossing Augustynskiego, you come to the Small Armoury (1643-5) on Plac Wałowy, for which Jerzy Strakowski was responsible. Beyond here stands his Lower Gate (Brama Nizinna, 1626), one part of the system of fortifications that enclosed much of the city which existed in 1621-36, as planned by the Dutch engineer Cornelis van den Bosch.

From the main thoroughfare, Jedności Robotniczej (Workers' Unity) running into Okopowa, you can catch any northward bus or tram to alight at the Main Station (ask for Gdańsk Główny).

The station is in German neo-Renaissance style (1894-1900), which will not detain many purists; take S. Elizabeth's St (Ulica Elżbietańska) to the church of the same name. It is impossible to discover from the interior that S. Elizabeth dates from the 14th century, because of a complete reconstruction in 1846. Its rampant devotion to modernity can be judged from a white screen, on which verses of the hymn being sung during my visit were flashed up in black, making hymnals obsolete.

S. Joseph's Church was erected from 1467-1518, with a short intermission for the Reformation, then the façade was eventually finished in 1681, but the interior is modern. Immediately adjacent, S. Elizabeth's and S. Joseph's gave me the impression of jostling churches encountered elsewhere only in some parts of Italy.

The charming House of the Pelplin Abbots at no. 3 (1612), attributed to Abraham van den Block, nestles on the bank of the Radunia canal. The house survived World War II. Pelplin is a small town not far from

Gdańsk. Corner of the Pelplin Abbots' House, with S. Catherine's in the background above the Radunia canal

the west bank of the Vistula south of Tczew, with an abbey founded in 1274; its church (1280-1320) will repay a visit.

I next followed the Radunia along Na Plaskach to Ulica Korzenna, where the Old Town Hall ascends like any other Hanseatic Rathaus, and indeed bears the polonised name Ratusz. Low Countries Renaissance architecture has been elegantly transposed to the Radunia. A Gothic Town Hall of about 1380 was replaced in 1587-95 by this assembly hall of great distinction, the concept of Antoon van Opberghen, with sculpture by Willem van der Meer of Ghent and Willem van den Block, from Malines like the architect. The shape is nearly square, 24 metres x 22, and the Flemish-style hall is unobtrusively covered by two parallel hip roofs. The façade was constructed in veneered brick with discreet stone ornamentation, the brickwork being replaced in the 19th century. Six entrances led to cellars from which the Town Council sold mead, beer and wine. The ground floor originally housed the staff, kitchen and coach-house, while the first floor divided into official accommodation and the Great Hall for official functions. The Prussians, who occupied Gdańsk from 1793, remodelled the Town Hall as law courts, but in 1910 the Town Hall reverted to its original use, and the Great Hall revived its style, and was almost untouched by the last War. Currently, the magnificent building serves as the Voivodship Social and Recreational Centre.

The main entrance portal, between herms, shows the White Eagle (Poland's national emblem), with the arms of King Sigismund III. Within, precious architectonic details from wealthy burghers' houses have been preserved: a mannerist arcaded stone wall from Ulica Długa 45 (1560), and in the director's room a baroque ceiling and fireplace of 1642 from Ulica Podwale Staromiejskie 69-70. The ground floor provides exhibition space, and the cellar is usually (though not during my visit) open for coffee.

Two mills survive on the Radunia, one on each flank of S. Catherine's: the Little Mill dates from about 1400, but only the walls remain; the Great Mill (on the street of the same name, Wielkie Młyny) arose in 1350 and ground up to two hundred tons of grain a day until it was wrecked in 1945. As I entered I was deafened by pop music and the demonic clatter-ping-screech of a jungle littered with dead-eyed teenagers and whirring fruit machines. The Great Mill is an amusement arcade. I bought a Pepsi-Cola from a gum-chewing youth inside the door, and listened to his implausible Elvis shrug-and-slur on-off dialogue with a tight-cardiganed chick on a bar stool. Outside the Great Mill, a black-leather jacketed spiv of thirty tried to prise me loose from some of my dollars, and a courteous man twice his age, with slight stubble, slight limp and slight wall eye tried, ever so slightly, to interest me in a guided tour of German Danzig. 'Do you find a lot of German tourists who want to look around?' I enquired. 'Very many', he nodded. 'Most people who come to the city lived here before the War, so they are disorientated, and sometimes cannot believe they are in the street where they were born, even after I take them there. Other people visited Danzig twenty, thirty years ago and cannot be persuaded that they have come back to the same place. It is as though they were living in a dream then.' 'Or now', I added. 'Or both.' I thought of the bizarre return to his birthplace of Günter Grass, thirty years ago.

The most compelling work of art to emerge from Gdańsk-Danzig in recent years is Günter Grass' novel *Die Blechtrommel* (1959), translated by Ralph Manheim as *The Tin Drum*. Born in Danzig in 1929, without graduating from secondary school, Grass devoted himself to writing, sculpture and stage design among other activities, before rocketing to fame with this remarkable, obsessive novel about young Oskar Matzerath (reaching the age of sixty in *Die Rättin*) who lives through the traumas of German Danzig and the Free City up to World War II, beginning with tales of his grandmother. Chapter 2 of Book II, 'The Polish Post Office', brings to life the Nazi siege of the Polish Post Office in Gdańsk, at Ulica Obrońców Poczty Polskiej. Withstanding this attack, concerted on 3 July to take place simultaneously with the Westerplatte attack on 1 September, fifty post-office workers with rifles and hand grenades held off an attack for nearly fourteen hours. In 1958 Grass discovered that two of the postal workers had survived, though their names had been engraved on a memorial tablet. Grass interviewed both of them, who were earning more in the shipyard; he 'spoke in graveyards with tombstones that made me nostalgic, sat as I had as a boy in the reading-room of the municipal library, leafing through piles of the *Danziger Vorposten*. I smelled the Mottlau and Radaune. In Gdańsk I was a stranger, but in fragments I rediscovered everything: bathing establishments, walks in the woods, brick Gothic, and the apartment on Labesweg between Max-Halbe-Platz and Neuer Markt; and revisited – on Oskar's advice – the Church of the Sacred Heart: still the same old Catholic fug.'

Yet somehow S. Bridget's Church has not *quite* the same old Catholic fug, since the visit to Poland of Pope Jan Paweł II. His statue outside this huge, harmonious brick church of three naves bears the provocative slogan TOTUS TUUS: everything is yours. Many a Sunday morning, the national mass fills the church to overflowing, and one of the participants is Lech Wałęsa, the celebrated free trade union activist, who rose to world renown with his steadfast insistence on workers' rights during the brief and glorious episode when Solidarność challenged the Party's total control over all aspects of secular Polish life. Reverberations last throughout the week, until the next national mass. S. Bridget is called after the saint whose relics were sent from Rome and, in 1374, exposed in a former chapel. A convent and church started in the 14th century was completed by a southern nave in 1514 and a steeple in 1616.

S. Catherine's, properly 'Little Kate's' (Katarzynka), arose over a long period, too. The brick presbytery was begun in 1326, and within a hundred years the three-nave church and steeple were complete, though the latter was raised in 1486. The baroque dome of 1634 has been repaired in recent years. Anton Möller the Elder (1563-1611) painted the mannerist Crucifixion shortly before his death, with a contemporary view of Gdańsk in the background. Matthäus Gletker is the sculptor of the baptistery's marquetry and allegorical figures (1585).

Take a moment to enjoy the 17th-century plebeian house at the

Gdańsk. Small house on the corner of Ulica Katarzynki, with Jacek Tower

corner of Katarzynki and Podmłyńską and the elegant House of the Preachers (1602) with a façade by Antoon van Opberghen. Continuing along Podmłyńską, you come to the isolated guard tower of S. James (Jacek) which is all that remains of an early 15th-century defensive system. If you take Podwale Staromiejskie towards the Fish Market (Targ Rybny), ending at the northern guard tower called the Swan, from the same period as Jacek Tower, you come to the Holy Ghost Hospital. At Ulica Grobla 4, a 14th-century church was pulled down, making way for the hospital in 1647. The building has been remodelled as teachers' lodgings.

For all the achievements of those who rebuilt Warsaw, it may be that the single most imaginative enterprise of post-War reconstruction in Poland has been the remarkable ensemble running from Upper Gate to Green Gate along Gdańsk Long Street and Long Market, a brilliant success of the mid-16th century, with a multiplicity of later surprises, some quite inspired but none at all in the slightest dull, widening in a delicately peculiar curve towards the Town Hall.

Behind the authentic façades, not all is as it seems, however. Many poky interiors have been replaced by modern apartments, and squalid hovels built within backyards were never rebuilt, thus increasing areas for playgrounds and gardens. Fragments and details rescued from rubble have been reused wherever possible; old prints provided an exact blueprint for revival. We start at the Upper Gate (Brama Wyżynna), once moated with a drawbridge, its façade rebuilt in 1586-8 by Willem van den Block, the father of Abraham, architect of the Renaissance Golden Gate (1612-14), separated from the Upper Gate by the Front Gate (1593) by Antoon van Opberghen.

At the northern side of the Golden Gate stands the Gothic Mansion of the Brotherhood of S. George (1487-94), a society of patricians. The architect was J. Glotau. The effeminate little tower on the roof has a metal statue of S. George whose helmet bears the white eagle and arms of Poland.

Long Street curved gently, idiosyncratically into its present form as long ago as the 13th century. The town centre first sprang up here in the middle of the 14th century, but only with the prosperity of the Hanseatic League and the arrival of merchants from Lübeck did the intellectual, mercantile and landowning city leaders commission the great houses that we see today from the most talented architects of Germany, Holland and Flanders, with eloquent additions by local artisans. Tall and slender, with neat rectangular windows to match, the houses express their greatest individuality in gables and lofts, attics and stucco at higher levels, where northern skies play skittishly with sun, cloud and shadow. No. 12, designed by Jan Benjamin Dreyer in 1776, belonged to the town councillor of Flemish origin Jan Ophagen. Across the street, nos.

69 and 70 offer an unobtrusive contrast, in the eclectic style of the late 19th century. On the corner of Ulica Pocztowa at no. 22 a post-war Post Office tactfully retains the ambience of Renaissance Gdańsk with its red plaster and sandstone. No. 28, Konstantin Ferber's House, was created by Sebastiano Serlio in Renaissance style for Mayor Ferber about 1560.

No. 35 is a Renaissance mansion of 1569 by Johann Kramer of Dresden, known as the Lion's Castle: its porch incorporates some original sculptural elements. The vestibule was closed at the time of my visit, but a print by Johann Karl Schultz appears in *Gdańsk* (1978) by Maria and Andrzej Szypowscy. No. 30 possesses a splendid façade of 1563 by Flemish sculptors. No. 45, grandly entitled the House of the Kings of Poland, is a 16th-century mansion converted into tourist accommodation. No. 47, the Museum of the History of Gdańsk, above the handy Café Palowa, was the Main Town Hall, first erected in Gothic brick before 1360, and expanded several times beginning in 1379-82. The ascent to the tower looks demanding, but amply repays the effort of climbing eighty metres above old Gdańsk. A northern wing was added in 1593-6, while the grand external porch and stairway by the Swedish sculptor Daniel Eggert dates from 1766-68. Gutted in 1945, the Town Hall has risen from its ashes and its carillon peals every hour part of a patriotic song: 'We shall never abandon the land of our fathers'. The Great Council Chamber, named the 'Red Room' since the 18th century, has an interior of 1593-1611, including a fireplace by Willem van den Meer, and woodcarving by Simon Herle. The paintings are by Jan Vredeman de Vries, Izaak van den Block and Anton Möller of Königsberg (now Kaliningrad). In 1560 a spire surmounted by a gilded statue of King Sigismund Augustus was erected, and a replacement was set up in 1950. My most vivid recollection of the Museum must be Möller's extraordinary 'Rent Penny' (1601), with its lovingly detailed backcloth showing Long Market, Long Street, and this very Town Hall. Crowds in front of the Artusz Mansion on Long Market throng the lower section of Izaak van den Block's stirring 'Apotheosis of Gdańsk' (1608) in the centre of the ceiling of the Red Room.

The Royal or White Hall is the scene of ceremonies and festive occasions. A gallery devoted to 'Slavic Gdańsk and Gdańsk under the Republic' is followed by the heartbreaking yet inspiring story of the 'Destruction and Liberation of Gdańsk' in 1945. A leaflet similar to thousands dropped on Gdańsk's German defenders carried an appeal from the Soviet Commander: 'Further resistance is pointless... and would lead only to your death and to the death of hundreds of thousands of women, children, the aged and infirm. I appeal to you for immediate surrender'. But the Nazis fought on and Gdańsk became almost mortally injured. Before World War II the population had been 240,000; in 1946 (after all Germans had been moved to Germany in accordance with the Potsdam Treaty) the numbers had fallen to only 117,000. Perhaps its tower and steeple are too large for the slim, light Town Hall, but when you take a sparrow's-eye view of the Long Market all is harmony and pastel colours: orange, green, cream, brown, white, pink. Above the sun-dial of 1589 and 15th-century clock we can look down on Long Market and the Green Gate (east), across to Holy Trinity Church and the National Museum (south), Long Street and the Golden Gate (west), and S. Mary's Church and the Archaeological Museum (north).

Long Market will be the heart of your stay in Gdańsk, for the variety and elegance of its porches and the houses which rise behind them like many-storied fantasy dwellings. Porches were devised above cellars

Gdańsk. Długi Targ, with Town Hall and Neptune Fountain

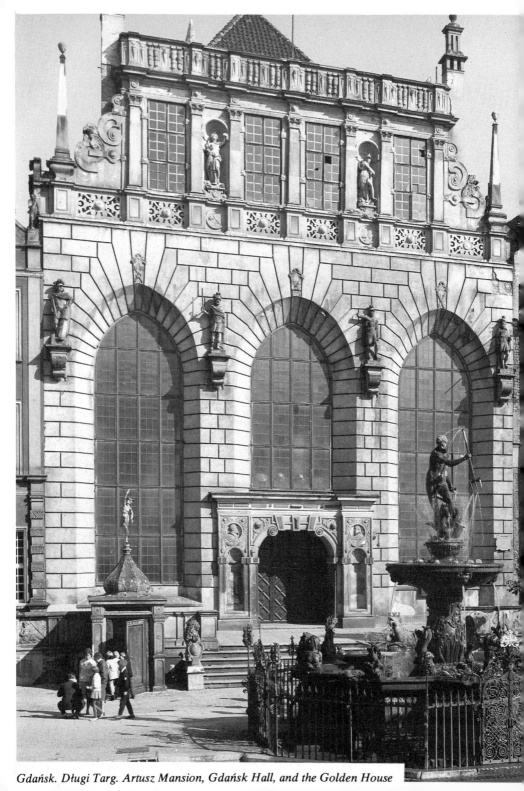

Gdańsk. Długi Targ. Artusz Mansion, Gdańsk Hall, and the Golden House

where merchants kept their goods. Feast-days and firework displays were celebrated in this aristocrat demesne, where urban pavilions are floodlit on summer nights. In 1607, John Green brought his players from England to give outdoor performances here. At no. 19 you can still find accommodation (in the Hotel Jantar) of budget type: Jan Matejko lived here in 1877.

Boisterous Polish marines jostled, soft-punched and elbowed each other self-consciously in front of a companion's camera as they grouped below Neptune's Fountain, the sea-god cast by Danish sculptor Peter Husum (1613) and the whole designed by Abraham van den Block. Sculptures round the base and the present pool are due to the German Johann Carl Stender (1757-61).

The north side of Long Market, past the Town Hall, glitters with wealth and style. The Artusz Mansion, once the ceremonial hall of the city guilds, had a Gothic interior of 1476-81, with a mannerist façade of 1617-8 by Abraham van den Block. The porches and entrances of this mansion and its neighbours at 46-7 are originals of 1760 by Johann Heinrich Meissner (1700-70), possibly the most notable rococo sculptor on these Baltic shores. No. 43, called the Gdańsk Hall, has an 18th-century gable above a Gothic façade. No. 41, the Golden House, must be the most attractive Renaissance mansion in the city, executed in 1609-18 for Mayor Johann Speimann to designs by Abraham van den Block. The four elegant storeys are surmounted by a balustrade with four life-size mythological figures. Friezes at other levels illustrate Roman history. At the House of Books, Długi Targ 62-3, I scoured the shelves for the works of Polish writers whose critical minds and questing imaginations have provoked discussion and argument: Zagajewski, Herbert, Miłosz, Przybyszewski, Witold Gombrowicz, Bruno Schulz. But none of them is to be found on the shelves of Polish bookshops today, whose stock is determined by Government censors, explicitly or implicitly. If all interesting, original, experimental writing is barred from bookshops, how does the questing mind discover key texts?

One way is to import books from emigré houses such as Instytut Literacki, 91 avenue de Poissy, Le-Mesnil-le-Roi, 78600 Maisons-Laffitte, France, publishing exclusively in Polish. New authors appear first in their monthly magazine *Kultura*.

Another way for young Poles to find out about literature written for the sake of literature, as opposed for some Party-defined message, is to borrow books from older people, and pass them from hand to hand, either in originals, or in photocopies. But photocopiers are registered with the state – as printing presses are, and as typewriters too once were – so that in theory one may photocopy only approved texts. In this, as in all else, the underground is so close-knit and widespread that the secret police make only token raids, and know that the battle for the Polish mind is lost, at least in this generation, when the victories of Solidarność still glow radiantly in people's minds and hearts.

A third method is to find access, through visiting friends or relatives, to translations into languages read by the older generation (mainly German and English) or the younger generation (mainly English and French), but this is naturally more effective in prose work, such as *The Captive Mind* of Miłosz, than in poetry, such as Zbigniew Herbert's or Tadeusz Różewicz's. Poems are, as in the Soviet dominions, learnt by heart and can be recited by everyone from taxi-drivers to railway ticket-inspectors, one of whom produced from memory for me Wiktor Woroszylski's poem 'Slavery'. A few years ago a translation of the Qur'an into Polish appeared in an edition of ten thousand copies or more, but it was snapped up so quickly by the voracious bookbuying public (and especially by the Muslim minority, descendants of marauding Tatars, in the south-east) that within a matter of days the whole edition was sold out and no amount of cajoling or browbeating could produce an extra copy from a bookshop. The same happens to many books once the word gets out.

So I did not despair too keenly at the absence from the bookshops even of such masterpieces as Bruno Schulz's *Sklepy Cynamonowe* (1934), translated by Celina Wieniewska as *The Street of Crocodiles* (1963; paperback, 1980). Or Witold Gombrowicz's *Ferdydurke* (1937), translated by E. Mosbacher (1961).

Gombrowicz satirises three main targets: false interpretations of the 'prophetic' or 'Messianic' nature of Polish literature; the 'virile' nature of the peasantry, whom Gombrowicz castigated as merely boorish; and the so-called 'progressive' urbanites, whose cult of the modish and modern makes them in his eyes merely ridiculous.

Bruno Schulz's two collections of stories (the other is *Sanatorium pod Klepsydrą,* 1937, translated by Wieniewska as *Sanatorium under the Sign of the Hourglass,* 1979; paperback, 1980) transmute the provincial world of Drohobycz (now called Drogobych, in Soviet Ukraine, south of Lwów) into a magical world of images, where the grotesque accompanies the workaday world hand-in-hand, disconcertingly. Born in 1892, he was shot in 1942 by a Nazi jealous of the Jewish writer's friendship with another German. Everyone who has tramped through dismal suburbs of Cracow, Warsaw, or any other Polish city will recognise Schulz's Drohobycz. 'Already for some time our town had been sinking into the perpetual greyness of dusk, had become affected at the edges by a rash of shadows, by fluffy mildew, and by moss the dull colour of iron'.

Porches above cellars dignify the so-called 'royal' houses on the south of Long Market, where successive monarchs stayed while in Gdańsk. Andreas Schlüter the Younger designed at least two of these: no. 3

Gdańsk. Długi Targ. The 'Royal Houses' opposite Artusz Mansion

(c.1670) and no. 20 (c.1685). We have come full circle: to the Green Gate from which harbour cruises can be taken. For evening entertainment in the Triune City, we could go back to the nearby Coal Market for the Teatr Wybrzeże. Other plays may be seen at Gdynia's Teatr Dramatyczny, Ulica Bema 26 or at Sopot's Teatr Kameralny. For music, Sopot in Summer has Opera-in-the-Woods and Gdynia the Music Theatre at Plac Grunwaldski 1. But on no account miss the State Opera and Baltic Philharmonic on Aleja Zwycięstwa 15.

As well as a joyous *Córka źle strzeżona* (a ballet I slowly construed as *La fille mal gardée* while counting out my 250 złoty or 60 pence for a

Gdańsk. Baltic Theatre and Philharmonic Hall

ticket), I managed to obtain a seat for a *Traviata* sung in Polish. Or nearly Polish: the guest singing Violetta, Christina Rorbach, sang in the original Italian. If Cracow Opera can sing the work totally in Italian, why cannot the Baltic? The question is not simply academic, for when Alfredo urges his new love ardently to meet him tomorrow, his 'Na jutro!' is here echoed by her 'Domani!', which damages Verdi's musical effect. The spirited musical life of Gdańsk could be exemplified by the month I was there: Moniuszko's *Halka* and *Straszny Dwór*, *The Barber of Seville* and *Madama Butterfly*, the ballets *Jurand* and *Coppélia*, and concerts by the Leningrad Philharmonic and the BBC Scottish

Symphony Orchestra. Like the Coast Theatre, the Baltic Opera House is modern in age and feeling, airy, spacious, and choosing glass for light where the traditional European red and gilt, velvet and stucco palace would repudiate the outside world with thick stone walls and weighty portals.

Living in Oliwa in a pleasant room with access to a lavish bathroom, in a semi-detached house surrounded by trees and gardens, I could enjoy early morning strolls in the Cathedral park. Back in 1958, Günter Grass had returned to the park of his childhood, and found what he had lost: 'Goldfish and swans, Mama and Jan Broński in the famous Whispering Grotto. Afterwards, more goldfish and more swans, clearly working hand-in-glove with a photographer'. A grandmother wheeled a

Gdańsk. Oliwa. Semi-detached urban houses in Ulica Asnyka

pram solicitously through the leafy glade. Two soldiers whispered, lounging by a lime-tree. Ducks waddled and flapped, on the scavenge for a few crumbs. A short man in a faded brown suit scuttled past with a briefcase, reminding me of the White Rabbit in *Alice*. The park, now named after Adam Mickiewicz, has a symmetrical sector laid out in 1760; I preferred (I admit) the English-style sector to the north, laid out in 1782. Oliwa Zoo, in a forested area called the Hill of Joy (Dolina Radości), stays open from about 9 to 8 in Summer and 10 to 3 in Winter: but as always check these times beforehand. To explore a modern Polish housing estate, cross to seaward for the Przymorze Estate (1959-1973), intended for 60,000 residents: three nine-storey blocks were given by the city of Leningrad to the dockworkers of Gdańsk.

Oliwa Cathedral has developed over the centuries from the first little brick oratory of about 1200, extended within the next fifty years by a transept and three naves. Further expansions in the 13th and 14th centuries provide the cathedral we see today in broad outline, though of course numerous details have changed, and the main, west door is baroque, from 1668. Swedish invaders looted many church possessions, including the organ and pulpit. Mediaeval objects were lost when the church was burnt by citizens of Gdańsk. The present organ (1763-88) by the west front is used for concerts throughout the year, and rehearsals enhanced my tour of the interior, which started at the crossing between transept and nave, by the small organ, used for magical echo effects during recitals. Proceeding to the ambit, a tombstone of Chamberlain Hulsen (1760) is the work by Meissner, and a black marble plaque (1615) to the Pomeranian princes can be seen at the entrance to the transept. A tiny Abbot's Chapel is reached by stone stairs.

Try to obtain permission to enter the presbytery, for the main altar (1688) with an altarpiece of the 'Adoration of Mary' by Andreas Stech (1635-97), son of the painter Heinrich Stech of Stolp. The rococo pulpit (*c.*1750) is decorated with scenes from the life of S. Bernard, while painted friezes honour those connected with the church up to 1580, when the paintings were made. The stalls (1604) are splendidly carved. Returning from the presbytery, you will see in the northern arm of the transept late 16th-century mannerist stalls, an original wooden main altar of 1606, and a stone altar of 1635.

As at Wilanów or Łazienki, at the Abbots' Palace in Oliwa I was bemused by the ideology of a socialist workers' state that spends so munificently on the upkeep of palaces once owned by kings or great magnates of the churches. The older palace, a 15th-century Gothic mansion, has been partly reconstructed as a scientific institute. The magnificent rococo residence of 1754-6, also burnt by the Nazis in 1945, was commissioned by Abbot Jacek Rybiński, who also endowed the pulpit in the cathedral. Occasional chamber recitals are held in the music room, but the main function of the palace these days is museological. The ground floor depicts the life and homes of Pomeranians, and one has to don silly sloppy slippers (as in the Maritime Museum) to protect highly polished wooden parquet floors from high heels (which, as Henry Reed would have said, 'in my case I have not got'). It is all worth the stern words from stout lady custodians to see colourful dressers, chests and wardrobes from Kashubia, weaving and tapestries, and a ludicrous wooden rocking goose from Elbląg. You can learn more about the Kashubian minority at the Kashubian Ethnographic Open-Air Park at Wdzydze Kiszewskie (open daily

Gdańsk. Oliwa. Abbots' Palace, now a museum

except Mondays, like most museums in Poland); the Kashubian Museum at Ulica Ludowego Wojska Polskiego 1, Kartuzy; and the Museum of Kashubian-Pomeranian Literature and Music, Ulica Sobieskiego 239, Wejherowo. Wejherowo is a station on the frequent electric-train service from Gdańsk via Gdynia.

I was informed that the upper floor of the Palace was closed, though staff were in fact moving upstairs and downstairs without apparent difficulty. Politely I expressed my interest in the upper floor, requesting to meet the director or a delegate. 'By all means,' came the reply. 'But she can only speak French.' I must have looked as incredulous as I felt, but as usual I humoured my interlocutor, and spoke to the pleasant young lady who emerged from an office in the language of Diderot. Open sesame! Flopping like a wounded penguin in my overshoes up the stairs, I came on paintings well worth the effort. Here is the 'Tragedia Gdynska I' (1979) of Maksymilian Kasprowicz (1906-86) and the superrealism of 'Bread' (1975) by Włodzimierz Kamiński (b.1935). Western artistic trends that one might expect to see confined to open-air markets or private galleries have found their awkward place in the august rooms of the Abbots' Palace: the op art of Jan Ziemski (b.1920) in 'Interferencje' (1974), the *frottage* of Bohdan Borowski (b.1923) in 'Motyw z Wybrzeża V' (1975), and the Delvaux-like 'Z ognia przybędzie pan' (1973) by Henryk Waniek (b.1942). The 20th century being the age of the modern international movement, without frontiers of race or nation, religion or historical necessity, it is a shock to see a 'Pietà' of 1973-4 by Z. Grzywacz. More consonant with our adventurous times are 'Horyzont I & II' (1975) by Marian Bogusz (1920-80); the flowing forms of Małgorzata Lutomska (1948-83) in 'Kompozycja Brązowa' and dense structures in 'Reminiscencje Morza' (1976) by Andrzej Śramkiewicz (b.1951).

A day out in Sopot could begin at the electric rail station called Sopot Wyścigi (Racecourse). Even if no races are planned that day you could wander along Ulica Polna to the sea shore by Plac Rybaków. Poles, French and Germans alike have treated Sopot (Zoppot in German) as a quiet seaside refuge for centuries, even before its first documented mention in 1283, but it was only with the arrival of a French doctor, formerly with the Napoleonic armies, Jean-Georges Haffner, that the coast's potential was realised, and baths, beaches and hotels sprang up like mushrooms almost overnight: the baths in 1823, and the Spa House a year later.

The new northern and southern baths date from 1903-4. A horse bus service ran north from Gdańsk to Sopot from 1823. The Grand Hotel rose in 1927, just north of the Molo, a pleasure pier of 516 metres, and so the longest on the Baltic. A pedestrian precinct, Monte Cassino Heroes Street, leads from the pier and Polish-Soviet Friendship Square

Sopot. Beach

to the main thoroughfare between Gdańsk and Gdynia, here called 20 October (Ulica 20 Października).

Alight at the main Sopot rail station for the accommodation bureau, labelled 'Biuro Zakwaterowań', Ulica Dworcowa 4: the Hotel Dworcowy is situated opposite the station, but you might prefer to stay on the beach, more expensively, at the chic Orbis Grand, Ulica Powstańców Warszawy 8-12: you can imagine giggly young things dancing the Charleston, and picking at delicacies in the restaurant overlooking the Baltic. The Shah of Iran stayed there, so you might like it too. Architecture is not Sopot's strength: a neo-Gothic chapel of 1870 in elm-green Ulica Powstańców Warszawy; in Ulica Czyżewskiego the last of the manor houses of the early 19th century, at first a Burski property, then a Sierakowski; and an art nouveau building of 1904; at Ulica Dzierzyńskiego 21, near the modern church of S. Michael (1968). Inland from the northern baths and tennis courts, near the northern end of Ulica Bieruta, a mound is surmounted by remains of an 8th-10th century Slavic castle, with a fortified embankment. The Summer Theatre is situated south of this, but the Opera-in-the-Woods lies to the west, across the main road, not far from the Soviet monument on Olympic Hill. Created in 1909, the Opera-in-the-Woods was modernized with a receding roof in the early 1960s, and seats up to five thousand. Transport after performances is arranged both to Gdańsk and to Gdynia.

A tiny village from its first mention in history, in 1253 up to the present century, Gdynia became a city of the future when, in 1922, the Polish Parliament resolved to create a new port, since the Free Port of Gdańsk no longer provided Polish naval or mercantile interests with an adequate outlet to the sea. Construction of the port began in 1924 and, with the exception of war years, has continued ever since. In 1939, the Nazis expelled fifty thousand people and executed more than twelve thousand in the Piaśnica woods, between Krokowa and Wejherowo. Gdynia was freed by the Red Army in March 1945, though the port had been devastated by enemy action. The electric train can be taken from Gdańsk as far as Orłowo, if you want to stroll in a typical residential district landward; or to Wzgórze Nowotki (seaward).

But most visitors will leave the train at the Main Station (ask for Gdynia Główny) for the woods to landward, or the port. 'Gotenhafen' in German, Gdynia can best be seen from Kamienna Góra, accessible from Ulica Mickiewicza. The Southern Pier juts out into the General Zaruski Yacht Basin, overlooked by the Marine Fishery Institute and the Higher Maritime College, with an aquarium and Oceanographic Museum, rounded like a whale where it faces the bay. The Baltic exhibition on the third floor has a relief map illustrating the topography of the seabed, and faunal distribution. Four dioramas on the second floor reveal marine life in four different zones: the littoral, pelagial depths, tropical regions, and oceanic abysses. The aquarium displays fauna from the Baltic, borealic, temperate and tropical seas, as well as freshwater fish from the tropics and subtropics.

On your way from Kamienna Góra to the Southern Pier, stop at the Naval War Museum (as usual, closed on Mondays) at Bulwar Nadmorski, a boulevard created in 1965-9. Beginning with the earliest years of Slavs in the Baltic region, the museum explores the rise of the Teutonic Order, the Polish Navy in the 16th-17th centuries (models of *Wodnik* and *Rycerz Św. Jerzy*), and in the present epoch, concentrating on the Navy in World War II. Even when the museum is closed, an open-air sector adds a chill to the warmest Summer's day with antiaircraft guns, bombs and rockets.

Associated with the Naval War Museum is the *Błyskawica*, a destroyer decked out with a permanent display in the stern to illustrate Poland's millennium as a seafaring nation, with especial reference to World War II. Also on the Pomeranian Quay is the three-masted frigate *Dar Pomorza* used since 1969 as a training ship. Made in Hamburg in 1909, it has flown the Polish flag since 1930. You can visit the ship while it remains in port from 10 to 4 every day but Monday. The guided tour, though only in Polish, is well worth an hour of anyone's time. Nearby you can take a steamer for a cruise round Gdańsk Bay, or Świnoujście (for Szczecin) or Ustka (for Słupsk). A motor-boat chugs you round Gdynia Bay for half-an-hour.

Harbour cruises pass the pier of commercial trawlers fishing the Atlantic (Molo Rybne), the Coal Pier (Molo Węglowe) and the Passenger Pier (Molo Pasażerskie). The TS/S *Stefan Batory* plies once a month from here to Copenhagen, Hamburg, Rotterdam, London and Montreal. Cargoes are handled on docks IV and V, while dock VI is the scene of shipbuilding and refitting by the Paris Commune Shipyard.

A film festival had attracted an international audience to the Teatr Muzyczny, opposite the Orbis Gdynia Hotel. I took coffee and cakes in the hotel's café 'U Marysieńki'. A receptionist assured me that a single room cost 16,000 złoty (£40 or US$60) a night, with breakfast, and a double 21,000 złoty (£50.25 or $77). This interested me, because a young teacher to whom I had spoken on the beach told me that her salary amounted to 20,000 złoty a month, and in ten or twelve years she could aspire to 30,000 złoty, and these were figures before the price rises of 1988 made life even more expensive. A month's electricity for a three-roomed flat in 1987 came to about 2,000 złoty in Summer or 3,000 in Winter, with a further 1,000 złoty a month for gas throughout the year, and 10,000 złoty for a whole Winter's coal supply: these prices rose by more than double in 1988.

You can reach the pine-scented peninsula of Hel by boat direct to Hel

Gdynia. General Mariusz Zaruski Basin, with the Oceanographic Museum and Aquarium

from Gdynia, or by road through Puck and Władysławowo, touching at Chalupy, Kuźnica, Jastarnia, and Jurata. Hel has its own register of private accommodation at Ulica Stefańskiego. Beaches make a heaven of Hel, but there is a small museum too, in a disused 15th-century Gothic church. Puck also has an interesting Gothic church, of the 14th century in the main, with parts from the mid-13th.

Similar beaches can be found along the Vistulan Peninsula, eastward from Gdańsk. This Amber Coast run from the central bus station in Gdańsk to Krynica Morska takes about an hour, and beaches even closer to the Soviet border become progressively more empty as you travel eastward. The route passes the former Nazi concentration camp of Stutthof, now Sztutowo, where a Museum of Martyrdom commemorates 65,000 dead, including Jews and Christians alike: Poles, Russians, Belgians, French, Lithuanians, Danes, Norwegians and Hungarians. The efficient, logical organization of this death camp mystifies anyone for whom savagery is synonymous with chaos. Here is the neat villa of the camp commandant; a well-made guardhouse; a tidy Command Office; symmetrical barracks and hospital; the unobtrusive gas chamber and crematorium. Should we seek to remember such barbarity? Should we strive to forget man's inhumanity to man in the effort to forge a new future? Reader: I leave you with neither quick answers, nor simple, plausible statements. I leave you only with the questions.

III WARSAW

It is a mystery why Warsaw, like Madrid, took so long to become national capital, given its central location. In fact, it was merely the residence of the Dukes of Mazovia until their line died out in 1526 and Warsaw was annexed to the Polish Kingdom. Significant till then as a market town and trading entrepôt, Warsaw developed into a true capital only in 1609 under Sigismund III (1566-1632), to whom the monument opposite the Royal Castle was erected in 1644, a bronze by Clemente Molli dominating its surroundings much like Nelson's Column in Trafalgar Square.

'The siege has lasted a long time', ponders Zbigniew Herbert in his *Report from the Besieged City* (1987).

'In the evening I like to wander near the outposts of the City
along the frontier of our uncertain freedom
I look at the swarms of soldiers below their lights
I listen to the noise of drums barbarian shrieks
truly it is inconceivable the City is still defending itself
the siege has lasted a long time the enemies must take turns
nothing unites them except the desire for our extermination
Goths the Tartars Swedes troops of the Emperor regiments of the Transfiguration
who can count them
the colours of their banners change like the forest on the horizon
from delicate bird's yellow in spring through green through red to winter's black...'

And if your memory goes as far back only as the Warsaw Uprising, 1 August to 2 October 1944, a glance through Norman Davies' two-volume history, *God's Playground* (1981), will draw attention to the ceaseless turmoil for the mastery of Warsaw from the seventeenth century until the arrival of the Soviet troops on 1 February 1945, since when the country has been controlled by the U.S.S.R. and those loyal to the U.S.S.R.

Prussians, Austrians, Swedes and Russians: all have attempted to seize control. Carl Gustaf of Sweden held the city for a year from 1655; Augustus II and III of Saxony embellished the city between 1697 and 1763; the Russians took command in 1764 and installed Stanislaus August Poniatowski as 'their man in Warsaw', a King who created

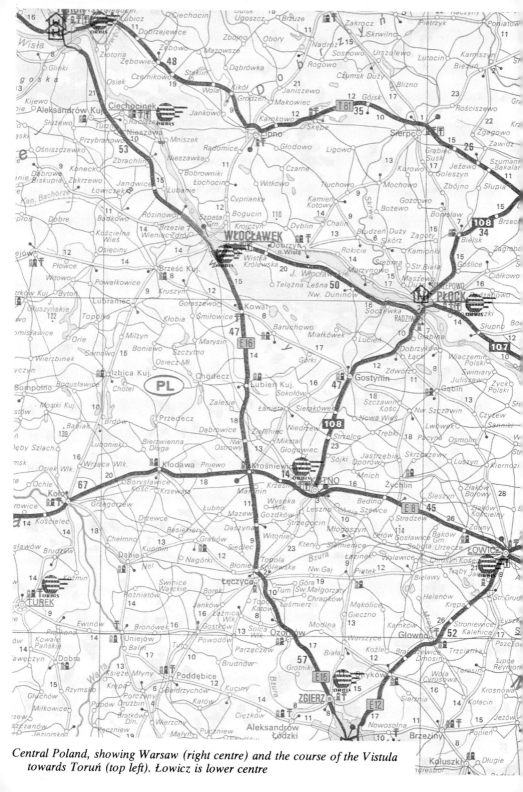

Central Poland, showing Warsaw (right centre) and the course of the Vistula towards Toruń (top left). Łowicz is lower centre

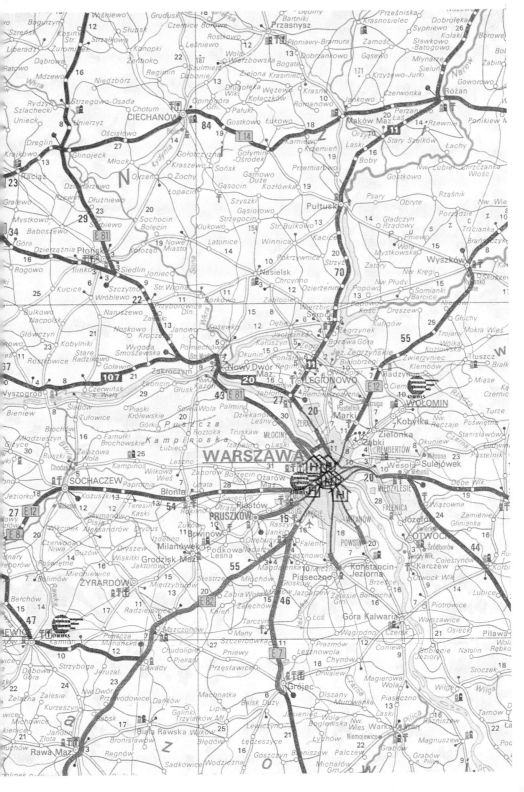

almost single-handed in a single generation the city of great mansions and palaces that we can admire today on the 'Royal Way' to Wilanów. In 1795, the city was granted to Prussia in the Third Partition; in 1806 it was occupied by Napoleon; in 1809 by the Austrians; in 1813 by the Russians. Polish insurrections against the might of Russia were savagely put down, rebels being killed or deported in huge numbers to Siberia. Honest men found themselves torn between underground activities against the state, or exile. We know much more about the latter, for they were able to express themselves openly. After the insurrection of 1863, by contrast, an entire district was razed to the ground, to be replaced by a vast citadel created as a place of torture and execution for Poles. 'If the City falls but a single man escapes', murmurs Herbert, 'he will carry the City within himself on the roads of exile: he will be the City.' From 1918 to 1939 Independence was achieved, in a new state called the Polish Republic, or Rzeczpospolita Polska, and the population rose to 1.3 million.

Nazi air attacks on Warsaw brought the city quickly into Axis hands and, despite heroic resistance, 800,000 Varsavians lost their lives in the War. The Ghetto Rising of 1943 lasted four weeks and ended with the death or deportation of more than 400,000 people, and the total destruction of the Jewish quarter. The Warsaw Rising, on the left bank of the Vistula, lasted nine weeks from 1 August 1944, and anyone left alive after the killing of 15,000 Polish soldiers, the wounding of 20,000 more, and the massacre of 150,000, was expelled by the Nazis, who plundered any remaining objects of value, and destroyed about 85% of the city's buildings, and 90% of its factories and industries. So that the Warsaw we see today is a phoenix risen almost literally from ashes.

Post-war Poland is about a fifth smaller than pre-war Poland, losing 46.5% of its territory to the U.S.S.R. but gaining most of the former German province of East Prussia, the whole area up to the rivers Odra and western Nysa (in German Oder-Neisse), and Szczecin, the Baltic port on the west bank of the Odra. The balance changed from a majority living by agriculture (60% in 1931) to a minority (38% in 1961) with a compensating rise in those living by industry, resulting in a steady drift from the countryside to the cities.

By elections on 19 January 1947, Communist tactics (violence against the Polish Peasant Party; repression of Karol Popiel's Labour Party), Poland became a one-party totalitarian state, and it is in the light of a Soviet satellite that the nation must be seen today. The Soviet bookshop on Nowy Świat in Warsaw is one tangible evidence of this unilateral style of leadership, just as the teaching of Russian in schools is another. Warsaw's skyline is overwhelmed by the massively tall, monolithic Palace of Culture and Science on Plac Defilad, 234 metres high, a gift from the Soviet Union in the years 1952-5. You can take a lift to the thirtieth floor, said by a Polish writer to offer the most beautiful panorama in Warsaw, because it is the only one from which the Palace of Culture is not visible. It also houses four theatres, three cinemas, and a Congress Hall as forbidding as the Palace of Congresses in the Kremlin.

Over the last generation, Poles have become increasingly restive with their submissive rôle. In the early 1970s, Poland's economy enjoyed the third fastest growth rate in the world, benefitting from great investment projects financed by western credit. But an economic crisis loomed, and huge food prices were announced by Gierek in June 1976, provoking strikes and riots throughout the country, notably at the Ursus Factory in Warsaw, and three-quarters of the nation's largest factories were hit more or less severely by strikes. Within twenty-four hours, the price-rises had been rescinded, but the mood was ripe for concerted action by the people. The Committee for the Defence of Workers (KOR) was formed that year against all odds, and the future Pope cried out against political murders such as that of Stanisław Pyjas of KOR in May 1977. 'We are still very far from the liberation of the workers for which they themselves have fought for one and a half centuries', sermonised the Archbishop of Cracow. 'Having liberated themselves from the capitalist pagan economy, they have fallen prey to the materialist pagan economy and the people, slaves before, are slaves today'. The free trade union Solidarność burned bright like a shooting star in 1980, only to be extinguished as rapidly, in 1981, with the imposition of martial law. The banning of Solidarność is a question on which most Poles feel strongly. Reputedly amassing ten million members at the height of its influence, an intellectual with whom I spoke in Warsaw suggested that it now has 'around nine million' unofficial members. Since the work force runs to about fourteen million people and there is no mention of the former union in the press, radio or television due to party censorship, the visitor should be aware of a dimension to Polish life absent from newspapers, conversation with tourist guides, and conventional chatter. But somehow the atmosphere has become heady with the *prospect* of greater toleration, even if the practice falls very far short. The Soviet Government has requested confidential documents on the recent history of Poland so that yet another rewriting can take place, but this time with a glimmer of objectivity based on a smattering of *glasnost*, or openness.

The first place to explore is Castle Square, with the Sigismund Column. My host queued at the ticket office before nine o'clock, emerging an hour later for admission at 10.35. Burnt by the Nazis in 1939 and blown up in 1944, the Castle immediately became a focal point for reconstruction, as with so much of Warsaw. On the day after Warsaw had been won back, Bierut vowed, 'We solemnly swear that on

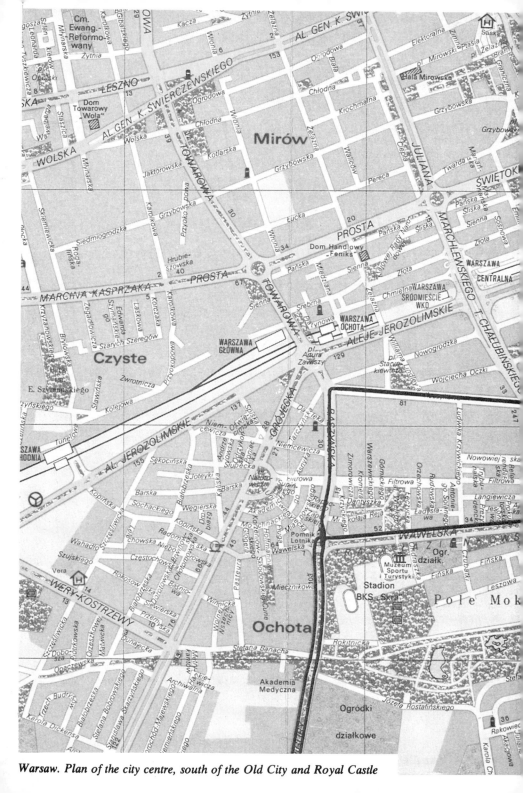

Warsaw. Plan of the city centre, south of the Old City and Royal Castle

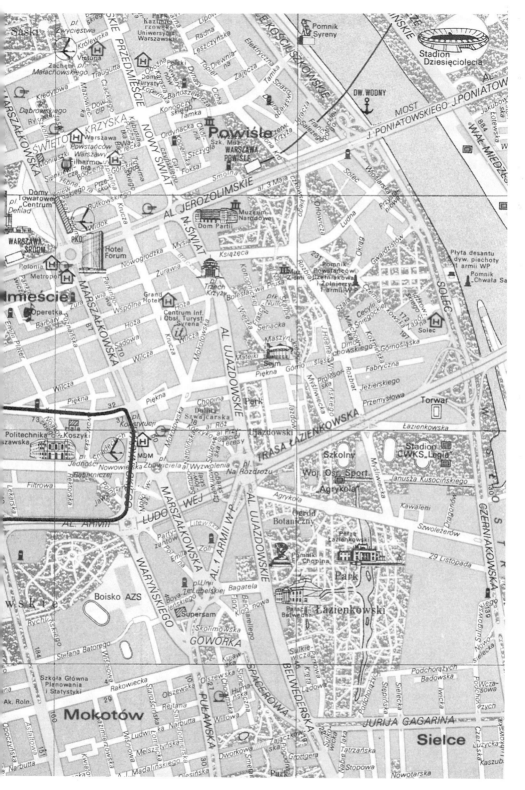

the graves of the heroes of Warsaw, on the ruins of our fairest buildings, we will, Warsaw, make efforts of which only we who love you are capable, and erect a monument worthy of your historic fame'. The new 'People's Council' established a reconstruction commission known as Biuro Odbudowy Stolicy, set up in the old Russian military hospital. The population had been devastated from 1¼ million in 1939 to scarcely twenty thousand, all on the right bank of the Vistula. Every bridge had been knocked out, and the city had no functioning sewage, water or electricity. The will of the Polish people to rebuild Warsaw proved so tenacious and urgent that the trams were running again in five months and the population had swollen to six hundred thousand in three years. There is something inherently human about the doggedness with which Varsavians set about rebuilding their homes much as they were in the eighteenth century, at least as far as the façades are concerned. Ulica Marszalkowska, for instance, looks like any modern wide street, but it has been enlarged by combining it with a street that once ran parallel to it.

The Royal Castle was the last piece in the restored jigsaw, having enjoyed unprecedented care and attention to detail during the works which lasted until 1981.

The Oval Gallery possesses splendid Flemish tapestries to designs by Michiel van Coxcie (1548-53) and Italian *cassoni* of the 17th century, when the tradition had declined from its Renaissance apogee. A portrait gallery has paintings of Charles II of England (English School) and Ferdinando de' Medici. Great paintings by Jan Matejko (1838-93) capture the atmosphere of national pride and despair. 'Tadeusz Rejtan at the Diet of Warsaw' (1866) shows the statesman from Nowogródek protesting in shame and disgust at the Diet's approval of Poland's partition in 1773. 'Batory at Pskov' (1872) witnesses the moment of glory in 1581 when Stefan Batory, King of Poland from 1576 to 1586, claims victory over the Muscovites. The Senate Hall exhibits a royal throne in a neo-classical setting. Matejko's 'Constitution of 3 May 1791' (1891) celebrates the adoption of a constitution as a result of the so-called 'Four-Year Diet'; it features King Stanislaus Augustus Poniatowski surrounded by reformers and supporters of the new constitution, in procession from the Castle to S. John's Cathedral.

The Gallery of the Four Seasons is named for tapestries signed by François Glaize. Exceptional stucco work distinguishes the Room of the Royal Horse Guards. You may recall André Le Brun (1737-1811), sculptor of 'The Flaying of Marsyas', from his 'Judith' and 'David' in San Carlo, Rome. Possibly the most interesting room of all is the Bellotto Room, in which the nephew and pupil of Canaletto (whose name he used in a deliberate attempt to confuse) demonstrates his topographical accuracy, to the point where these paintings were used by

Warsaw. Royal Castle.

architects planning the city reconstruction after World War II. Bellotto (1720-80) parted from his uncle by 1746, travelling in northern Italy before appointment in 1748 as court painter to Friedrich August II, for whom he painted faithful representations of Dresden and other towns in his domains. After a time in Vienna and Munich, Bellotto settled in Warsaw, where he painted a sequence of memorable, beautiful views of Warsaw and environs between 1767 and 1780, the year of his death in his adopted home. I delighted in a panorama of Warsaw seen from Praga (1770), the breathtaking perspective of 'Ulica Długa' (1777), and a charming delineation of Wilanów (1776). A small chapel has a Caravaggiesque oil, and the Old Audience Hall two Greek red-figure vases. A library filling the dressing-room contains not only the expected Biblia Sacra, but also Marmontel and Rousseau. The Knight's Hall has sketches of 1888-9 for large historical paintings which Matejko never executed. In chronological order, these are 'Christianity arrives in Poland, 965', 'Coronation of the first Polish king, 1001', 'Reception of the Jews, 1096', 'First Diet of Lęczyca, 1182', 'Defeat at Legnica, 1241', 'Second Conquest of Ruthenia, 1366', 'The Beginnings of Cracow University, 1361, 1399-1400', 'Pagan Lithuania accepts Christianity, 1387', 'Renaissance Humanists in Cracow, 15th century', 'The Golden Age, 16th century', 'The Election of Henri de Valois, 1573', and 'The 3 May Constitution, 1791'. Matejko's choice of grand themes is itself a theme for contemplation in front of these vivid, impressionistic scenes, crowded with vigour, colour, incident and majesty. Symbolism vibrates like sound waves across history: here are no dry, academic studies mincing towards formal acknowledgment by royal sponsors, but Balzacian, even Stendhalian crowds: a veritable 'Comédie humaine' rising to the potent level of a 'Chartreuse de Parme'.

And the Marble Room continues the theme of Polish royal history, with the gallery of small portraits and a large portrait of Stanislaus Augustus Poniatowski III, the last by Marcello Bacciarelli, a Roman painter born in Rome in 1731, who was appointed court painter at 22, when the future King of Poland was still Elector of Saxony.

As I sauntered from the Castle round to the Tin-Roofed Palace (Pod Blachą) at Plac Zamkowy 2, a group of three nuns pattered by twittering like black birds. I recalled Mayakovsky's 'Vozdev pechen'ie kartochki lichek' ('with small baked-potato faces looking up').

Until I explored Warsaw day by day, on foot and with frequent pauses to allow senses long enough to focus, concentrate, compare, I had never considered it primarily a city of mansions and palaces. The authorities have not rebuilt the Brühl, Jabłonowski, Kronenberg and Rzyszczewski mansions, nor the Saxon Palace. Some remained intact after the Nazi demolition of 1939 and 1944: the Belvedere, Dziewulski, Janasz,

Natolin, Karnicki, Radziwiłł, Sobański, Ursynów, Wielopolska, and Wierzbicki. But most were destroyed, and could be rebuilt only by careful study of old plans and photographs, and with huge expenditure, which the State provided. None of these great houses could be sited within the Old City, for reasons of space, but most date from the 17th and 18th centuries, following the southward line from the Castle to Krakowskie Przedmieście, Nowy Świat, Ujazdowskie, and Belwederska towards Wilanów. Others are scattered along Miodowa and its byroads, such as Senatorska and Długa. Earlier mansions possessed ample courtyards, but towards the end of the 18th century and throughout the 19th, architects started to build along street fronts, varying the popular neo-classical style with a more neo-Renaissance approach.

Pod Blachą was erected for the armourer Wawrzyniec (you may not recognise the Polish form as 'Lawrence') Reffus in the early 1650s, but the baroque appearance Pod Blachą wears today is due mainly to a transformation wrought by the powerful Prince Jerzy Lubomirski, Lord High Chamberlain, who bought the palace in 1720. Its most celebrated resident in Warsaw tales of gossip was Henriette de Vauban, mistress of Prince Joseph Poniatowski, who lived there between 1798 and 1806 during the Prussian partition. Known as 'the old parrot' for leading the life of a bird in a gilded cage, Vauban became insufferable for her airs and graces, yet was evidently a 'tall, thin, highly experienced and by no means beautiful Frenchwoman'. She could bear not the slightest noise, hated fresh air and insisted on the daintiest dishes. She refused to get out of her closed coach even when returning a social visit to a great lady and 'Madame de Vauban's' visits' consisted in fact of the unfortunate recipient of Madame's civility being required to attend her in her coach!

From Castle Square you can take either Ulica Piwna or Ulica Świętojańska to Old Town Market Square (Rynek Starego Miasta). I suggest the latter, which once crossed the city, with Ulica Nowomiejska, from the demolished Cracow and Nowomiejska Gates. No. 1 Ulica Świętojańska is the Pigułczyńska House, inhabited more than three centuries ago by Adam Jarzębski, author of *Gościniec* (1643), the first guide to Warsaw. The talented Jarzębski enjoyed the reputation of a fine builder and became court composer to Sigismund III.

Nearby is S. John's Cathedral; I attended a service for the installation of the new organ, and then roamed the ancient place, restored in 1956 after the ravages of war, when all that remained were the Chapel of Our Lord founded by the rich merchant Baryczko; a Renaissance tombstone (in the presbytery, the size of the original church of about 1339); and tombs in the crypts, commemorating the painter Bacciarelli, the writer Sienkiewicz, the pianist Paderewski, the scientist Gabriel Narutowicz, assassinated in 1922, two days after taking the oath, and the former Primate Stefan Wyszyński, who died in 1981 after three years in prison

(1953-6) for defending Roman Catholics from heavy-handed totalitarianism. Internally, the Cathedral has little of the atmosphere of Cracow's Cathedral on Wawel or S. Mary. The portal and high altar designed by A. Jabłoński, for example, date from 1963. Yes, the Baryczko Chapel offers a vision of the past, and the triple-aisled church has a stellar vault that harks back to Mazovian Gothic. But the heart of the cathedral is what is in the mind: one can imagine here the confirmation of the historic 3 May Constitution in 1791; generations of persecuted, humble passers-by taking part in Mass.

The Jesuit Church next door was similarly demolished by the Nazis, but you can see some objects saved. One is a Gothic crucifix of 1383; another a papal gift of a painting of Our Lady of Charity, Warsaw's patron saint. Below the church are foundations of houses razed by a great fire in 1607, and Gothic capitals. The cellars when I visited were furnished with a display glorifying the Pope's tour of Poland in 1987. Most Warsaw churches have pinned to a notice-board somewhere one or more portraits of Pope John Paul II, the former Archbishop of Cracow. These churches still seem to reverberate with the joy and pride of having a Polish Pope, the Vicar of Christ on earth. In some strange way the first triumphal return of John Paul II at Warsaw Airport on 2 June 1979 seemed to compensate for so many of Poland's losses, hardships, even tragedies over the centuries. His visit was timed to commemorate the nine hundredth anniversary of the murder of S. Stanislaus, but he also visited the concentration camp at Auschwitz, the Piast shrine and See of Gniezno, with its eighth century ramparts, and the shrine of the Black Madonna of Częstochowa. From then on, the jailed and ageing Cardinal Wyszyński, respected and firm though he had always been, was to be replaced in the hearts and minds of Catholic Poles by a leader internationally much more important than any temporary, temporal head of state.

Continuing towards Old Market Square, note at no. 31 the 18th-century Czempiński House, a ship on the sea sculpted in sandstone above the portal. Then prepare to have your breath taken away by the vision of Old Town Market Square, restored in general terms as it was during the 17th century, though it dates back in fact to the 13th. The northern side is named for Jan Dekert, Warsaw's civic leader during the Four-Year Parliament. He, like Franciszek Barss and Hugo Kołłątaj, was involved in the Forge salon (Kuźnica) during the Enlightenment. The east side of Rynek is named after Barss, the west side after Kołłątaj, and the south side after Ignacy Zakrzewski (1745-1802), the civic leader during the Kościuszko Revolt of 1794.

Since you normally approach Market Square from the Castle and Cathedral, our tour will start on the Zakrzewski side. No. 3 (The Barber's) was owned in the 17th century by a celebrated hairdresser called Juchta; no. 5 (The Oczko House) was owned in the 16th century by the court physician Oczko, and is now a restaurant well worth a visit; no. 7 (The Gilded House) belonged to the Baryczko family, deriving its name from its decorated façade; no. 13 (The Lion House) belonged to the Czempiński family and as well as its rococo lion now boasts a sundial on the flank wall overlooking Zapiecek Square and a painting by Zofia Stryjeńska of 1928.

On the Barss side no. 2 is the Small Monastery, having belonged to the Jesuits before the Barss family; 4-6 is a DESA art gallery; 8-10 a CEPELIA folk-art shop; and 18-20 the Adam Mickiewicz Museum of Literature. During my visit, the major display was devoted not to the eponymous national poet, but to the contemporary writer Edward Stachura, born in France in 1937, widely travelled in Syria, Mexico and Norway, and author of such works as *Fabula Rasa* (Olsztyn, 1979). A table indicated opening times of other Warsaw museums, including the Historical Museum a few steps away, on the northern side of Rynek. 'No', emphasised a guard at the Historical Museum, sunning himself on a rickety chair, 'the museum is closed for two years. Under repair.' 'Then why,' I enquired, 'do you not tell the museum over the road to change their list of opening times?' 'I don't need to,' rejoined the attendant. 'They know already.' And accusingly, after a weighty pause: 'Everybody knows'. He added in conversation later that a film showing the devastation of Warsaw and its post-war reconstruction would be available to visitors well before the whole museum is refurbished, and this film – already familiar to earlier visitors – is well worth seeing.

Across Rynek young families were lapping delicious, cheap ice-cream, and inspecting the open-air display of drawings and paintings by young artists. Cafés and restaurants make Rynek a popular meeting-place.

The Dekert side's exteriors are also worth close attention. No. 28 is the 17th-century Falkiewicz House, with sculptured saints adorning the attic. No. 32 is another Baryczko property (like no. 7) and when open gives a representative idea of a 17th-century patrician mansion, with an old printing press still in use in one of the rooms. The City Museum also owns the other houses: no. 34, the former Szlichtyng House, and no. 36 the House of Jacopo Gianotti, distinguished in overseas trade, personified by the head of a negro boy set in a roundel on the façade. No. 38 is the Talenti House, once the property of the royal secretary and later of a nobleman called Maciej Kurowski. No. 40 is the Montelupi House, later a printing works.

The last side is named for Hugo Kołłątaj (1750-1812), a secular radical and reformer who earns lasting respect as a founder of the 3 May Constitution. The aim was to strengthen the executive authorities and reform the legislature, army and treasury, and confer charters on towns.

Warsaw. Old Town Market Square

Like Stanislaus Staszic (1755-1826), he argued that the gentry had become too powerful, while the monarchy was circumscribed and the peasantry and petit bourgeoisie were virtually powerless. Kołłątaj lived for a short time at no. 21, the Klucznikowska House, built in 1608 by the Mayor, Pawel Zembrzuski, now occupied by the Krokodyl restaurant. My favourite building in the whole of Warsaw is no. 27, next to the former Fugger residence at no. 25. It is the Fugger Wine Shop, used from 1590 by an earlier wine merchant, and taken over by the Fuggers in 1810. Dating from the 15th century, it was restored in the 17th century and at the end of the 18th century assumed the neo-classical façade recently reconstructed. Elegant stucco dances across the three cream upper floors, shadows playing different games throughout a sunny day. A winery museum within could be visited, but on no account forego the delight of the magnificent arcaded courtyard. No. 31 is called S. Anne's House, after the 16th-century sculpture of S. Anne on the corner, but it is one of the oldest houses in the Old Town, dating from the 14th century (ogival blind windows and corner abutments), with a Renaissance attic and façade and early Baroque portal.

Stroll behind the Kołłątaj side of Rynek to parallel Ulica Piwna ('Brewery Street'), formerly known as Szynkarska and Marcinkańska, a mediaeval street from the early 14th century, with some Renaissance elements but a preponderance of the baroque, restoration having eliminated more recent additions. No. 13 was the Hospital of the Holy Spirit (represented by a dove on the façade) established in 1444.

Time for a coffee and cake? Ulica Piwna is the place: Pod Herbami at 21-3, Kmicic at 27, Zapiecek at 34, or Gwiazdeczka at 38-40.

S. Martin's Church and Augustinian Monastery were founded in 1352 by the Duke of Mazovia. Originally Gothic, the church was destroyed by fire in 1478, 1669, 1888 and most recently by the Nazis in 1944. Augustinian friars lived here until their dissolution in 1863 by the Russian Tsar. After World War II, the church and monastery were rebuilt, and interior design by the nun A. Skrzydlewska in a modern style offers an uneasy compromise between exterior and interior. Warsaw's intellectuals visit S. Martin's: the atmosphere is clear and invigorating in the centre of the church: almost like an Alpine valley. Black nuns darted about with flowers, messages and candles, rebel angels within Communist walls. Crossing Ulica Świętojańska again, you come to an idyllic tiny square called Kanonia, irregular in shape with 17th-century homes of the former Canons of the Warsaw Chapter; do not miss the house on the corner of Kanonia and Ulica Jezuicka with part of a Gothic window bay and a Renaissance plaque.

Crossing the pigeon-plagued Rynek once more, you have a marvellous view over the Vistula and the suburbs on the other bank

Warsaw. View from the Old Town down to the Vistula, with the Stara Prochownia Theatre (centre)

from an outcrop at the end of Ulica Celna. The isolated building below and towards the Vistula is the Stara Prochownia Theatre at Ulica Boleść 2.

From Świętojańska and the Kołłątaj side of Rynek, take Ulica Nowomiejska northwards to the New Town. At no. 1 'New Town' Street stands the former home of the distinguished civic leader Jan Dekert, while an original Gothic portal can be seen at no. 5. The great Barbican was the creation of a Venetian architect in the mid-16th century, defending the Nowomiejska Gate and the northern flank of Warsaw. Restoration has taken place with bricks similar to those used by Gothic builders. Within the Barbican you can find a magic amulet

Warsaw. Barbican

shop, an amber shop hinting at the Baltic's proximity to the north, and galleries from which views across the dry moat to Praga and the Vistula constantly change. Painters and craftsmen display their wares in the open air.

There are three kinds of shopping in Warsaw, as in other Polish cities. The majority of shops, with some goods artificially expensive (because of fluctuating shortages) and some artificially cheap (because of government subsidies), are staffed by apathetic shop assistants working long hours for scant wages, who often stand idle when cupboards are bare, while being overworked during rush periods when goods suddenly become available. In *A Warsaw Diary* (1984), Kazimierz Brandys notes two queues, in July 1981, one for cigarettes and one for vodka. In May soap and vinegar had been available; now nothing. A barter system had been set up by the ingenious, exchanging cigarettes for soap, vodka for cigarettes, and soap for vodka. Rationing applied to sugar, flour, kasha, meat and butter. Standing in a queue for a box of matches, an old woman told the stranger behind her, 'Last week I cried three times, for reasons of state'. The churches were full, the shops empty.

The second kind of shop is the PEWEX, DESA, CEPELIA type of hard-currency store intended for foreigners and for anyone else with dollars or Deutschmarks to spend.

The third type is the open-air market, like souvenir stands on main streets in Zakopane, or artists exhibiting in Warsaw's Rynek Starego Miasta. At Ochota, a district of south-west Warsaw, every Sunday the "Skra" stadium is crammed with goods of every description, from mink coats to empty bottles of Haig Whisky or Coca Cola. People sell what they can, or what they must, sometimes for złoty, but more frequently for dollars, which a young woman escorting me suggested was almost an official currency in Poland, in 1987. Technically illegal, these markets provide a vital artery for the lifeblood of Poland's economy, which staggers from crisis to crisis. The doctrinaire economy stipulates full employment at all cost, but this can only be achieved by economic ruin, since wages of unproductive employees have to costed in prices, which thus rise to uncompetitive levels, and must consequently be subsidised if they are to become affordable. But these subsidies in turn have to be added to the national debt.

I took lunch at the milk-bar 'At the Barbican', which takes up part of the ground floor of the former Marshal's Guardhouse. Hot milk, bean soup, and mushroom omelette cost me 35 pence (55 US cents), but I hardly noticed the food because of my intriguing conversation with a student. He complained about having to do two years' national service (only medical students are exempt), and about the faceless uniformity of life in a bureaucracy, where prospects for promotion are based not on expertise or hard work, but on whom you know and 'keeping in with members of the nomenklatura'. Since repression results from showing dissatisfaction, the student knows no alternative but to go underground (since the official demise of Solidarność) or to earn a regular meal-ticket with the forces of repression, such as the army, police or secret service. The government does not represent the underprivileged, who are taught that the State is acting solely on their behalf, but only the government, which is controlled by the Party, which is controlled by the Soviet-style Politburo. As a dissident, he showed considerable unease in speaking to me in fairly fluent English, but considered a desperate cause worth the risk. He tested the two old ladies and three labourers lunching near us (and thus able to overhear) by saying provocative English words, but detected no reaction, so continued. 'We are told in schools that the Soviet Army liberated Warsaw. I found out from a friend of mine – because my parents were confused, and anyway came from Szczecin after the War – that Komorowski's Polish Secret Army tried to save Warsaw's million, two hundred thousand people *from* the invading Soviets as well, but the Soviet Army waited until the last moment, delaying entering Warsaw until the people were dead or evacuated.'

Nearby is the Church of the Holy Spirit, opposite the entrance to Ulica Mostowa ('Bridge Street'), built by Italian architects in the early 18th century, and thus baroque in manner. Of the baroque interior, only the altar is original. A banner within reads in Polish '276th Warsaw Pilgrimage on Foot to Jasna Gora', the tradition of the Black Madonna having begun in 1711. An earlier 15th-century church built by Janusz the Elder was transferred to the city authority but after the Swedish Wars the Order of Paulines settled here, creating a new church and a new monastery.

On the corner of Ulica Długa stands a tiny one-room house which is also a 'Ruch' kiosk: the smallest registered property in Warsaw, almost dwarfed by a hot-dog van parked alongside. No. 7 is the Raczyński Palace, 18th-century home of Alderman Jakub Schultzendorff designed by Tylman van Gameren but altered out of all recognition by the Bishop of Kujawy and later owners until it passed to the Raczyński family and from 1827 to the Kingdom of Poland, who used it as a Ministry of Justice. During the Warsaw Rising, the palace became a hospital, but – restored after the War – it now serves as the Central Archive. The corner of Długa and Miodowa is occupied by the Church of the Piarist Monks, Orthodox Cathedral from 1834 but since 1917 the garrison church. From here you have an opulent view of the Krasiński Palace (1678?-1682), created by Tylman van Gameren of Utrecht for Jan Dobrogost Krasiński, Starost of Warsaw. Andreas Schlüter sculpted two figures of the Roman tribune Marcus Valerius Corvinus (with a giant Gaul on the front elevation; driving a chariot on the garden elevation) because the Krasińskis claimed descent from Corvinus. It has to be said

Warsaw. Ulica Długa 1, a small house now a 'Ruch' kiosk

that the Krasiński's magnificence outshone every other palace in Warsaw at the end of the 17th century, and the Crown Treasury Commission acquired it in 1765; it burnt down in 1783 and was rebuilt again within a year by Domenico Merlini. Acting as Supreme Court between the two World Wars, it now accommodates in elegance and splendour the special collections of the National Library.

Continuing westward along Ulica Długa, you could visit the Archaeological Museum at no. 52, the nearby Lenin Museum on Aleja Świerczewskiego 62, but on no account should you miss the Four Winds Palace, at Długa 38-40, because this is the home Krasiński used from 1685-98 before his great palace was ready. The charming four-storey

Warsaw. Krasiński Palace, now part of the National Library

mansion is called after allegories on pillars between the palace and the street. After passing through the Dückert family (1801-91), the Four Winds eventually came to the Ministry of Health and Social Welfare, who restored it after the War.

Retracing my steps along Długa, I turned left into Ulica Freta, the nearest Polish can get to 'Freiheit' (the German for 'freedom'). Here at nos. 8-10 is the Church of S. James ('Jacek'), a Dominican stronghold created between 1612 to 1638 on the model of S. John's Cathedral. Stylistically, the ogival windows, vaulting and chancel are Gothic, while the façade and naves are early baroque. A steeple was added in 1753. At no. 12 a mural of 1954 depicts 'Bricklayers of the Old Town,

132

Warsaw'. No. 13, with only one storey, escaped war damage and thus exemplifies original 18th-century architecture. No. 16 commemorates the work of a former resident, the Nobel Prizewinner Maria Skłodowska-Curie, its museum being open currently every day but Monday and Thursday.

The New Town Market Square strikes a false note because of its irregularity, after the Old Town Square in Warsaw or in Cracow. The New Town Hall succumbed to the demolition craze of the early 19th century, and after World War II reconstruction tended to restore the square to its appearance at the end of the 18th century, a conceit happily reinforced by the banning of vehicles and effective, simple street lighting by lanterns. I bought apples at a fruit-stall run by a private farmer, with flowers from his garden neatly arranged in vases. I found it an endearing part of Polish life that a 'Kwiaciarnia' (florist's) can flourish on most streets, and in most market squares. Even the least pretentious restaurant will festoon its tables with fresh dahlias, fuchsias or chrysanthemums.

The Church of S. Casimir, in its modest way, dominates Warsaw New Town Square just as S. Mary's prevails over a corner in Cracow. The Nuns of the Holy Sacrament came here from France in 1687, and their successors seem elfin-small below this immense dome on an octagon. Designed by Tylman van Gameren, the baroque Greek-cross church was dedicated by Queen Marysieńka Sobieska in celebration of King Jan III Sobieski's victory at Vienna in 1683. Virtually nothing is left of the Queen's pious plans, for in 1944 a thousand people were killed inside during a bombing raid. All we have from before the raid is Mattielli's rococo tombstone of 1746 in memory of the King's daughter Marie-Caroline de Bouillon.

Near the church two old women sat companionably talking in low tones, with subtle gestures, reminding me of the couple in Anna Świrszczyńska's poem:

'The two of us sit in the doorway,
chatting about our children and grandchildren.
We sink happily
into our old age,
like two spoons
sinking
into a bowl of steaming porridge.'

I followed Ulica Piesza to the tiny Church of S. Benon, created by German builders in the 1620s, overlooking the Vistula. Bizarrely utilised as a metalwork factory in the early 19th century by the English company Morris and Evans, its last pre-War use was also as a cutlery works, owned by F. Bienkowski. Why visit so many churches, often of questionable artistic taste or architectural distinction? One answer must be that it enables one to see half of the Polish personality at work, the socialist-politicizing personality being denied by notions of secrecy or confidentiality. Piety is not sentimental *only*, though that element exists of course; it is also grimly assertive, decisive, a definite stance taken up. It is feminine: at least seventy per cent of worshippers I saw were women, usually either middle-aged or old. This is mainly because younger women are working; girls are at school. Working women can be home by 3 or 4 in the afternoon; schoolchildren might be home by two. Piety is also nationalistic, perceived as a necessary bulwark against Lutheran Germans and Swedes and Orthodox Russians in earlier times, and against Marxist-Leninist East Germans and Soviet Russians in these troubled times.

The oldest church in the Nowe Miasto is that of the Visitation, founded in 1411 and last rebuilt in Gothic style, with a high steeple, and within a stellar vault, ogival windows, and polychromes uncovered during restoration. Its belfry has an authentic 16th-century base, with reconstruction in the upper part. Returning from the Vistula view along Ulica Kościelna, on the right-hand side is the 18th-century Przezdziecki Palace, and on the corner the 18th-century Mokronowski Palace, now the Museum and Library of the Warsaw Musical Society. Turn the corner and you come to the most elegant primary school I know: in the Sapieha Palace, Ulica Zakroczymska 6. The patrician Jan Fryderyk Sapieha acquired the original manor-house in 1725, pulled it down, and created to designs by Jan Zygmunt Deybel a late baroque residence (1731-4) amplified by two new wings (1736-46). Acquired by the Kingdom in 1817, the palace was converted into a military barracks and became home to the 4th Infantry Regiment. Ignacy Komorowski noted in his *Memoirs of a Cadet Officer* that the regiment was celebrated for its perfect drill and its 'assortment of rogues and rascals, frauds, humbugs, swindlers, and even thieves'. As usual, what you see is not what you think you see, but a post-war reconstruction: a mirage that you can touch.

Across the Traugutt Park northward rises the Russian-built citadel of the early 19th century. Near the entrance (facing the Vistula) you can visit the Museum of the History of the Polish Revolutionary Movement.

A quick taxi ride along Bonifraterska brings you back to Miodowa 17-19, the Archbishop's Palace (ask for Pałac Borchów). After various transfigurations, the palace was acquired by the Lord Chancellor to the Crown, Jan Borch, in 1768. He commissioned Domenico Merlini to convert the façade to the neo-classical manner then in vogue. It became a café, restaurant and hotel until the Government bought it in 1837, but it is still nowadays the Primate's residence, as it was from 1843. Fittingly dignified, it has a tiny door scarcely bigger than the ethereal windows.

Several burgeoning trees obscure the view from the wrought-iron gateway. At no. 15, the Ministry of Health and Social Welfare occupies a palace named for Ludwik Pac, whose restoration plans were finished in 1828. A first residence on the site (before 1697) belonged to Prince Dominik Radziwiłł, Lord Chancellor of the Grand Duchy of Lithuania, which Tylman van Gameren extended in baroque style, and Marconi (for Pac) added a new building and two wings. A bas-relief frieze facing Ulica Miodowa depicts Titus Flaminius proclaiming freedom to the Greek cities at the Corinthian Games. Neo-Renaissance and neo-classical features on the exterior might appear misguided when assessed with Gothic and Moorish components within, but the ballroom is a gem of just proportions, and the Great Hall on the first floor – reminiscent of the Roman Baths of Caracalla – is a dazzling achievement. I wondered, in this Hall, how it was possible for a 'socialist' government to lavish untold wealth and expertise on aristocratic buildings of the past, when so many present-day Poles have to manage in tiny, ugly high-rise apartments, crowded together, without any architectural distinction and even so numerically inadequate to meet the demand.

The question recurs in the context of the Branicki Palace at Miodowa 8, now the Ministry of Higher Education, Science and Technology. The Wettin dynasty from Saxony ruled Poland in the first half of the 18th century, a period when the traditional bourgeois home of Warsaw no longer formed the dominant residence, giving way to the mansions of political, financial and ecclesiastical leaders, as well as the palace of the royal family.

The Grand Hetman Jan Klemens Branicki owned seventeen mansions, including the palace in Białystok renowned among his contemporaries as the Polish Versailles.

Beyond the Branicki Palace, facing the former Bishops' Palace (now the Central Board of the Aeronautics Industry), we come to the Małachowski Residence, Ulica Senatorska 11, with a more impressive elevation on to Miodowa. In its present form, it dates from 1888, though annexes were constructed in the late 18th century, and it was originally built by Józef Lupi shortly after 1731, and purchased by Jan Małachowski, Lord High Chancellor, in 1750. Its restoration is another excellent example of taste, tact and harmony.

Emerging on to the Royal Way, we enter Krakowskie Przedmieście, which I once translated in a lesson as 'the suburbs of Cracow', a howler locating the street in the wrong city. The name really signified 'the outskirts towards Cracow', for this thoroughfare remained outside the Old City and led to the capital, then Cracow. In the 15th century, central Warsaw was named the 'Old City' to distinguish it from the New City then rising on the high river bank to the north. Gradually, mansions and palaces of the wealthy bourgeois and church dignitaries spread southward, the rate of development accelerating in the early 17th century after Sigismund III had moved his capital to the centre of Poland. In the 19th century, Ulica Nowy Świat ('New World Street') filled up with middle-class houses. In the 20th century, workers' housing estates spread across the stretch south from Łazienki Park to Villa Nova, or Wilanów as the palace is known in Polish. Socially, therefore, the Royal Way from the Castle towards Wilanów reflects urban development down the scale, with the space given to each class reducing street by street.

As a writer, I was invited for morning coffee and a visit to the reference library at the Writers' Union, no. 87 Krakowskie Przedmieście, known as the Leszczyński Residence (for whom it was designed by Fontana in 1754) and the Prażmowski Residence, after the original manor erected here in the late 17th century for the Primate of Poland. Viewing the Castle Square through the fine rococo façade, in plush chairs and sheltered from the crowds outside by thick patrician walls, the only sound I heard was the turning of an outdated Romanian newspaper's pages in the hands of a visiting lady journalist from Bucharest. A charming, slightly flustered librarian proudly showed me the excellent reference library, readers' chairs empty as pews in Albania, and her collection of press cuttings. I checked to see the most popular writers – Mickiewicz, Słowacki, as I thought – and least popular: those who had offended the regime and consequently find little or no mention in the press: Zagajewski, Herbert, Szechter. No cuttings are taken from foreign papers, whether in Polish or other languages, so the value of a good idea is stultified in practice.

At no. 83, the souvenir shop 'Lalka' *(The Doll)* is named after the great realist novel of 1890 by Bolesław Prus, and the shop itself attempts to give a loose impression of the haberdasher's shop run by the novel's chief character, Stanisław Wokulski. The real 'hero' of the novel, however is Warsaw itself, just as Madrid runs through the greatest scenes of Pérez Galdós, and London through so much of Dickens. Warsaw is a city steeped in memories, from the huge and vivid to the diminutive and vague. The Warsaw of 1878-9 that comes alive in the nearly contemporary pages of the orphaned Prus reawakens here in the shop called 'Lalka'. The pretty society beauty Izabela is harder to find nowadays: the plainly-dressed, determined career-woman has taken her place, and Prus' satire in his other great Warsaw novel *Emancypantki* ('The Emancipationists', 1894) has rebounded on the satirist, for Polish women have become more truly emancipated than he could have imagined possible.

At no. 79, on the corner of Miodowa, stands the neo-classical shop designed in 1789 by Zug for Roessler and Hurtig.

Warsaw. S. Anne's Church

The East-West motorway crossing the Vistula by the Dąbrowski Bridge underpasses Miodowa close by S. Anne's Church, founded in 1454. From this time we can see part of the southern face of the tower, the north portal, the presbytery, and the cloister gallery. The separate belfry was constructed in 1582, but rebuilt in neo-classical fashion in 1818. Rebuilding in the 17th century preceded a neo-classical façade of 1786-8, the four evangelists being the work of Monaldi. The interior is chiefly baroque, except for the neo-classical Chapel of Our Lady of Loreto, the only part of S. Anne's completely destroyed by the Germans in 1944. Warsaw's Bernardine monks lived in the adjacent monastery, and used S. Anne's as the church of their order until 1863, but for most

137

of the 20th century it has been the church of the University. Part of the former monastery and the arcaded guardhouse (no. 66) are used for the Central Library of Agriculture. At no. 64 stands the neo-Renaissance Citizens' Club (1861), the site of humorous episodes involving Stanisław Wokulski in *Lalka* by Prus, at present the headquarters of 'Polonia', the Society for Cooperation with Overseas Poles. No. 62 is the headquarters of CARITAS, the Roman Catholic charitable organisation, next to the Chapel of the Immaculate Conception, a distinguished work by Antonio Corazzi.

Opposite no. 56, once the Deanery and latterly a hostel for arts students, rises the Carmelite Church; neither it nor its contiguous monastery was devastated in the War. Internally, the baroque building dates from 1661-2, though the façade is a neo-classical addition of 1761-83 owed to Efraim Szreger. All three principal altars are baroque wonders by Tylman van Gameren, and there are smaller altars in the apse with baroque sculptures depicting the Marriage of the Virgin Mary, and S. Anne with S. James.

The Palace of the Council of Ministers, closed to visitors, at nos. 46-48, faces the Potocki Palace at no. 15 and the 1847 Potocki House at no. 17. The Council of Ministers meets in one of the most elegant, spacious architectural ensembles in Europe, redesigned by Aigner in 1819 following time-honoured neo-classical tradition to create a worthy residence for the most demanding monarch, though in fact it was commissioned for a Prince, Józef Zajączek, Governor-General of the Kingdom. It is also called the Koniecpolski Palace, after the Grand Hetman of the Crown, whose designer was Costantino Tencalla. Completed in its original form by 1655, it was acquired by the Lubomirskis in 1661; by the Radziwiłłs (after whom it is also named) in 1685; and by the Government in 1818. But it was Aigner whose magnificent conception extended the wings up to the main highway, converted the front elevation in neo-classical style and the garden elevation in Renaissance style, and remodelled rooms on the first and second floor. One of the memorable landmarks in Warsaw is the equestrian monument of 1826 to Prince Józef Poniatowski, based on an original in Copenhagen by the Danish sculptor Bertel Thorvaldsen (1770-1844), who took as his inspiration the Capitolian statue of Marcus Aurelius. 'Destroyed by the Nazis in 1944, it was replaced', as the plaque tells us 'by Copenhagen, the home of Thorvaldsen.'

A display hall and crafts shop can be enjoyed in the Potocki House on the other side of the street. The Potocki Palace next door houses the Ministry of Culture and Art. Its site, first occupied in 1643 by a Denhoff Manor razed by the Swedes, was subsequently occupied by a second Denhoff Manor designed by Giuseppe Piola in 1693. The Denhoff widow inherited the huge Sieniawski family fortune in 1729 and two years later married Prince August Alexander Czartoryski, thus creating the power base from which the Czartoryskis rose to become so influential in the Kingdom and abroad. They enlarged the manor house in 1760, transformed the exterior into baroque and rococo, and constructed side wings. The prevailing neo-classical fashion was followed in reconstruction to designs by Szymon Bogumił Zug during the 1780s by which time the palace had passed by marriage to the Lubomirskis; the Potockis acquired it in 1886, adding neo-baroque wrought-iron gates, and retained it until World War II.

Two large hotels face each other across Krakowskie Przedmieście: the Bristol at 42-44, and the Europejski at no. 13. The talented Marconi family was responsible for both, the Bristol having been erected in 1899-1901 on the site of the 18th-century Tarnowski Palace, and the Europejski in 1855-9 on the site of the Ogiński Palace.

Behind the Europejski extends the huge Plac Zwycięstwa ('Victory Square'), earlier Plac Saski, with the Saski Gardens to westward laid out in French baroque. 'Saski' refers to the Saxon Wettin dynasty ruling Warsaw in the early 18th century. Their palace, destroyed in 1944, has not been rebuilt, the only remnant being three arches of a colonnade (1838-42) around the Tomb of the Unknown Soldier (1925).

Polish baroque has been underestimated by virtually every writer on the subject, including Germain Bazin of the Louvre whose *The Baroque* (1968) includes only one painter and one architect working in Poland: Szymon Czechowicz (a pupil of Maratta) and Domenico Merlini. Yet the Church of the Visitation Nuns is a triumph of the fashion that becomes art in such visionary hands as those of Bernini or Borromini. It is believed that the Polish architect K. Bay was responsible for the Visitation's rebirth in 1728-33, following the burning by the Swedes in 1655 of the original chapel and nunnery within a year of their erection. Except for Sacheverell Sitwell's eloquently persuasive *Southern Baroque Art* (1924) and *Spanish Baroque* (1931) books by northern writers have tended to denigrate Italian baroque and its effervescent influences abroad, as though surfaces should in all cases be kept Lutheran-plain and Calvinist monochrome. But if we drop our prejudice and enjoy Caravaggio, the Carracci, Domenichino, Guercino – and Orazio Gentileschi, who brought Caravaggiesque exuberance to the Court of Charles I in London – we can appreciate more keenly the 'Visitation of Our Lady' painted by Thaddäus Küntz in the mid-18th century. Accept for what it is, and not in any spirit of carping, the boat-shaped Rococo pulpit by Jan Jerzy Plersch. After the 1863 Rising, all other orders were abolished except for the Visitants, who retained this nunnery, completed in the early 18th century. As it came unscathed through World War II, this corner of Old Warsaw retains a unique atmosphere, especially for those who realise that the boarding school in

Warsaw. Palace of the Council of Ministers

the nunnery educated girls and young ladies from the aristocracy. Listen for the ghostly soprano laughter behind the church, the same reverberations that resound from the Smolny Convent of St. Petersburg founded in the mid-18th century by the Empress Elizabeth.

Next to the Church of the Visitation Nuns is Warsaw University Library's Department of Graphic Art, nobly accommodated in the Tyszkiewicz Palace at no. 32 Krakowskie Przedmieście. Whenever public exhibitions are held, you may inspect the palace's interior, such as the glorious Shell Drawing-Room and sumptuous white Dining-Room on the piano nobile. Royal stables covered this site, until a palace was designed in 1786-92 for Ludwik Tyszkiewicz. Field Hetman of the Grand Duchy of Lithuania, he married a niece of King Stanislaus Augustus. Tyszkiewicz withdrew the commission from the architect Stanislaus Zawadzki with work in progress, replacing him with Jan Krystian Kamsetzer, responsible for employing the best stuccoists of the time in Paolo Casasopra and Giuseppe Amadio, and the painter Wawrzyniec Jasiński. The four atlantes 'holding up' the first-floor balcony on to the main street were made by André Le Brun and Giacomo Contieri in 1787. The palace passed to the Potocki family in 1840 and to the Polish Academy of Literature in 1933. As to the Collection itself, more than half of the collection numbering 100,000 items in 1939 failed to return after World War II. The foundations were the collections of King Stanislaus Augustus (acquired from the King's estate in 1818) and of Stanislaus Kostka Potocki, Minister of Religious Affairs and Education. Dutch, Flemish, Italian and French masters are widely, if unevenly, represented.

At no. 30, the Geography Department of Warsaw University occupies the former Uruski Palace (1844-7). A Baroque manor-house of the 1730s first occupied by Stanislaus Poniatowski, father of Stanislaus Augustus, was pulled down and replaced to designs by Andrzej Gołoński for Seweryn Uruski, Privy Councillor, and Steward at the Russian Court. Uruski's family lived in the two-storey central body of the neo-Renaissance residence, both three-storey wings with Corinthian columns on the façade being let as apartments. It passed to the Czetwertyński family in 1872, thence to the University.

Stanislaus Kostka Potocki, whom we have already met in the Tyszkiewicz Palace, joined forces with the enlightened and educated bourgeois writer Stanislaus Staszic (1755-1826) to press for the foundation of Warsaw University in 1816. Closed down for political reasons by the Russian authorities in 1831, a successor reopened for just another two years in 1861. A Russian-language university opened in 1869 in an attempt to russify a new generation of Polish intellectuals, but suffered a student boycott. So Warsaw University, embattled and working under severe restraints, effectively dates from 1915, even then being shut by the Nazis during their occupation, its only real period of expansion being the last forty years. The whole area used to be a royal game reserve and hunting park. The first building of any note in the precinct, the Royal Villa of 1634 commanded by King Ladislaus IV, was demolished by invading Swedish forces in 1655; in its place King Jan Casimir ordered a baroque palace (1660) known thenceforth as the Kazimierzowski, to designs by the polymath Tito Livio Burattini and Isidore Affaita. The King occupied it, since the Castle had also been devastated by Sweden, but it remained unoccupied after his abdication until King Jan III Sobieski bought it in 1678. Total reconstruction after a fire of 1814 included the provision of a neo-classical façade and conversion of the interior for use as a central library. Rebuilding after World War II has restored the Palace to its appearance about 1830. It functions now as university administrative offices.

Adjoining the imposing neo-baroque university gateway is the Hospital of St. Roch, 14th-century patron saint of those stricken by the plague. A charity hospital founded by Rev. Bartłomiej Tarła early in the 18th century, it is now headquarters of the Union of Polish Youth. Across the road, at no. 5, is the Czapski-Krasiński Palace, restored in the post-war period to its external appearance about 1750, but the interior enjoyed no such treatment, housing now the Rector of the Fine Arts Academy, the Fine Arts Library and studios. The history of the building as we see it today dates from designs about 1700 by the eminent architect Tylman van Gameren (c. 1632-1706), regrettably omitted from most general architectural histories such as Banister Fletcher's. Van Gameren created this design for Michał Radziejowski, Archbishop of Gniezno from 1687, as well as another for the Primate's baroque palace at Nieborów, 1690-6. But the palace's appearance today is due to Agostino Locci (architect of the Wilanów Palace), Karol Bay (also responsible for the Church of the Visitation Nuns as we have seen), and Kacper Bażanka, construction having taken place 1717-21. The palace passed through Czartoryski hands to the banker Riacour in 1732, thence to the Czapski family in 1736. Late baroque features were added 1752-65, and neo-classical features by Jan Krystian Kamsetzer in 1790. In 1808 the Krasiński family took on the fine residence and it became an artistic and literary salon under the sparkling influence of the wealthy, pro-Russian aristocrat Wincenty Krasiński. His son, the poet Zygmunt Krasiński (1812-59), felt frustrated under his father's influence, travelling and publishing his work abroad anonymously. His 'Undivine Comedy', translated in 1924 by H. E. Kennedy and Z. Umińska from his play *Nieboska Komedia* (1835), prophesied class conflict, with a hero prefiguring Lenin. The Chopin Society (Ul. Okólnik 2) is responsible not only for the Manor House of Żelazowa Wola, but for the Drawing-Room of Chopin's in an apartment they rented here from the Krasińskis.

Holy Cross Church dominates Krakowskie Przedmieście, with twin flanking towers and a massive baroque façade by Giuseppe Fontana (1725-37) and Jacopo Fontana (1756-60), with sculptures by Plersch of SS. Peter and Paul, Hope and Charity and two angels adoring the Holy Cross. The church itself is earlier, having been designed by Giuseppe Simone Bellotti (1679-96) for the same Primate, Radziejowski, who paid for the Czapski Palace. Both church and the adjacent monastery were intended for the Order of S. Vincent de Paul, whose founder was patronised by Queen Marie-Louise Gonzaga. The monastery is now the philosophy department of the University, but the Church interior remains in use, with a great main altar by M. Hankis of Elbląg (1700) reconstructed in 1960-72, adorned by an undistinguished modern painting of the Crucifixion by S. Komorowski. In one of the northern chapels you can find 'The Sermon of S. Vincent de Paul' painted by Szymon Czechowicz in 1730. In the Chapel of the Virgin Mary a Roman-style sarcophagus holds the remains of Prince Adam Kazimierz Czartoryski, who died in 1823. In the southern transept stands the altar of S. Felicissima (c.1698), designed by Tylman van Gameren for Cardinal Radziejowski; beside this the Cardinal's own tombstone has an impressive figure of the Cardinal (d.1705), carved in wood and covered with gilded copper.

Next door to the Church, and opposite Thorvaldsen's Copernicus Monument (1830), the elegant Staszic Palace proclaims itself as 'Societas Scientiarum Varsaviensis' above Corinthian columns and pillars extending up the first and second floors. Poznań's National Museum displays a portrait of Stanisław Staszic (1820) by Jan Gładysz. Staszic appears a pallid, hollow-cheeked humanitarian with gentle eyes, a view borne out by a far-seeing book, 'Warnings to Poland' (Przestrogi dla Polski, 1790), which urged a reduction in the power of the nobility. 'Make one nation of the nobility and the city youth', he urged. Staszic promoted the idea of the neo-classical building and sponsored part of the building cost, but from the first it was intended as home to the Royal Society of the Friends of Science, being erected to plans by Antonio Corazzi, 1820-3. The society itself was abolished by Tsar Nicholas in 1832, and the Staszic Palace became headquarters of the State Lottery, then a secondary school. After World War II it was restored to its neo-classical appearance, though the dome's shape was altered and side projections omitted. The Polish Academy of Sciences now occupies the palace, which 'closes' the view at the end of Krakowskie Przedmieście much as, if more flamboyantly, the Paris Opéra closes the Avenue de l'Opéra.

Southward the Royal Way wends towards Wilanów along Nowy Świat; westward lies Ulica Świętokrzyska; eastward Ulica Tamka dips towards the Vistula. A diversion is well worth while along Tamka to no. 41, the so-called Ostrogski Castle or Gniński Residence, superbly restored to its probable appearance in 1681, when a reduced design by Tylman van Gameren for Jan Gniński, Deputy Crown Chancellor, was constructed on a high embankment. The interior is less successful: a mishmash of baroque, rococo and neo-classical elements, but music lovers may wish to see the Chopin Museum or hear a concert in the hall. The Chopin Society also maintains its offices, archives and library here.

South of Gniński Palace rises the Paderewski Monument, to a pianist and composer also in 1919 briefly a Premier. Appropriately close to Paderewski's statue and Chopin's archive is the State College of Music, at Ulica Okólnik 8. Towards the Vistula a slight detour brings you to the Convent of the Sisters of Charity of S. Vincent de Paul. The Sisters came from France in 1651 by invitation of Queen Marie-Louise Gonzaga. The church of S. Casimir dates to the 17th century, while the present convent is of 18th-century date. This area was known as 'Vauxhall' in the 18th century, following attempts by a banker to create an amenity off Nowy Świat on the model of the London pleasure gardens. The street 'Foksal' is a polonisation of this name. Regrettably, 19th-century crowding made it necessary to divide Vauxhall Gardens into smaller lots, the most majestic of the new buildings being the Zamoyski Palace of 1873-7, now home to the Polish Architects' Association. Temporary displays of contemporary Polish art are arranged in the Foksal Gallery, on the ground floor of the left wing.

Nowy Świat buzzes with activity: its shops and restaurants retain a faint whiff of those elegant years at the turn of the century, before the cult of the proletariat insisted that everyone should at least try to conform to the lowest common denominator, and private property is somehow sinful, private ownership of land entirely unthinkable. This cult cannot ultimately succeed, because it runs counter to human nature and the evolution of human society, during which some institutions (such as hospitals or museums) may usefully pass into state ownership, while others (such as homes and attached gardens) should stay with an individual or the family. The first people to own property on Nowy Świat were farmers and smallholders in the 16th-17th centuries. Thereafter, the gentry and nobility created new places and mansions, but no 18th-century stately home has come down to us, and after World War II only six buildings remained. The others were rebuilt in façade to resemble their 19th-century forebears, but all the charming little courtyards and sheds (some of which we might admit must have been squalid with chickens, pigs, and foraging rats) were replaced with gardens.

Take a meal or a snack in the Społem first-floor restaurant at Nowy Świat 63, and look down unobserved at crowds swirling by, trams and buses sweeping past them in an endless stream. From my window seat I sipped coffee and guiltily ate a chocolate gateau, while trying to appear deep in solemn contemplation. A vivacious curly-haired woman was stroking the back of her hands erotically at a man who was explaining matters in grave detail. Two gloomy middle-aged men gazed without any great hope alternately at each other and at other customers to left and right. Twin girls competed in breathless demolition of strawberry ice-creams under the somnolent eye of their mother, a redhead dressed in unappealing dark brown jacket and skirt. A student with catarrh sniffed his way painstakingly through *Trybuna Ludu*, Warsaw's equivalent to *Pravda*: the Party newspaper to be seen with. Intended neither to be objective nor comprehensive, a Communist official party newspaper is there simply to propagate the party line, and we must not expect it to command the respect that an independent journal could claim, in the right hands. It would be more like *Hansard* if there were an opposition; but as there is none – for the Solidarność press is illegal – it is like nothing in the free world. But it is not only the press which knowingly distorts the truth in the interest of party discipline. Andrzej Wajda's film *Man of Iron* (1981) showed a radio reporter following instructions by trying to discredit strikers and their leaders in Gdańsk. He can be bought, and so can all other radio, television, film and stage workers, says Wajda. Such intellectuals, who are leaders of objectivity in the West, suffer only contempt from students and workers in Poland, after the short period when such heroes as Maciej Szumowski *(Gazeta Krakowska)* and Mieczysław Rakowski *(Polityka)* were permitted a degree of free comment. Many deserve praise, however, for brilliantly allusive satire masquerading as straight reporting. The greatest prose stylist is probably Ryszard Kapuściński, whose *The Emperor* (seemingly reportage on Haile Selassie) and *Shah of Shahs* (superficially nothing but an account of the last Shah of Iran) concealed wicked barbs aimed at leaders in his own society.

Nowy Świat no. 51, the Jabłonowski Palace, dates from the mid-18th century; its ground floor has a DESA souvenir shop. The composer Karol Szymanowski lived at no. 47 from 1924 to 1929. You can enter the Hołowczyc Palace at no. 35, because its Hunting Museum is open several days a week. The palace was commissioned from Antonio Corazzi (1820) by Szczepan Hołowczyc, Archbishop of Warsaw, and its Doric portico looms dramatically above the busy street and the ground-floor patisserie run by the Blikle company since 1869.

Every building in Nowy Świat possesses its own charm or dignity. No. 25 is a neo-classical house of 1829, the residence from 1951-3 of the eminent Jewish poet, translator, novelist and anthologist Julian Tuwim (1894-1953), whose adventurous spirit and love of the Polish language's quirks and foibles produced an output at once lyrical and grotesque:

146

adoration of Woman, and despair at the inability to seize and understand any individual woman. No. 19, the Kossakowski Palace, illustrates what a mid-19th century mansion could look like when restored. In 1848-9 Henryk Marconi redesigned the old Ollier residence of 1784 for the landowner Ladislaus Pusłowski. The four Muses in the centre of the second floor are Clio (History), Thalia (Comedy), Urania (Astronomy), and Erato (Love Poetry), the work of Paweł Maliński (1851). The Kossakowskis' house-warming ball in 1859 became the talk of the town, but bad times always follow the good; it became an apartment-house in 1905, then an ice-skating rink, a roller-skating rink, and eventually the Colosseum Cinema. The former palace now houses the state enterprise providing services to foreign diplomats.

A former Branicki residence can be seen at Ulica Nowy Świat 18-20, where an earlier home was transformed in Renaissance style to designs by Henryk Marconi, with a left annex and right annex, the latter (at the junction with Ulica Smolna) being a charming old-fashioned pharmacy, preserved in mid-19th century style. The home itself passed in 1899 to Ksawery Branicki, who also owned Wilanów Palace at that time and, though immensely wealthy, was also immensely mean. As President of Warsaw's Hunting Club, he used to dine there frequently and insisted on a specially cheap dish for ten kopeks: smoked sausages with horseradish sauce, which the less rich but more discerning members would not touch. Before World War II, the residence became the British Embassy, but now makes a palatial home for the Registrar's Office.

The busy junction with Aleje Jerozolimskie leads westward to Warsaw Central Station and eastward past the National Museum across the Poniatowski Bridge to the suburbs of Grochów and Saska Kępa. Why should a street in Warsaw be called 'Jerusalem'? The answer lies in the 18th century, when a Jewish colony created a 'New Jerusalem' on the western limits of Warsaw, and this road led to it, though it was not so amply widened until the 1820s.

The end of Nowy Świat is marked by Three Crosses Square (Plac Trzech Krzyży) and the Pantheon-like Church of S. Alexander, the masterpiece of Chrystian Piotr Aigner (1818-25), whose S. Anne we have seen at the opposite end of the Royal Way. The rotunda was enlarged in 1886-94 by the raising of its dome and the addition of two steeples and a nave to the southern side. Within, the most remarkable exhibit is a marble of Christ Entombed brought here in the late 17th century. The huge building on the eastern side of the square is the Institute for the Blind, Deaf and Dumb (1827). Down Ulica Książęca (towards the Vistula) you come first to the presbytery of S. Alexander (1902), the sole building in the street not destroyed in the War, and then to open spaces once elaborate gardens landscaped in the English style by S. B. Zug in 1776 for Prince Kazimierz Poniatowski.

From Three Crosses Square the southward road, with 28 chapels along the route, was known as the Way to Calvary, as far as Calvary Hill, now the Botanical Gardens, with a Chapel of Christ's Tomb demolished in 1770. Then the road was expanded to link the city with the palaces of Ujazdów, Łazienki and Belvedere. Gradually, throughout the nineteenth century, patrician mansions and palaces arose along the Aleje Ujazdowskie, as the boulevard came to be known. Nowadays it is above all a diplomatic quarter, with a modern United States Embassy at no. 31.

Antonio Corazzi left a rich heritage of great buildings in Warsaw, none more harmonious than the Kulikiewicz Residence at no. 49. The Doctors' Club at no. 24 stands out for the huge figures of Atlas shoring up the balcony. No. 24 is popularly called 'The Giants', and nos. 12-14 is 'The Artichoke'. This is the Marconi Palace, designed by Leandro Marconi in 1869, and now used by the North Korean and Mongolian Embassies. No. 39 is the Karnicki Mansion (Józef Huss, 1877), a three-storey Renaissance residence lightened by *loggie* on the upper two floors which survived the War intact. The original owner, Jan Karnicki, served as Privy Councillor, Secretary of State, and Senator of the Russian Empire.

Henryk Marconi had the good fortune to be the last architect to design a great private villa on Aleje Ujazdowskie: for Stefan Dziewulski the lawyer, at nos. 33-5. Created in 1913, it combines the Renaissance style with German Eclecticism. It too remained unharmed by the Nazis, and was sold after the War to become the Bulgarian Embassy.

The Rau Residence at no. 27 belonged to the industrialist Wilhelm Rau, for whom Leandro Marconi designed a neo-Renaissance mansion in 1868; after post-war rebuilding it became the Swiss Embassy.

The Poznański or Lesser Palace at no. 6a, facing the Rau Palace, is a mid-19th century masterpiece by Francesco Maria Lanci in the shape of an H. The Renaissance villa commissioned by Stanislaus Lesser is now headquarters of the Freedom-Fighters' Union, an association of war veterans. Farther along Piękna towards the Vistula you will come to the Institute of Nobility, of the mid-19th century, appointed the seat of the Parliament, or Sejm, in 1918, and after renovation it was demolished during the War, rising in expanded form.

On the southwest corner of Piękna crossroads with Ujazdowskie rises the Szleszyński Mansion, named for a captain of the Polish Engineers, Stanislaus Szleszyński, who paid for its design by Antonio Corazzi and its construction in 1826; he also planned the 'Swiss Valley', pleasure gardens known as Dolina Szwajcarska. The splendid porticoed two-storey Renaissance villa houses the Yugoslav Embassy, next door to the Hungarian Embassy at no. 21, the former Rzyszczewski Residence.

The British Embassy can be found on the corner of Aleja Róż in the Wielopolski Residence, called after Marchioness Eliza Wielopolski, who reconstructed an 1870s residence in 1904. It was undamaged during the War, unlike the adjoining Sobański Residence at no. 13, created for the philanthropic Sobański family by Leandro Marconi (1876), but now housing the Front for National Unity.

Still southward, beyond the square called Plac Rozdrożu, the eastern side of Ujazdowskie counts among its historical treasures the once-glorious Ujazdów Castle, with a park designed on French principles, Botanical Gardens (1818), and an Observatory (1820-4, C. P. Aigner), but the prize is Łazienki Palace, distinguished by the highest grade in the international list of historical monuments.

The original late 17th-century Łazienki, or bathing-pavilion, belonged to the Lubomirski family. On that site King Stanislaus Augustus erected a neo-classical Summer Palace in 1775, to plans by Domenico Merlini. The surrounding park, originally hunting grounds attached to Ujazdów Castle, has remained substantially as it was when laid out in 1764-95 under the direction of the King, whose sensitive but firm taste imposed a new Polish Renaissance style recognised by historians as the 'Stanislaus Augustus' style.

Łazienki Park is so glorious, with its studied irregularity, hillocks, sudden vistas, Gothic Orangery, Egyptian Temple, Roman Rotunda (based on the mausoleum of Caecilia Metella on the Via Appia), that the visitor could be bewildered. Enter the park just north of Belvedere Palace, on Aleje Ujazdowskie, and stroll downhill turning right at the third or fourth pathway, so you pass the White House on your left or right. My advice is to start with the Palace-on-the-Isle, which will take longer than you think, then the Theatre-on-the-Water, Orangery Theatre, and White House, before finishing with the Myślewicki Palace, and the Café Trou-Madame in the New Guardhouse.

After buying a ticket at a booth nearby, where the rudest lady attendant I have ever met invited unfavourable comparison with Attila the Hun in one of his more uncontrollable rages, I was asked to wait for five minutes more until the next party assembled. Having already queued for forty minutes, such adamant bureaucracy rankled, but... It was all worth it, even to stand on the terrace, between allegorical statues of the Vistula and Bug, and watch ducks swimming aimlessly to and from the Theatre, modelled on that of ancient Herculaneum. Little children had brought crusts from home to crumble into the water above their quacking admirers. Their unspoken feelings are echoed by Marshal Lubomirski's original sentiments, couched in cordial Latin above the entrance: 'Haec domus odit tristitias, amat pacem, fundit balnea, commendat rura et optat probos': 'This house detests melancholy, loves peace, offers a bath, commends country living, and desires the virtuous'.

149

The 1780s is a great period in Polish architecture: the unified appearance of the Summer Palace is due not only to imaginative architects working for a monarch of sensibility, but also to sculptors capable of fulfilling plans in the spirit of the time: two satyrs (now moved to the terrace entrance) by Plersch; another two, against the recessed wings of the façade, by Le Brun; a fifth, on the way to the Theatre, by Contieri; and a copy of the Borghese gladiators on the northern terrace, also by Contieri.

Łazienki Palace's interior consists of two styles: the early phase of the 1680s is represented by Tylman van Gameren's vestibule, with pebble-dashed walls then much in vogue for grottoes and country gardens.

On the ceiling of the vestibule, the King placed the royal initials SA (Stanislaus Augustus) and the initials of his ducal predecessor at Łazienki SL (Stanislaus Lubomirski).

Dutch tiles from the time of Tylman van Gameren panelled the Bacchus room, proving that this too formed part of the first baths; some (to the right, above the door) are original, but the remainder are post-War Polish copies. The ceiling painted with a Bacchus and Venus scene by Plersch (1778) fell victim to the Nazis. The Bacchanalian theme recurs in the splendid Jacob Jordaens painting of 'Silenus with Bacchantes' above the fireplace. I recalled dalliance in Boccaccio's *Decamerone*, and those mysteriously evocative lines from the erotic Song of Songs:

'Descendi in hortum meum, ut viderem poma mea convallium, et inspicerem si floruisset vinea, et germinassent mala punica': 'I descended into my garden, to find apples in the hollows, and to see if my vines had flowered, and if my pomegranates had come to bud.'

Portraits of Lubomirski and the King, jointly responsible for Łazienki, are by an unknown Polish painter and Giovanni Battista Lampi (1751-1830) respectively.

The last baroque room is the Bathroom, once complete with tin baths by Tylman van Gameren, and still adorned with splendid bas-reliefs, though Plersch's Diana ceiling fresco has disappeared. The motif of water is repeated from Diana's bathing with nymphs to Andromeda's patient awaiting of Perseus; from the Danaïds' punishment (filling a bottomless tub) to the escape of Arion on a dolphin. Rococo furniture includes French candelabra of the 1730s and a Polish table and Polish chairs from the 1760s.

Now we come to the neo-classical eloquence of Łazienki, openly expressed in the Ballroom (1788), with decorations finished five years later. The design by Jan Krystian Kamsetzer stresses the magic of Summer light with abundant windows on two levels, white stucco, marble sculptures, and an absence of the clutter which we found in the

Bathroom. A brilliantly simple axis of two chimney places enhances one's view of two large male sculptures: a copy of the Farnese Hercules (the lost original being by Lysippus, *fl.* 328 B.C.), and a copy of the Belvedere Apollo (the lost original being by Leochares, *fl.* 366 B.C.). Below these, respectively, are Centaur and Cerberus; and donkey-eared Midas with the satyr Marsyas, all by André Le Brun (1737-1811), who was also responsible for the bas-reliefs flanking the orchestra pit: Apollo and Daphne (left) and Hercules and Deianeira (right).

Plersch painted tempera panels showing the four elements (near the pit) and three ages of Man, three Fates, three times of day, and three seasons of the year, Spring having been omitted.

Three ground-floor rooms were intended to accommodate the royal collection of art: the Portrait Gallery, the Hall of Solomon, and the Picture Gallery. The Portrait Gallery now displays works by Marcello Bacciarelli, the Hungarian Adam Manyoki (1673-1756), and the Swede Per Krafft the Elder (1724-93), whose portrait of Izabela Lubomirska must be singled out for especial praise. Kamsetzer's bronze chandelier has come from the Raczyński Palace on Ulica Długa.

Solomon's Hall was named after paintings by Bacciarelli destroyed by the Nazis in the fire of 1944. Bacciarelli's idea was to compare the temple-builder of the Old Testament with the secular builder of neo-classical Warsaw, not neglecting the Biblical monarch's reputation for wisdom, all made explicit by showing facial likenesses in King and court. Merlini is the architect of this golden showpiece, and Kamsetzer the decorator, with marble cherubs by Le Brun.

Green provides a restful keynote colour for the exciting Picture Gallery. King Stanislaus Augustus purchased over 2,500 paintings through a network of agents in the West, preferring Dutch masters, among them Rembrandt and his circle, and Flemish artists such as Brueghel, Van Dyck and Rubens. Looting has deprived the gallery of its three Rembrandts and many other treasures. If you want to see the missing Rembrandts you can find them in Vienna (Count Lanckoronski's Collection: the *Portrait of a Scholar* and *Young Girl at a Window*, both of 1641) and in New York (Frick Collection: the breathtaking *Polish Rider* of 1655). But why regret absences among so many new friends?

Every painting here belonged in the King's own collection: *A Man in a Hat* by Nicolaes Maes, a cheerful *Inn Scene* from David Teniers, and *Sir Francis Bacon* by Frans Pourbus the Younger, all on the south wall; on the east wall, *Guillaume de Vair and Aldermen* by Pourbus, and Querfurt's *Imperial Cavalry Engaging the Turks*. The west wall, faithful like the other walls to the 18th-century mode of hanging paintings close together, has allegorical representations of *Old Age* and *Oblivion* by Johann Karl Loth, a 17th-century Bavarian artist active in Venice (where he was called 'Carlotto') and Vienna; and *Sir Charles Williams* by the 18th-century Bohemian portraitist Anton Raphael Mengs. Williams, then British Ambassador to Russia, enjoyed the acquaintance of King Stanislaus Augustus.

The Chapel's reconstruction is flawed: the original stuccoes were red (not yellow) and the capitals composite (not Corinthian). Copies of antique sculptures adorn the ante-chamber. The King's Dining-Room formed part of the Lubomirski establishment, but it became stamped with the personality of Stanislaus when a baroness commissioned a 'Roman' bust of him (from Domenico Cardelli) to set beside busts of Caracalla, Julius Caesar, Galba and Hadrian. Did Stanislaus, I wonder, read, heed and inwardly digest Gibbon's *Decline and Fall of the Roman Empire* (1776-88), comparing the gradual dissolution of the Roman frontiers, like sheets of paper, singed at the edges before disintegrating at the centre, with threats to Poland? I stared at the bust of the King whose tenancy of Łazienki seemed so secure, yet proved so tenuous. General Suvorov put down the 1794 National Rising led by Kościuszko, then seized the eastern suburb, Praga, and murdered many of the inhabitants. Warsaw capitulated; the King was exiled and ordered to abdicate. The Kingdom of Poland (with Lithuania) was suddenly no more, and the new Republic carved up by three butchers: the Russians, now installed in Vilna (the modern Vilnius, capital of the puppet state Lithuania); the Austrians, new masters of Cracow; and the Prussians, who will control Warsaw in anticipation of the Nazi occupation during World War II.

Think on these things as you enter the imposing Rotunda, which survived the fire intact. For Stanislaus intended this magnificent adaptation of Lubomirski's grotto to become a Polish pantheon, as we can see from the noble citation from Lucan's 1st century *Bellum Civile*: 'Utile mundo editi in exemplum' ('Placed as an example for the use of the world'). The Roman emperors chosen are Marcus Aurelius, Titus and Trajan (from ancient originals) and the four Polish Kings in full-length statue form: Casimir the Great (1333-70), Sigismund I (1506-48), Stefan Batory (1575-86) and Jan III Sobieski (1674-96). Plersch's paintings of the four times of day on the dome had been covered by Bacciarelli's paintings of the four virtues (Clementia, mercy; Themis, justice; Mars, courage; Minerva, wisdom) but these last have been relocated on the first floor.

These upper apartments, residential and private, have been completely reconstructed post-War. In the vestibule a number of interesting paintings include *Apollo and Daphne* by the 18th-century Florentine Benedetto Luti, and Bacciarelli's *Monk in Brown*. The two landscapes attributed to Andrea Locatelli, the 18th-century painter influenced by Claude, could be greatly enhanced by proper cleaning.

The Small Gallery glows with a genre scene by Jan Steen, and among other Dutch masterpieces are portraits by Dou, a *Card Game* by Metsu, and a *Inn Scene* by Teniers the Younger. When Max Friedländer suggested that 'To draw is to measure, to paint is to weigh', I thought immediately of the animated scenes in Jan Steen, whose characters may be anonymous but seem to bulk their actual weight and shape in these half-lit interiors garrulous with anecdote.

A balcony room has been created by dividing part of the Small Gallery. Here is a selection of rococo furniture and ornaments, with a Bacciarelli portrait of King Stanislaus.

The Royal Study possesses Bernardo Bellotto's view of Łazienki, a faithful yet glowing depiction of the bath-house as seen in the 18th century; turn to the windows and there is a panorama extending in the opposite direction, an almost tangible time-warp.

An 18th-century Polish neo-classical four-poster bed is contemporary, but not the original bed in the Royal Bedroom. Friedrich Anton Lohrmann's portrait of Anna Szaniawska, one of the King's mistresses, shows Łazienki gardens in about 1780. Royal mementoes in cabinets include weapons, Belvedere pottery, and a miniature portrait.

The Royal Dressing-Room shows some second-rate paintings, including *A Man in a Black Hat* over-optimistically attributed to Nicolaes Maes, and a *Temptation of S. Anthony* from the Breughel workshop. I preferred idiosyncratic Berlin porcelain figures of a Jew, a Russian and a Pole.

The Library's contents were destroyed by a 19th-century fire, so the furniture is unconnected: a Per Krafft portrait of the King, an 18th-century Parisian armchair by Jacob, and an 18th-century Polish secretaire seem cleverly at home. It's a shame that the public is not allowed into the Librarian's own room next door, for this was the sanctum of Jan Chrzciciel Albertrandi, whose Christian names polonise 'Giovanni Battista' or John the Baptist. Albertrandi's name and reputation deserve honour: it was he who founded in 1770 the significant literary magazine *Zabawy Przyjemne i Pożyteczne* ('Pleasant and Useful Games') to raise poetic standards in Poland, using the example of Horace and Poland's own Renaissance writers; it was he, as founding President of the Society of Friends of Learning in Warsaw (1800), who proclaimed that – after the demise of the Kingdom he had served – there was 'only one way left to serve the homeland: science and skills'.

Through a narrow corridor we accede to the Valet's Rooms, in which nothing remains associated with Franciszek Ryx, the valet in question. The study has paintings by Bacciarelli *(Stanislaus Sołtysek)*, Per Krafft *(Portrait of a Boy)* and Nicolaes Maes *(Portrait of a Woman)*. I was intrigued to find a Self-Portrait by Antoni Albertrandi (1730-1808), court painter from 1765 and member of that intellectual family originally from Italy which contributed so much to Polish life. Antoni not only ran a private art school, but composed a poem about art in five *canti*. Polish furniture of the late 18th and early 19th centuries indicate how far cabinetmakers had come since the aristocracy had begun to commission their compatriots in preference to French, German and Italian craftsmen. More of the Polish workmanship can be seen in the adjacent vestibule and bedroom.

Exotic theatres have been a delight of mine since I saw Mozart's *Don Giovanni* performed at Baalbek, Turgenev's *A Month in the Country* at Tampere's moving auditorium, and Verdi's *Aïda* in the Roman Baths of Caracalla. So I did not miss the chance of a classical play at the Theatre-on-the-Water at Łazienki, concealed lighting revealing not only actors and 'ruined' columns on the stage, but also rustling leaves on trees in the background. How enchanting it must have been to attend the inaugural performance here, on 7 September 1791 (the same year as Mozart's *Magic Flute*), for the ballet *Cleopatra*. We have drawings, by the court painter Jean-Pierre Norblin de la Gourdaine, of triremes, sailing in towards the stage during the naval battle scene.

I took a cold drink and ice-cream at the Café called Trou-Madame after a ball game played in the Summer pavilion, built in 1780 to a design by Domenico Merlini, with decorations by the ubiquitous Plersch. In 1830 Kubicki redesigned the pavilion, with a new guardhouse added on the west side, in the neo-classical mode. From Trou-Madame I walked across grass towards the famous White House. A sad, hungry-looking policeman sitting on a bench waved a gun at me in admonition: I was clearly in breach of an unpublished law but I regret to state that I paid no more attention to the enforcer than to the law, and smiled disarmingly at his scowling gestures as he stood up and waved his weapon, strangely impolite in a nation scrupulously proud of his courtesies.

Merlini's White House has come down to us almost intact from 1774, which makes it the first permanent building in Łazienki Park.

From the vestibule we reach a splendid dining-room with murals of 1777 by Jan Bogumił Plersch depicting times of day, the four elements, and the works of man, based on the grotesqueries of Raphael's *loggie* in the Vatican, itself an inspired recreation of the sensibility behind Roman frescoes. The Aphrodite in a niche is of Roman date, not an 18th-century copy. The Chinese Drawing-Room, within the Oriental movement which captured the hearts and minds of Europe during the Enlightenment, has murals *à la chinoise* by Plersch. Next door, the Chinese Bedroom has paintings reconstructed from originals by Jan Ścisło (1729-1804), a pupil of Bacciarelli. Birds and butterflies inhabit these walls as well as the surrounding gardens. On the four-poster bed two carved pigeons kiss, a symbol of love like the bow and arrows of Cupid, enmeshed in a maze of allusions from Apuleius to La Fontaine, whose *Amours de Psyché et de Cupidon* (1669) was set in the garden of Versailles, itself a prototype for Łazienki.

An octagonal boudoir is again decorated with landscapes by Ścisło and Plersch. Off the Chinese Bedroom, a passage takes us to the toilet with 18th-century bidet and to two dressing-rooms with Polish furniture of the time, together with a French commode of 1750 supporting two Chinese vases. The *Portrait of a Boy* is by Per Krafft.

On the first floor, a hallway leads to an ante-chamber of the western apartment, its walls decorated with flowers and scenes of myth and legend. The 18th-century porcelain is Meissen. The study, bedroom and two dressing-rooms are also ornamented with floral patterns, with 18th-century Polish and French furniture. The eastern apartment is less interesting, evocative only for Lampi's portrait of *Ksawery Branicki and his Sons* in the bedroom.

Domenico Merlini's Old Orangery incorporates a concert hall and sculpture gallery, but it is his 18th-century royal court theatre that attracts particular attention. Intended solely for court use, it opened on 6 September 1788 and remains virtually undisturbed by time and the Nazis. The main auditorium seats about 210 spectators, with nine additional boxes. Above the cornice more 'boxes' are filled with a buzzing audience painted by Plersch, a highly successful mural comparable with Plersch's ceiling: a tondo depicting Apollo (King Stanislaus again!) on a quadriga surrounded by genii. The four medallions in the corners of the ceiling indicate the four greatest playwrights according to His Majesty: Sophocles, Shakespeare, Molière and Racine. *Trompe l'oeil* effects include 'marble' walls, beams and pillars, but really everything is made of wood. It was presented in 1791 for public use to Wojciech Bogusławski, who had founded in 1785 the first permanent theatre in Vilna, then in Polish Lithuania, now Vilnius in Soviet Lithuania. The King had founded French, Italian and Polish stages in Warsaw as early as 1765. Like Molière, whom he translated, Bogusławski became at once actor, writer, director and impresario. His political plays, such as *Proof of the Nation's Gratitude* and *Cracovians and Highlanders,* achieved great resonance in the hearts and minds of Polish audiences, inclined to read a Polish political allegory into whatever they see or hear, and Polish writers who realise this and can phrase their speeches the more subtly as a result.

I felt saddened when a Polish tour leader told his group, 'Of course the theatre is never used nowadays'. With a monarch as Apollo and statesman gazing down at you from an imperial ceiling? Of course the theatre is never used.

If you cross the bridge by the King Jan III Sobieski Monument, and continue past the Hermitage on the main wide path, a right turn will bring you to the Great Outhouse and the elegant Myślewicki Palace. The former served as kitchens and servant-quarters, and afterwards a school for officer-cadets. The Palace, by Merlini, was built in 1775-6 initially for the King but, after he had moved into Łazienki, it passed to his nephew, Prince Józef. An attractive façade has sculptures of Flora and Zephyr by the Roman Giacomo Monaldi (1730-97). A vestibule gives on to a dining-room with murals by Jan Bogumił Plersch: Piazza San Marco, disturbingly broken by a window, and the S. Michele Bridge and the Casino of Pius VI in the Vatican *en face*. The bathroom has its original stuccoes and sculptures by Piersch. Off another anteroom we come to the Landscape Room, named for a mural by Jan Ścisło. From the bedroom we reach a circular Cabinet, tastefully adorned with Chinese vases, following the European taste for Chinoiserie which affected Łazienki most obviously in the decade from 1775.

The best time to visit Łazienki is when it opens, at 10 a.m., because the palaces, White House and Orangery Theatre, as well as the exotic garden in the New Orangery, and provisional exhibitions in the Old Guardhouse, close at 3 p.m., and attendants eager to get away will hustle you out well before actual closing time.

Wilanów too requires a whole 'day' starting at 10, and the cry 'all tickets gone for today' can resound as early as 11 a.m., the idea being not to allow too many people in at once.

On leaving Łazienki, enjoy a view of the exterior of Belvedere Palace, home of the Chairman of the Council of State, patrolled by vulture-eyed soldiers. Bizarrely palatial for a modern leader of the proletariat, Belvedere escaped destruction during the War: it stands as a tribute to the neo-classical taste of Grand Duke Constantine, Tsar Alexander's brother, who commissioned Jakub Kubicki to convert a late baroque residence into the neo-classical masterpiece we see today, dating from 1822. Before then, the site had been built on by Krzysztof Pac, Lord High Chancellor of the Duchy of Lithuania, whose small home was completed in 1663. This was replaced in 1740 by a baroque palace in two storeys, purchased in 1767 by the King, who hoped (until his funds ran out) to build a large palace there. Instead, he opened the Belvedere porcelain factory, which occupied one annex. After the time of Constantine it remained Russian property until World War I, when it passed to the German Governor-General Hans Hartwig von Beseler. Marshal Józef Piłsudski lived there for a few years, followed by President Stanislaus Wojciechowski, then Piłsudski again (1926-35). Governor-General Hans Frank lived there towards the end of World War II.

Southward again, Ulica Belwederska merges into Aleja Sobieskiego, an area once 'countryside' beyond Warsaw, with 18th-century brickyards where huge housing estates are now sited. Buses going south will drop you off at Ulica Idzikowskiego, from which it is less than a quarter of a mile to Tylman van Gameren's Church of SS. Anthony and Boniface, founded in 1687-9 by Marshal Stanislaus Lubomirski to become his mausoleum. Andreas Schlüter created the altar to Tylman's design, the altarpiece being an anonymous painting of S. Anthony presented to the Marshal by the Venetian Baron Ottavio de Tassis. Poor-quality paintings on the left of the presbytery show how this *S. Anthony* was rescued from Venice-in-flames, removed from the Piazza San Marco, and brought to the Marshal's Ujazdowski Castle. Another cycle of paintings depicts the building of the Czerniaków Church. Far superior are frescoes of the Triumph of S. Anthony by Francesco Antonio Giorgioli (1655-1725), a Swiss artist active in his homeland, in southern Germany, and in Rome; his brother was one of the stucco artists responsible for the angels, acanthus leaves, and other elaborate decoration. Giorgioli's frescoes in the cupola portray an angelic concert, while other anonymous frescoes concern events in the life of S. Anthony of Padua. An altar on the left hand side has a *Lamentation* flanked by S. Joseph of Arimathea and S. Mary Magdalene in a triptych ascribed to the Fleming Pieter Cock van Aelst (1502-50). A coffin above the crypt is said to contain the remains of S. Boniface, presented to Marshal Lubomirski in 1687 by Pope Innocent XI.

Tylman van Gameren also designed the associated Bernardine monastery (1687-93), cassated in 1863 but permitted to operate again from 1945. Across the street an old granny in black trudged slowly ever forward, with a heavy shopping-bag weighing her down symmetrically, cleverly, so that her left side did not bear too much weight, nor her right side. Conserving energy, looking straight ahead, her thin gray hair wisping in a gust of wind, she plodded evenly ahead, beyond the threat of war or party Diktat, her mind busily registering what she would do over the next ten minutes, the next hour, the next meal, for the rest of the day until bedtime. Then she could sleep.

The end of the Royal Road brings us to the Wilanów Palace and Park. A first mansion was started here in the mid-17th century by Bogusław Leszczyński, then Deputy Chancellor of the Treasurer, but King Jan III Sobieski, elected monarch in 1674, considered it ideal for a retreat from the noise and congestion of Warsaw, and acquired the estate in 1677, instructing his Chief Architect Agostino Locci to begin work on a palace within a matter of weeks, and by mid-1679 a one-storey mansion arose, with two outbuildings to create a courtyard. Both patron and connoisseur, as well as military genius, Jan III followed the example of Louis XIV by establishing his own complete atelier, though Wilanów's insatiable requirements dictated that many paintings, furniture and other major items had to be imported, while other precious objects were

Wilanów. Rear view, with gardens and lowering clouds

received from other courts in Europe and abroad.

Opening hours and days at Wilanów can never be predicted; for example, the Orangery was closed during my visit though advertised open, and the Palace may currently be seen only four days a week, though the park is generally open from ten a.m. till sunset. Check with your hotel or in the current *Warszawski Informator Kulturalny* (a few złoty at any kiosk). Son et Lumière shows are held in the Summer, and plays, concerts and lectures enjoy that extra sense of occasion in aristocratic surroundings. Slightly the better of the two restaurants is the Kuźnia Królewska ('Royal Smithy'), but the Zajazd pod Dębami ('Oak Inn') I found equally atmospheric, with excited visitors from all over Poland comparing notes.

Painters in the Wilanów atelier included the Frenchman Claude Callot (1620-86), Jerzy Eleuter Szymonowicz-Siemiginowski, Michelangelo Palloni (1637-c.1710), and the Neapolitan Martino Altomonte (1657-1745), who germanicised his name to Martin Hohenberg on being invited to the Polish Court. Locci's workshop included stuccoists, sculptors, and craftsmen in every field of interior design. The overall conception relied on a 'Sarmatian', or idealised Polish, interpretation of Roman Baroque, and the geometrical garden was also derived from Italian models. Revelations of a new age in Poland? A certain self-confidence and insouciance, indicated by the monumental figure of John III, as victor over the Turks, placed in the Grand Hallway, and by the general tone of artistic creativity, and the constructive use of leisure in pursuit of beauty and debate.

In Wilanów's next great period, Elżbieta Sieniawska, wife of Commander-in-Chief Stanislaus Herakliusz Lubomirski, extended and embellished the palace from 1723 to 1729, first in the hands of Giovanni Spazzio, then from 1726 in those of Jan Zygmunt Deybel. Stucco scenes from Ovid and from battles to decorate the new façade were produced by Jan Jerzy Plersch, Piero Comparetti and Francesco Fumo, who also adorned the interior. Now velvet wall hangings arrived from Genoa, and splendid gilt mirrors were set above Italian marble fireplaces. The old wooden parish church of S. Anne was removed to a site opposite the inn, by the approach from Warsaw.

After its short-lived occupancy by Augustus II (1730-3), Wilanów came into the hands of Isabella Czartoryska, who married the Grand Marshal, Prince Stanislaus Lubomirski. A new orangery arose parallel with the palace, to the north, and neo-classical baths replaced old stables. The Hill of Bacchus, to the south, changed its aspect to rococo, with carefully-placed sculpture, arbours for sly assignations and benches from which to admire changing seasonal views. Stanislaus Kostka Potocki and his wife Aleksandra, daughter of Isabella, inherited Wilanów in 1799: a fortunate occurrence for the palace which had been wrecked by Polish and Russian soldiers billeted there. Potocki, enormously wealthy, determined to recreate the glorious years by discovering and buying back as many dispersed objects as he could trace, adding others by determination and endless enquiry, and eventually, in 1805, opening a public gallery, designed by 1802 by Aigner. He also built up a private library of great value, and converted the gardens into a landscaped park *à l'anglaise*, removing from the east side the flower parterres and box-trees, and altering the southern, rococo, garden with its Chinese elements, into an English park. To the north, he added a 'Chinese' Summer pavilion, a 'Roman' bridge and a monument to the Battle of Raszyn, absorbed in a strange if anachronistic equilibrium within a Romantic garden where Lord Byron might have felt at ease.

By contrast I cannot imagine anyone feeling at ease with the unhappy Potocki Mausoleum (1826) for Stanislaus and Aleksandra by their son Aleksander, designed by Henryk Marconi and sculpted by Konstanty Hegel and Jakub Tatarkiewicz, inappropriate in the vast courtyard of Wilanów as the Albert Memorial seems in London.

Further changes to the palace and (chiefly) to the garden were made in 1855-6 by Boleslaus Paweł Podczaszyński, who added fountains in the courtyard and on the upper terrace. Henryk Marconi altered the church of S. Anne into neo-baroque.

In 1892 Wilanów passed to the Branicki family but, despite brave attempts at maintenance, the fabric deteriorated and the gardens with it, culminating in Nazi devastation and pillage. Extraordinary efforts by the Polish State have ensured that Wilanów has been preserved in its eclectic glories, original paintings from the 17th and 18th centuries emerging from below later layers of paint and 19th-century plaster.

The front elevation, a frozen apotheosis of King Jan III, his family and his victories, is inscribed 'Quod vetus urbs coluit, nunc nova villa tenet', 'What the ancient city cultivated, the new villa possesses', contrasting the glories of Rome with those of Wilanów. At the apex, the sun shines on the Sobieski coat of arms, underlined by the language of the Caesars: 'Refulsit sol in clipeis'. Figures of the muses exemplify Jan's devotion to the arts of peace, as well as the arts of war.

While viewing the interior, remember that time and its assassins have worked their worst on precious movables like paintings and vases: so much has disappeared, or is replaced in faithful copies or in comparable examples of the period!

It is immediately obvious that Wilanów started life as a country mansion, because in baroque town palaces the main reception rooms were situated on the *piano nobile,* or first floor. More modest villas required immediate access to grounds and gardens, and it is in this paradoxical context that we should envisage Poland's grandest palace.

A sign *Cisza!* ('Silence!', pronounced 'chee-sha') invited us to view the palace with a species of ecclesiastical veneration, another odd relationship to monarchy and its paraphernalia, in a socialist state, matching meticulous reconstruction of city palaces for primates and nobles.

The central part of the palace has a great hallway giving on to a drawing-room, with the royal bedchambers at the sides, mostly dating from the time of Jan III. The north wing's interiors appear much as they were during the Potocki period, in the 19th century, while the south wing consists chiefly of rooms for Augustus II and subsequently for Isabella Lubomirska. We end our tour with the exquisite Chinese rooms and major Polish Portrait Gallery on the *piano nobile*, by comparison incongruously modest.

The great hallway, originally a dining-room, was decorated by Baumann in neo-classical fashion to Szymon Bogumił Zug's designs, ceiling and frieze being by Henryk and Karol Marconi.

Frescoes in the northern gallery illustrating the tale of Cupid and Psyche, from the *Metamorphoses* of Apuleius, were carried out by Michelangelo Palloni in 1688, complementing those in the southern gallery. Szymonowicz-Siemiginowski painted frescoes of the four seasons: Autumn in the Queen's Antechamber; Spring in the Queen's Bedchamber, Summer in the King's Bedchamber, and Winter in the King's Antechamber.

Italian Renaissance ceramics mingle with Delft and Limoges wares of the same period and later; the walls shimmer with Genoese velvet; the Queen's Antechamber also possesses an outstanding portrait of Louis XIV by Hyacinthe Rigaud (1659-1743), *le Roi Soleil* being candidly a model for Jan III throughout his career as warrior and connoisseur. The Queen's Cabinet displays recently-uncovered 17th-century frescoes based on the *Metamorphoses* of Ovid. Genoese velvet covers the walls and Saxon tabourets in the Queen's Bedchamber, which is dominated by a French four-poster bed.

Beyond the central great hallway we come to the Dutch Cabinet, so-called from Jan III's priceless collection of Dutch masters, now vanished; instead we have a reception room as it would have appeared in the period of Augustus II. Louis Silvestre (1675-1760), whose 'Perseus and Andromeda', 'Diana', and 'Venus at her Toilet' adorn the Queen's Bedchamber, also painted the *trompe l'oeil* ceiling in the Dutch Cabinet, glorifying the Saxon dynasty, and 'Venus and Mars' and 'Venus and Cupid' above the Dutch Cabinet's doors.

In the King's Antechamber, nobody should overlook an enchanting *Salomé* from the prolific Cranach workshop, or a magnificent 18th-century Florentine escritoire. If the King's Bedchamber seems a trifle out of character, perhaps the reason is a Perso-Turkish tester above the bed. Copies of three famous paintings by Rembrandt outface more of Silvestre's mythological scenes: 'Nymphs and Satyr', 'Bacchanalia', and 'Amphitrite, Sea-Goddess'.

The Chinese Cabinet provides yet another glimpse into the European fashion for *chinoiserie*, and especially for gilt lacquer. The less said about the neo-Renaissance Chapel of 1852 the better. The King's Library, better considered as a study, possesses portraits of King Jan III and his wife Queen Maria Casimir, and second-rate paintings by European artists. Devoted to literature and philosophy, the frescoed ceiling depicts artists, thinkers and poets in portrait medallions, with their names inscribed, among them Plato, Horace, Sarbiewski and Solon.

Sarbiewski? Maciej Kazimierz Sarbiewski (1595-1640), writing only in Latin at a time when his adopted Rome gave refuge to humanists from Hungary, Czechoslovakia and other lands who communicated in the languages of Virgil or Dante, earned lasting fame as the 'Christian Horace', and received a laurel garland from Pope Urban VIII. Fifty-eight editions of his works appeared between 1625 and 1892; he became mentor to a generation for his religious, patriotic and nature poems. He preached Crusades against the Turks, and translated into Latin Jan Kochanowski's stirring *Wieczna Sromota* ('Eternal Shame') on the invasion of Podhale by the Tatars.

In the north wing, the ground floor has a crimson tinge, from the Crimson Drawing-Room (with 18th-century decoration and 19th-century furnishing) named for its Italian damask, to the Grand Crimson Room utilised by the Potockis as a Gallery of Foreign Paintings. A Jordaens 'Cortège of Bacchus' seems strangely muted, compared with the master's usual exuberance, but a Polish effect is created here by a very large canvas by A. Viviani and the Fleming Pieter van Bloemen: 'The Polish Ambassador's Entry to Rome, 4 August 1680'. Much more attractive is a little classical landscape by Andrea Locatelli (1693-1741). The Small Crimson Room, once called the Landscape Room, now displays minor 17th-century Italian and Flemish genre scenes, and Polish furniture of Biedermeier taste. The so-called Etruscan Room shows objects, by no means all Etruscan, from antiquarian collections.

In the south wing, a remarkable White Hall (1730-3) was designed by J. Z. Deybel for Augustus II as a Banqueting Hall, with ample use of mirrors for brilliance. More royal portraits deck the walls: Augustus III, Augustus II, and the former's consort, Maria Józefa; the best portrait in the Antechamber nearby is a Bacciarelli of the splendid Isabella Lubomirska, who inhabited these apartments: tapestries in her drawing-room come from Brussels (17th century) and Beauvais (early 18th century) and her original four-poster bed languishes lonely now in her bedroom.

Though normally closed to the public, the private bathroom used by Marszałkowski was unveiled for me. Palatial in green and white marble, it is memorable for peacock feathers in the curtain concealing the bath.

In the first-floor Gallery of Polish Portraits, nobles of the 17th century are depicted in so-called *portretów trumiennych*, small-scale coffin portraits unique to Poland. Look for instance at the hexagonal Barbara Domicela, (*c.*1674) a frank brunette with a translucent bodice, and Stanislaus Woysza (1677), firm-chinned, white-haired. Official paintings of the monarch's family and noblemen range from the heroic to the cosy: Broderus Matthisen's 'Stefan Czarniecki' (1659) or Jan Tretko's 'Jan III' (1677) on the one hand, and stiffly-grouped 'Sobieski Family' by an unknown court artist. The best artists represented are Martin Kober (a dazzling 'Anna Jagiellonka'); Bartłomiej Strobel (the grave, statesmanlike 'Jerzy Ossoliński' and an effete, sardonic 'Young Magnate' of 1636, whose real interest is an abundance of bows, lace and fine embroidery); and Daniel Schultz (the mature, deceptively straightforward Stanislaus Krasiński, easily mistaken at a distance for a plain man).

Late 17th-century *trompe l'oeil* frescoes create an atmosphere of art and beauty around Venus, in the Quiet Room; an interior apotheosis of Jan III, more intimate than the façade of course, decorates the Faience Room, the tiles being Polish copies of Delftware, medallions depicting the four elements; Flora (*c.*1725) reigns over the Three-Windowed Room, with medallions of the four seasons. The Middle Room exemplifies a late 18th-century manorial interior in Mazovia, with a beam ceiling, and furniture from Poland, England and the Low Countries. Its royal provenance is betrayed by Jan III's coat-of-arms (and his Queen's) on the ceiling and equestrian portraits of their sons. The Ante-Chamber has restored *trompe l'oeil* decorations by Józef Rossi, court painter to Sieniawska in the third decade of the 18th century, with contemporary baroque furniture; you can find Rossi's self-portrait in the south-west corner.

Agostino Locci's rooms have been reconstructed much as they must have looked in the 1670s, while he was master-minding the earliest, most modest palace. Renaissance and baroque furnishings from Italy are surrounded by charming minor canvases, mainly from the Low Countries and Italy. An Al Fresco Room is so designated because of its 18th-century decorations. The fashion for court negroes at that period is personified by a negro carrying a parrot cage. The Pastel Study is named for the choice collection of pastel portraits showing those connected with Wilanów including Jerzy Potocki and Isabella Lubomirska, née Czartoryska. Among the pastellists are the Frenchman Louis Marteau (1715-1805), court painter to Stanislaus Augustus, and his pupil Anna

Rajecka (1760-1832), an admirer of Greuze.

Our visit ends in the principal section of the Polish Portrait Gallery, covering the period from the mid-18th century. Two canvases by Bellotto attract immediate attention, but the best works here are 'Józefa Amelia Potocka' by Jan Lampi (1751-1830), 'Stanislaus Potocki' by Alexander Roslin (1718-93), and 'Zygmunt Krasiński' by Ary Scheffer (1795-1858).

Poster art has enjoyed a surge of creative power and craftsmanship in Poland since the 1950s, representing the antithesis of the Stalinist concept of art as a political tool of proletarian consciousness. Instead, it delights in the surreal, intuitive, subjective and playful, running riot in free association and internal logic or dislogic. Once an ephemeral sheet, the poster in Poland has achieved classic status, with displays at home and abroad. The first National Poster Biennale was organised in 1965 in Katowice, and since 1966 the International Poster Biennale has been held in Warsaw. A Poster Museum was established in 1968 at Wilanów's former riding-school and coach-house (ask for the Muzeum Plakatu w Wilanowie) and may be visited every day but Monday and days after holidays. Do not miss the theatre posters by Franciszek Starowieyski or Jan Sawka; exhibition posters by Leszek Hołdanowicz or Jan Lenica; safety posters by Maciej Urbaniec or Marcin Mroszczak; circus posters by Waldemar Świerzy or Tomasz Rumiński.

My taxi back from Wilanów dropped me at Ulica Puławska 113, the Ksawery Dunikowski Museum, enjoyable as much for its surroundings as for its contents. The Królikarnia Residence's name denotes a 'rabbit-farm' organised here during the reign of King Augustus II Wettin. Then in 1779-86 Domenico Merlini designed a residence, kitchens and annexes for Count Charles de Valéry-Thomatis, Court Chamberlain to King Stanislaus Augustus. If the Królikarnia looks familiar, cast your mind back to Palladio's Rotonda at Vicenza. The Chamberlain not only opened his gardens to the public, but allowed an Italian restaurant to feed those intent on dining out in style. The attractive residence appealed to collectors and connoisseurs of means, such as Prince Michał Radziwiłł, occupant from 1816 to 1849, who also owned Nieborów and Arkadia; and Ksawery Pusłowski, whose family kept the residence until 1939. Ksawery Dunikowski (1876-1964), whose works and possessions are now shown within the Królikarnia, makes not the slightest appeal to me, but others might respond to the heavy posturing of 'Boleslaus the Bold' (1916-17) here, or his sculptures (1927-9) for the Cathedral in Katowice. But does *anyone* really respond to the socialist realism of his 'Silesian Insurgents' on Mount S. Anne near Opole?

Your evenings in Poland could be spent at clubs, discos, bars, cafés, wine-cellars or restaurants. Concerts, films, plays, operetta, ballet and

Warsaw. Great Theatre. Puccini's Turandot

opera can normally be enjoyed: check the week's *Informator Kulturalny* for times and places. This can be seen at any 'Ruch' kiosk or hotel lobby. Tickets may be purchased in advance from the Tourist Information Centre, Ulica Krucza 16; SPATiF, Aleje Jerozolimskie 25; or at the theatres themselves. The National Philharmonic Hall is situated at Ulica Sienkiewicza 12.

Theatre Square (Plac Teatralny) has both the National Theatre and the Great Opera and Ballet Theatre (Teatr Wielki means the same as 'Bolshoi'). The Wielki should not be missed on any account, for it represents yet again, as we have seen repeatedly with the variety and multiplicity of restored palaces, that will towards the imperial, grandiose and majestic so characteristic of totalitarian states. The vacuous rhetoric of the *Nike* monument facing Warsaw Opera House, and the vast parade-ground style of the square itself add to one's impression of being overwhelmed. The human scale is abolished, not simply diminished as in the Place de la Concorde or Times Square.

Antonio Corazzi's original façade in three tiers dates from the early 1830s, the first performance being given in 1833: it was *Il Barbiere di Siviglia*. The first great period of the Wielki is that of Karol Kurpiński, director until 1840. He composed the national ballet *Wedding in Ojców*, and introduced to the Polish operatic stage the works of Rossini, Weber, Boieldieu and Cherubini. The second great period was that of the father of Polish opera, Stanislaus Moniuszko, whose control of the Wielki ran from 1858, the Warsaw première of *Halka* (first seen in Vilnius, 1848), to his death in 1872. Some of his works still figure in the repertory of the many Polish opera houses, but most of them are rarely performed. You may be lucky enough to see *Halka*, a plain tale of a highland girl, or three other works on Polish themes: *Hrabina* ('The Countess', 1860), *Verbum Nobile* (1861), and *Straszny Dwór* ('The Haunted Manor', 1865), the last-named closed down by the Censor after its first few performances for its patriotism. Moniuszko's *Books of National Songs* had to be retitled *Books of Home Songs* for similar reasons of Tsarist suspicion, and became as popular in his homeland as the mazurkas and polonaises of Chopin.

The third zenith of the Wielki came under the leadership of Emil Młynarski, from 1898 to 1902 and 1919 to 1929. It opened after the War on 19 November 1965, continuing under the direction of Zdzisław Śliwiński until 1979. A smaller auditorium open intermittently since 1968 concentrates on modern and experimental work, or unconventional staging of classics. The present director is Robert Satanowski, in whose current season I noted the ballets *Pan Twardowski*, *Giselle* and *Insatiability* (the last after the novel by Stanislaus Ignacy Witkiewicz translated by Louis Iribarne, 1985). Operas included Kunad's *The Master and Margherita* (after the novel by

Bulgakov), Szymanowski's *King Roger,* Berg's *Wozzeck,* Mozart's *The Magic Flute,* Puccini's *Turandot,* and Moniuszko's *Straszny Dwór,* a repertory far superior to that of the Royal Opera House, Covent Garden, during the same season. I saw Verdi's *Macbeth* with Jerzy Artysz and Ryszarda Racewicz as the murderous monarchs, and Donizetti's *Lucia di Lammermoor,* starring Christina Rorbach and the Greek-born Paulos Raptis as the ill-fated lovers, both performances conducted by Andrzej Straszyński. Production was straightforwardly Romantic, without the designer-producer's capricious dominance that has damaged recent Western productions, from a perverse *Aïda* in Frankfurt, to the notorious *Flying Dutchman* and *Rienzi* in London.

Beforehand, I had roamed the splendid Theatre Museum, open in the middle of the day on three days a week, as well as an hour before performances and during intervals. A special display featured the influential work of Leon Schiller, director of the Bogusławski Theatre in 1924-6, great years which saw the staging of new social plays by Tadeusz Miciński *(Prince Potemkin)*, Stefan Żeromski *(The Rose)* and Zygmunt Krasiński *(The Undivine Comedy).* The permanent museum has a drawing of Szymanowski (1922) by Witkacy, paintings of the actress Irene Solska by Wojciech Gerson (1895) and by Wojciech Kossak (1908), and a charming portrait of the unforgettable actress Helena Modrzejewska (1840-1909) by Elviro-Michael Andriolli.

Do not miss the chance to see a play in Polish, for the theatrical tradition is as vital today as in the days of Sigismund III's Royal Theatre in the Castle, seating over 1,000 spectators. Jerzy Grotowski's *Towards a Poor Theatre* has provoked worldwide reaction; Tadeusz Kantor's theories and practice remain effervescent; and the acting tradition still forms an artistic bridge between private conscience and public outcry denied in politics by the one-party system. 'Acting between the lines' has always been a national tradition, eagerly studied by those without representation in the Sejm or in effective, legal trade unions. The Dramatyczny and Studio stages can be seen in the Palace of Culture. The Narodowy on Plac Teatralny has a chamber stage called the 'Mały' ('Small') at Ulica Marszałkowska 104-122. The principal Teatr Polski at Ulica Karasia 2 has a small stage at Ulica Foksal 16, where I saw a play on the early life of S. I. Witkiewicz, before 'Staś' (as the play is called) became known as 'Witkacy', to distinguish him from his dominant father, played in this production of Jerzy Jarocki's play by the celebrated actor Gustaw Holoubek, also the producer. Silent, attentive, gripped: Holoubek's audience was perfect.

The Teatr Nowy at Ulica Puławska 37-9 was giving Roger Vitrac's *Wiktor* and Bogusław Schaeffer's *Grzechy Starości* on its larger stage, and an adaptation of Dostoevsky's *Brothers Karamazov* in repertory with Różewicz's *Odejście Głodomora* on its chamber stage.

Other theatres include the Syrena, Ulica Litewska 3, the Ateneum, Ulica Stefana Jaracza 2, and the Powszechny, Ulica Zamojskiego 20. But the best atmosphere I found on any Warsaw stage was at the State Yiddish Theatre, Plac Grzybowski 12-16, named after Ester Rachel Kamińska. Brilliantly colourful and noisy like any 19th-century *shtetl* (Bełz or Słuck), the stage glittered with authentic costumes and resounded with sentimental songs (Gołda Tencer in 'Majn Yidisze Mame'), tragedy (from a poem about Treblinka by Icchaka Kacenelson), gaiety ('Biri Bom'), drama (from Sholem Aleichem) and pathos – in a monologue by the director Szymon Szurmiej, author of the evening set so long ago: *Świat moich Marzeń*. The 'World of my Dreams' presented fragments of Yiddish life in Central Europe against a backcloth of Chagall and tenderness, good humour and hard times. The evening was held completely in Yiddish, but earphones are provided for a simultaneous Polish translation. Anyone with Low or High German can make out 70% of the songs and dialogue, and even if you have no German background, or no Jewish background, the sense of occasion is unforgettable. Who could ever have imagined that here, rising from the terror of the ghetto's screams, we should see an officially-supported theatre celebrating the Jews of Ukraine and Poland, Byelorussia and Rumania? The audience, sprinkled with Americans and Western Europeans, rose in ovation as the curtain fell. We were giving praise to Jews whose families had been decimated by hatred, villainy, betrayal and racial theories meticulously put into practice.

The following morning I waited patiently outside Warsaw's Jewish Cemetery, Ulica Okopowo 49-51, reputedly the largest in Europe, not far from the Roman Catholic cemetery of Powązki.

'No more Jewish townships in Poland', noted Antoni Słonimski, on hearing about the Nazi holocaust. But there are townships of the dead, and deserted villages: Karczew, Sieniawa, Lesko, Szydłowiec, Krynki, Chrzanów. Names tolling like funeral bells. The cemeteries persist, open books testifying to great men and women, as well as to fields of the unknown. Lazar Ludwig Zamenhof is buried here. Creator of Esperanto, he could not know that his international language would flicker faintly through the decades but fail in its intention because of linguistic pride – and also because few could accept a language in which every plural ends in *j*. Here are the graves of Chaim Selig Słonimski (grandfather of the poet Antoni), who edited the scientific journal *Ha-Zefira*; the historian Meir Bałaban; the great actress Kamińska, whose daughter Ida and granddaughter Ruth continued to work for the State Yiddish Theatre; the statesman Szymon Ashkenazi; the poet Jakub Zonszajn...

Amid the plain memorials, great Jewish artists have worked on superb monuments. I commemorate the craftsmanship of Fiszel

Rubinlicht, Henryk Sztifelman, Abraham Ostrzega, and Mark Antokolski. David Friedlaender, painter and architect, was the sculptor responsible for the monument to Dov Baer Szmulowicz (1826). One flank has a bas-relief of Praga, where Szmulowicz lived as a boy. Here is the palace King Stanislaus Augustus had given his father; a synagogue; a cemetery; boats near a bridge broken to symbolise death. The other side of the Szmulowicz monument depicts the city and river of Babylon, with the Tower of Babel, musical instruments pendent from the trees, and the citation from Psalm 137: 'By the waters of Babylon we sat down and wept, when we remembered Zion. We hung our harps upon the willows in the midst thereof'.

I stopped for a minute's silence before the grave of Mordechai Anielewicz, a ghetto fighter killed at the age of 29. Closed on Saturdays and Fridays after midday, the Jewish Cemetery can be visited every other day between 9 and 3. The sign outside 'Bez nakrycia głowy prosimy nie wchodzić na cmentarz', only in Polish, means 'We ask you not to enter the cemetery without a head covering': even a knotted handkerchief is acceptable. A grieving family flapped their arms in the air and around each other like awkward seals: embarrassed to be alive in the presence of such overwhelming degrees of death.

A taxi brings you eastward along Ulica Anielewicza, then right into Nowotki, the next main crossroads being Aleja Świerczewskiego. At no. 79 the Jewish Historical Institute has organised a museum and library documenting Nazi atrocities. Three old ladies from Pennsylvania, presumably close relatives, wandered distractedly, bemused by the multiplicity of objects and their captions in Polish. 'I don't understand', said one. And another, 'What does that mean?'. I could make no comment. What do they mean, these grainy monochrome photographs of shattered bodies and headless buildings, armbands worn like stigmata, and pallid faces awaiting sudden death? I don't understand now any more than I understood then, that mid-morning in Poland, in a cold museum staggering under the accumulated weight of horror.

We must never forget that the 380,000 Jews who lived in Warsaw in 1939 comprised a third of the city's population, and they lost not only their lives but virtually all the remnants of their culture and religion, such as their libraries, all but one of their theatres, the beautiful old synagogue in the Praga district across the Vistula, and the Great Synagogue in Ulica Tłumackie, designed in 1887 by Leandro Marconi. The only surviving synagogue is that named for its founder, Zelman Nożyk, dating from 1902 and now rebuilt to serve its tiny, melancholy congregation. A major celebrant of Jewish life in Warsaw up to 1939 is Isaac Bashevis Singer. His reminiscences, *In My Father's Court* (1966), recount Hassidic life in his father's rabbinic court before World War I in Ulica Krochmalna 10, in Mirów district just southeast of the Jewish

Cemetery. My favourite Warsaw novel is Singer's *The Family Moskat* (1950), translated from the Yiddish by A. H. Gross: the saga of a family like so many others doomed to annihilation by the Nazi onslaught. Another great novel of Poland before Hitler is *The Brothers Ashkenazi* (1936, translated by Maurice Samuel), by Israel Joshua Singer, Isaac's elder brother by eleven years.

The Lenin Museum at Aleja Świerczewskiego 62 occupies the grand Przebendowski Palace, also called the Radziwiłł or Zawisza Palace after later owners. Jan Jerzy Przebendowski, Lord Treasurer of the Crown, commissioned designs from Jan Zygmunt Deybel, and the palace was erected in late baroque style by 1729. In the late 1760s the palace was purchased by Roch Kossowski, who filled the same function as his illustrious predecessor. Kossowski's second wife was Barbara, one of the great Polish society beauties of her generation, the others being Julia Potocka and Rozalia Lubomirska.

Stanislaus Wasylewski narrates a scandalous tale of these three ladies, who dressed as Greek goddesses one night, entered Prince Pepi's bedroom, and quickly transmuted it into Mount Olympus. They waited behind a curtain until the door finally opened and Prince Pepi entered, with the actress Sitańska! The installation of a hagiographical museum devoted to Vladimir Ilyich, self-appointed champion of the downtrodden, in the sumptuous Przebendowski Palace, so lovingly reconstructed to its 18th-century splendour, will not be lost on connoisseurs of irony.

Rather than spending time on souvenirs of Lenin, the Western visitor would be well advised to concentrate on the collections of the National Museum, next door to the Polish Army Museum on Aleje Jerozolimskie 3. Check opening hours: they will be roughly 10-4 or -5, except for one morning closure (Thursday) on a day when opening is extended for an hour or so, and one all-day closure (Monday). A rough and ready *Kawiarnia* serves snacks and lunch: I took vegetable soup, two hamburgers and roll, and a tea and chocolate biscuit for 50 pence (US$0.80). The hideous museum building plumbs the depths of those desperate days of 1927-1938, when T. Tolwiński was mistakenly invited to fill the avenue with something stolid, bulky, and grey. As with the Palace of Culture, the theory is 'the bigger the better', neatly counterpunched with the boxing dictum: 'the bigger they come, the harder they fall.'

Seven public galleries solicit attention: Ancient Art (first-rate); Faras, Sudan (for Africanists); Mediaeval Art (second-rate); Modern Polish Art (first-rate); Contemporary Polish Art, from 1914 (second-rate); Classical Foreign Art (first-rate); and Foreign Art from 1800 (insignificant). Two uninspired Renoir sketches, a *Paysage dans le Jura* by Courbet, and poor examples of Segantini, Signac and Vlaminck demonstrate all too clearly how a shortage of hard currency will prevent the best-intentioned of Eastern bloc gallery curators from carrying out their job of buying new works. And, though the museum is so enormous, so much space is wasted that there are no permanent displays of Polish or foreign graphic art, coins and medals, or decorative art. In fact, without a Museum of Applied Art, you can really only obtain an overview of Poland's excellence in this field from Zdzisław Żygulski's *An Outline History of Polish Applied Art* (Interpress, Warsaw, 1987).

During my visit a temporary exhibition was devoted to socialist realism, with banal paintings, song and sculptures – though brilliant posters, each with one simple idea. Silent Poles shuffled round the display, many still wearing the dull grey clothes shown in photographs of the 1950s, when you had to wear approved boots, dark suit and dark socks to show solidarity with the earnestness of socialism. Seeing the doctrinaire shabbiness, I understood the fascination Poles feel for the otherness of rococo furniture, baroque palaces, sumptuous gardens in the manner of Versailles, grand opera. At the bookstall one of the rare workers (as opposed to intellectuals) I had seen in the special display enquired the price of the illustrated catalogue. 'Oh,' he murmured sadly, on hearing it cost all of £1.50 (about $3), and wandered off humiliated, unable to afford it...

The Polish Archaeological Expedition to Faras, in classical Nubia (modern Sudan), was permitted to bring back from the 1960-4 excavations murals, architectonic details and granite columns from the site. Artistically, the schematic wall paintings seem crude enough by standards of Coptic Egypt, the best work being a mid-8th century S. Anne and an Archangel Michael of *c.975*.

On the right wing of the ground floor, an Ancient Art gallery shows items from Egypt, Etruria and the Roman Empire, but its greatest treasures are Greek red-figure and black-figure vases: the Panathenaic Amphora depicting a horse-race by the Berlin Painter (*c.480* B.C.); a stamnos showing the struggle of Hercules with Antaeus by the Aigistos Painter (*c.460* B.C.). A superb sculpture of the 2nd-3rd centuries A.D. portrays Hermes and the Rams. Many of the objects are deposited by the Louvre on long-term loan.

Polish mediaeval art, occasionally derivative, has many appealing qualities, particularly when enriched by the German sculptural tradition, as in Silesia. Outstanding in this gallery is an early 16th-century Silesian high-relief wooden sculpture showing S. Luke painting the Virgin, with the Christ-child playing on the floor in the foreground, from the Church of S. Mary Magdalene in Wrocław. From the Poor Clares' Convent in Głogów comes a great Silesian triptych: Ecce Homo, Christ Carrying the Cross, and the Crucifixion. A late 15th-century sculpture of S. Margaret from S. Catherine's, Gdańsk indicates the high level of Pomeranian craftsmanship at this time. Hans Suess of Kulmbach painted the Legend of S. Stanislaus (1514-18) for an altar at Pławno. A Małopolska *Pietà* of *c.*1450 shows the wounds of Christ dark against his sallow body, cradled in the awkwardness of death against the comfort of his Mother, sorrowing angels placed farther back to add depth.

'Wollen Sie Geld wechseln?', muttered a man's voice behind me. He could have been 35, with anxious brown eyes, an office-worker or civil servant judging by his soft hands. 'Nein, danke', I replied without turning away. He offered three times the official rate of exchange for dollars, sterling, Deutschmark. Perhaps he wanted to buy something in a hard currency shop, acquire a car more quickly than if he could offer only złoty, or take a one-way excursion to West Berlin. Once there, Poles can claim social security payments. They are supposed to work part of the year for the entitlement, but many don't. Złoty are not saved because, with inflation running at 20), and interest on savings varying from 6-15), there seems no point in saving. Moreover, there are never sufficient consumer goods around to meet demand so, when they do turn up, they are bought anyway, the excess resold at a profit on the black market. In the end I had to leave the room to prevent a scene for, though he would have been entitled to possess hard currency, I should have been liable to deportation or a jail sentence for changing money unofficially.

The Polish Modern Art Gallery earns its reputation as the leading home of 19th century Polish art by reason of its collections of Piotr Michałowski (1800-55) and Antoni Brodowski (1784-1832), father of the painters Tadeusz and Józef; and their successors Rodakowski, Simmler, Gerson, Kotsis, Chełmoński, the brothers Maksymilian and Aleksander Gierymski and of course Matejko. Among the 'Young Poland' group, note Malczewski, Mehoffer, Wyspiański and Wojkiewicz.

Matejko dominates the room because he patriotically equated large canvases with great aspirations. Surprisingly, his talents for drama, movement and disciplined placing of characters to avoid overcrowding all combine to achieve his intention. Some of his works, including many of his finest, can be found today in Warsaw Castle, where there is so much space. But do not miss the brilliant 'Stanczyk' (1862), in which the royal jester broods over the loss of Smolensk (1514) while the Court of Sigismund I revels at a royal ball.

The art of Poland since 1914 has been polarised between the official schools, proletarian in theme, traditional in style and treatment; and the unofficial, responding either to internal necessity or to external trends, such as Cubism, abstraction, and the rising tide of naïveté.

Italian art is well represented because aristocrats in earlier periods travelled to Italy and purchased good examples while they were still to be found, examples which later came into the State's hands, and thence to the National Museum. Urgent cleaning and conservation measures need to be taken, because in some cases (like the Pinturicchio 'Madonna and Child') centuries of grime and varnish virtually conceal the artist's intention. Memorable finds include a polychrome sculpture of 'Madonna and Child' by Antonio Rossellino, Lorenzo Veneziano's 'Madonna, Child and Bernardino', a Crucifixion by Taddeo di Bartolo, and two works by Cima da Conegliano: a *Pietà* and 'Christ among the Doctors'. A fine portrait of Lorenzo Giustiniani has been attributed to Gentile Bellini, and a portrait of a Venetian admiral to Tintoretto. Alessandro Magnasco – a painter wildly underrated because misunderstood – is represented by 'Magic Lantern', gipsy scenes, and a typically magic landscape, demonised by the force of the painter's personality. Ferdinando Arisi's monograph *Gian Paolo Panini* (1961) makes no mention of the 'Roman Ruins' and 1743 'Christ among the Doctors' by this great *vedutista*, so it was a joy and privilege to find and celebrate works unknown to Arisi. By contrast, the Bellotto paintings in Warsaw have become world-famous, and there is no need to dwell further on their documentary excellence. Other fine Italian works include 'S. Francis before the Pope', 'Christ with the Crown of Thorns' and 'The Flight of Egypt' by Francesco Solimena, 'The Apostles' Communion' by Luca Giordano, and 'Lucretia' by Antonio Carneo of Udine.

French art is represented by a portrait of Richelieu by Philippe de Champaigne almost invisible under dirt, a splendid 'Guitarist' by Greuze, 'Queen Maria Leszczyńska' by Jean-Marc Nattier, and an equestrian portrait of Stanislaus Kostka Potocki by Jacques Louis David.

The Low Countries can be seen at their best in 'The Choice between Youth and Old Age' by Jan Steen. A girl touches a young man's knee while avidly staring at an old man's wealth, desiring the best of both worlds. A 'Portrait of Maerten Day' given to Rembrandt in years gone by may fall victim to scrutiny by the Rembrandt Study Group, but the still life by Jan Davidszoon de Heem (1606-84) and another two by Willem Claeszoon Heda (1594-1682) are uncontestable. Jan Lievens has a magical 'Boy Fanning a Flame' and Roelant Savery a charming 'Noah's Ark'. Best of all is probably a 'Lazarus Raised from the Dead' in Carel Fabritius' vibrant chiaroscuro, Lazarus radiating the *chiaro*.

The Polish Army Museum presents a curious example of that predilection to show one's own country as glorious, 'right or wrong'. But which country? The very notion of Polish nationality remained tenuous until 'The Polish Republic' was established in 1918. And what is the 'Polish Army'? Is it an army that speaks Polish? Hardly, because the

Battle of Grunwald (1410) was won by Russians, Czechs, Lithuanians and Muslim Tatars as well as Poles. Does it comprise Polish nationals only? Certainly not, for the same reason. During World War II, was it the Polish underground force fighting the Nazis: the Home Army, under the orders of the Polish Government-in-Exile in London? Not quite, because other underground forces operated simultaneously, including the People's Army, Communist-run, which did not recognise the emigré Government; and the right-wing National Armed Forces, which would not submit itself to Home Army orders. Another Polish Government-in-Exile had been established in Moscow to take power once the Red Army had swept over a Warsaw devastated by the Germans, and this Polish Committee of National Liberation was already powerful in Lublin in 1944. Nowadays, the Polish Army is the military arm of the P.Z.P.R. in a one-party state which does not allow the people the luxury of voting for other parties because it is certain that in a free election it would lose power just as the Government referendum of 1987 (the first time that the people had been openly consulted since 1946), resulted in defeat for their proposals on price rises – the factor that had toppled previous governments with the threat of mass revolt.

Supposing you choose to surrender the chance of examining the Polish Army Museum in the same complex as the National Museum, but you still have a couple of hours left before closing, you could spend a couple of hours in the National Ethnographical Museum on Ulica Kredytowa 1, then the early evening wandering in the public park called the Saxon Gardens, where Królewska (north of Kredytowa) meets Marszałkowska. The National Ethnographical Museum was founded in 1888, but its 30,000 objects were systematically destroyed by the Nazis in 1939 and the dismal task started again in 1946. It is housed in the former Land Credit Association headquarters, designed by Henryk Marconi in the 19th century, and rebuilt in the same style 1962-72.

Special exhibitions are held on the ground floor (during my visit, the folk sculptor and glass-painter Bednarz Bronisław) and on the first floor non-European cultures can be seen. The African section includes crafts (basketry, weaving, ironworking), costume, architecture and furniture.

The second floor starts with folk crafts, such as ceramics, metalwork, and weaving, proceeding to textiles, carpets, costume, painted dowry chests, spinning-wheels, and musical instruments such as horn and bagpipe. Folk crafts in wood include shelves and spoon-racks, tables, stools and chairs. Naive artists are represented, among them Bronisław Krawczuk and Teofil Ociepka. Pride of the Museum is the folk costume collection, with more than 14,000 items, mainly of a ceremonial nature, since everyday wear did not vary much throughout Poland. Regional diversity matches the mediaeval divisions: Great Poland, Little Poland, Mazovia and Silesia, while many minor differences can be found from parish to parish. The main materials were linen, wool and leather; the principal fabric types being the striped fabric called *pasiak*, the geometrically-patterned fabric, and the double-warp carpet. If you want to see colourful folk costumes being worn today, try festivals such as Easter or 22 July (National Day) in Kurpie, Podhale (the High Tatras accessible from Zakopane), Łowicz, Opoczno and Sieradz. See for instance the delightful costumes from Łowicz: red, orange and most recently blue-green.

Excursions from Warsaw provide an interesting contrast. Eastward lies Białystok (190 km) and the forest of Białowieza, the last virgin plains forest in Europe. Shared between Poland and the U.S.S.R., this forest remains the only European refuge of the bison, and wild boar, elk, deer, wolves and lynxes roam free. Special enclosures allow visitors to see bison, elk and wild horses.

Westward from Ulica Wolska we reach Błonie in 28 km, then at 49 km (Zosin) we turn right to Żelazowa Wola. Fryderyk Chopin (to give him his Polish name) was born here on 22 February 1810, and his museum-home can be visited daily from 9 to 6, except from 9 to 4, November-April. The period furniture is not the family's, but objects and manuscripts belonging to the composer are shown. The painted ceiling beams of the kitchen are characteristic of Polish country houses of the early 19th century. Sunday recitals are still given occasionally in the Music Room. The children's room displays family treasures among its Biedermeier furniture, while his mother's room has an alcove where the composer was born. In his father's room prints and plans are exhibited. The park was designed in its present form in 1930.

Past the town of Sochaczew (with the ruins of a 14th-century castle of the Dukes of Mazovia), we come to the country town of Łowicz, also with about 23,000 inhabitants. The Regional Museum at Plac Kościuszki 1 offers a fascinating cross-section of local crafts, including painted Easter eggs, ceramics, furniture, glass painting, and especially costumes. These are worn on Sundays throughout the year, but can be seen at their best during the festivals of Whit Sunday, Assumption Day, and Corpus Christi early in June. Don't miss the Collegiate Church of 1652-68 in Renaissance-baroque style by T. and A. Poncino, with the memorable sarcophagus of Archbishop Uchanski by Jan Michałowicz (1580-3).

A minor road from Łowicz brings you in 4 km to Arkadia, a delightful park, feminine to the point of felinity, commissioned by Princess Helena Radziwiłł (1778-1821), inspired by Isabella Czartoryska's park at Powązki (1774). Arkadia's Temple of Diana preserves frescoes by the notable rococo artist Jean-Pierre Norblin, who – here and at Powązki – manages to ensconce Watteau's vision in a Polish landscape. The pastoral idyll then permeating European literature, painting and early ballet is played out in Arkadia's Sybilline Grotto, Arcaded Gallery, Greek Arch: all the conceits and parkland views that we associate with Claude and Poussin, at one end of the artistic spectrum, and with Fragonard and Boucher at the other.

Another 4 km along the same road brings you to Nieborów, a palace administered by the National Museum in Warsaw. Designed for Archbishop Michał Radziejowski by Tylman van Gameren, who had been invited to Poland by the Lubomirskis, Nieborów rose into the astonished skies of rural Poland from 1690-6, and one never forgets the sonorous coincidence hereabouts that *niebo* is also the Polish word for 'sky' The palace later belonged to the Towiańskis, the Lubomirskis, the Ogińskis, and the Radziwiłłs, under whose imaginative and benevolent aegis it became a treasure-house of craftsmanship and art that we prize today, thanks to the painstaking efforts of the Polish State since it took over responsibility in 1945. In the palace, paintings by the Spaniard Jusepe de Ribera (1588-1656) and the Frenchman Louis Silvestre le Jeune (1675-1760) vie with splendid furniture and a fine grandee's library of 5,000 volume to attract one's attention.

Long after the palace's baroque style had become a period piece, Prince Michał Radziwiłł founded a majolica factory at Nieborów, in 1881: the last such enterprise by a great magnate. The works manager, a Frenchman of Polish origin called Stanislaus Thiele, had been lured from his position in the Ćmielow porcelain factory. Nieborów majolica (marked PMR) was inspired by wares from Nevers and Italian Renaissance ceramics. Characteristically blue and yellow, production from Nieborów concentrated on decorative objects such as *tazze*, vases, lamps, stove tiles, and *jardinières*.

Choose a fine summer's day for Nieborów, when the gardens appear at their ravishing best. A lapidarium includes pagan stone idols of the 10th-11th centuries, before Christianity took a firm grasp on the minds of Poland. Two late 18th-century orangeries can be explored.

A geometrical park extends behind the palace as far as the eye can see. Parallel with the park and palace complex, and separated from it by water, is a fine landscaped garden with ever-changing vistas, maintained as it was in the early 18th century.

The extraordinary contrast between the colourful folk art of a peasant cottage in nearby Łowicz, and the aristocratic dreamworld of Arkadia and Nieborów underlines the dichotomies evident at every step in Poland today. The state celebrates by investment in restoration and maintenance the great monarchical and aristocratic societies of earlier centuries, while openly reviling their politics. Yet the ordinary people of Poland, while undoubtedly better off than their ancestors, see themselves as poor relations to their contemporaries in the West, and subjugated to equally poor relations in the U.S.S.R., who are forced to import grains and advanced technology, because their doctrinaire system cannot manage creativity, spontaneity, and incentives for productivity. A result of full employment at all costs means low wages for all except the few so elevated in the hierarchy that their privileges are unassailable. In the deeply serious *Reflections on the Republic* (1971), Jan Szczepański could write, 'Our citizens identify democracy with anarchy while the men in authority, used to governing by terror, are helpless, for they do not understand democratic techniques of leadership'. He went on to explain that democratization could exploit social forces for everyone's benefit, strengthen the government and 'if the government solves the nation's problems wisely and efficiently, it can always rely on the majority of the people. There is a disparity between strong government and democracy only if we misunderstand both: equating strong government with despotism, and democracy with anarchy.' Many years later, the problems of Poland remain the same; the solution just as far off.

In the LOT aircraft back to London, a Polish stewardess announced over the intercom, 'The left-hand side of the aeroplane is for non-smokers only'. Under her breath, the Polish lady sitting next to me enquired as if to herself how the government-owned airline proposed to prevent the smoke crossing to the other side of the plane...

USEFUL INFORMATION

When to Come

My suggestion for those wishing to visit museums and castles throughout Poland is to choose the beginning or end of the tourist season, avoiding July and August if possible, when trains, buses, and accommodation of all sorts will be stretched to bursting point. Remember that Eastern bloc countries, lacking the supply-and-demand factor in Western nations and capitalist countries in Asia such as Singapore and Japan, do not expand their tourism potential to the limit for a complex variety of reasons. As always, one never loses one's temper or seeks to explain a foreign policy in terms of one's own preconceptions and prejudices, but seeks to accommodate oneself to the host country. This is particularly easy in Poland, where the vast majority of the people make every effort to be polite and understanding. Since most Poles prefer to take their holidays in July and August, I suggest you benefit from long June and September days. May is an excellent choice for the centre of the country (Warsaw, Toruń, Poznań) but might still be chilly in the Baltic region (Szczecin, Gdańsk, Frombork) and in the Tatra Mountains of the far south, near Zakopane. Winter sports are held in the Podhale region centred on Zakopane from December to March or April. Spring in the countryside can be as muddy as the Serbinow estate immortalised in Maria Dąbrowska's novel *Nights and Days* recently made into both film and television series.

Wear warm clothes (or have access to them) except during July and August, and keep a compact rolled umbrella handy, with a polythene bag to put it in when wet. Showers are frequent, and temperatures range from 60-80° Fahrenheit (17-25° Centigrade) in the period May to September, but can fall to -30° F in mountain Winters.

To make up your own mind when you would prefer to visit Poland, here are average Fahrenheit temperatures in each month for the three cities described in detail in this book:

	Cracow	Warsaw	Gdańsk
January	27.6	26.8	29.3
February	29.5	28.2	30.4
March	27.4	34.2	35.1
April	46.6	45.8	43.2
May	57.1	56.8	52.3
June	62.2	62.1	59.5
July	65.8	65.6	63.8
August	63.5	63.1	61.9
September	56.8	55.8	56.5
October	47.5	46.1	47.2
November	37.6	36.1	38.3
December	30.6	29.4	32.5

To convert Fahrenheit into Centigrade, subtract 32 from Fahrenheit, and divide by 1.8. The overwhelming reason for preferring the Fahrenheit scale in *Polish Cities* is that Gabriel Daniel Fahrenheit (1686-1736) was born in Ogarna Street, Gdańsk, even if he did most of his work in the Netherlands and Great Britain.

How to Come
American visitors can reach Poland through European airports such as London or Frankfurt, or direct from New York with LOT, the Polish national airline, which uses Soviet-made aircraft. A number of companies in London offer charter flights at a considerable saving. For instance Tazab Travel Ltd., 273 Old Brompton Road, London SW5 9JB, offers low-cost flights on LOT or British Airways in January to March (minimum stay 6 days and maximum 31 days), rising in April, May and October, and again in high season (June through September).

Orbis is the state travel bureau, headquartered in Warsaw at Krakowskie Przedmieście 13. A variety of package- and combination tours can be arranged through Orbis offices throughout the world. Polorbis Travel in London is at 82 Mortimer St., London, N.Y. 10036. Orbis also maintains offices in Amsterdam, East Berlin, Brussels, Budapest, Chicago, Cologne, Helsinki, Madrid, Moscow, Paris, Prague, Rome, Sofia, Stockholm, Tokyo and Vienna. LOT Polish Airlines maintains offices in those cities as well as in Algiers, Athens, Baghdad, Bangkok, Beirut, Belgrade, Benghazi, West Berlin, Cairo, Copenhagen, Damascus, Dubai, Frankfurt am Main, Geneva, Hamburg, Istanbul, Kiev, Kuwait, Leningrad, Luxembourg, Lyon, Manchester, Milan, Montreal, Sydney, Tunis and Zürich.

High-season charter flights on LOT are available from Gatwick and Manchester to Warsaw once a week, at weekends, and from Gatwick to

Cracow. Connecting flights in the U.K. are arranged by your agent, who can also offer onward connections in Poland to Gdańsk, Katowice, Koszalin, Poznań, Rzeszów, Szczecin, Wrocław and Zielona Gora.

Anyone holding a non-Polish passport is required to pay at least three times the fares paid by Polish nationals on internal routes only, and in złoty.

A most enjoyable coach trip taking two days (with overnight on the ferry) runs from Manchester - Nottingham or Birmingham - London - Harwich - Hamburg - Poznań - Warsaw, especially useful for those visiting Poznań.

The same applies to the train departing on Saturdays from Liverpool St. via Hook of Holland to Warsaw: this also calls at Poznań.

On balance I should *not* suggest bringing your own car to Poland, or even hiring one there. The handicap of encapsulating yourself against frequent encounters with Poles is not offset by convenience, because travel in Poland is a factor of which the country is rightly proud. Trains and buses are frequent, punctual, comfortable and very cheap. Express trains with reserved seats are especially recommendable. By contrast, local car hire is very expensive; you need an international and national driving licence, an International Green Card (for insurance) and petrol coupons, bought in hard currency from Orbis and guaranteeing a foreigner limitless supplies. Often you can go a great distance in the countryside without finding a filling-station or repair shop, however. Much better, for those outlandish places you wish to visit, to negotiate a figure beforehand with a taxi-driver.

Guided tours of Warsaw (with an English-speaking guide) take you by coach from the Forum Hotel (9.30 a.m. and 2.30 p.m.) with ten-minute intervals to pick up other passengers at the Grand, Victoria and Europejski on a sightseeing tour daily from May to September, and on Saturdays and Sundays throughout the rest of the year. The morning itinerary covers the Old Town, Historical Museum, and the Royal Way from Plac Zamkowy to the Belvedere. The afternoon itinerary substitutes Łazienki for the Historical Museum. Departures from the same four hotels take you on a guided tour of Wilanów.

Taxis have metres, and a government regulation currently authorises cab-drivers to multiply the figure on the metre by three, which incredibly remains a very good bargain. But since taxis are so cheap and hence greatly in demand, you might find it much quicker and easier to board a city tram or bus than to wait in a lengthy taxi-queue. Not many drivers speak English or German, so if you speak no Polish it is helpful if you show him your destination written or printed. The vast majority of taxi-drivers are honest, but if one forgets to set the metre going, do remind him by pointing to it; do *not* argue about paying three times the figure shown, for it is legally correct, and round up about 10% as a tip.

To use bus or tram routes, buy tickets at 'Ruch' kiosks near major stops. Insert the ticket into a little machine in the vehicle and pull a handle to punch holes in your ticket. There are no conductors: you are expected to do this yourself. Street maps can be found at bookshops marked *Księgarnia* and *Dom Książki*, or sometimes at 'Ruch' kiosks which sell newspapers, magazines, Polish cigarettes, matches, toys, souvenirs, combs, and a random selection of books ranging from children's stories to the works of Lenin or the playwright Sławomir Mrożek.

For those familiar with 'closed zones' in the Soviet Union, it will come as some surprise that Poland has no restrictions whatsoever on travel within its borders: indeed I was not waved away peremptorily from the Presidential Palace (the Belvedere) in Warsaw, or the sensitive Gdańsk shipyards: moreover, the horrific Oświęcim concentration camp (notorious in the West as Auschwitz) has been so carefully preserved as a warning to future generations that admission is free of charge to both Museum and Lager.

Accommodation

If you buy an expensive tour, you can expect to stay in an expensive hotel, such as the Forum Intercontinental, Victoria Intercontinental, or Grand Orbis in Warsaw; the Holiday Inn or Wanda Orbis in Cracow; the Hewelius or Monopol in Gdańsk; the Grand in Sopot; the Gdynia Orbis in Gdynia; or the Kasprowy Orbis or Giewont Orbis in Zakopane. There is only one good reason, unless one counts snobbery as a reason, for staying in these hotels, since the three-star and two-star hotels are just as clean, spacious and probably more friendly. That reason is to be sure of a private bathroom, but then most public bathrooms are spotless. For electric razors, and other appliances note that the power is 220 volts, 50 cycles, A.C.

By far the best way of living in Poland is with a private family, most of those on the established lists having at least one member who can speak English, French or German. In *Warsaw*, check at Syrena Accommodation Bureau, Ul. Krucza 17, open every day until 8 p.m. It is not unheard of for travellers arriving later to find freelance landlords helpfully offering a room just outside Syrena... If you find a room unofficially, register the fact at the Militia Registration Office for Foreigners. You pay the bureau in złoty, and they give you a receipt in two copies, of which one is retained and the other given to your host. This does not include any meals, even breakfast, but again, one can always come to some informal arrangement. In *Cracow*, check at Wawel-Tourist, Ul. Pawia 8, open every day until 9 p.m. In *Zakopane*, private rooms can be booked at the Tatra Region Tourist Office, Ul. Kościuszki 23a, open every day until 8 p.m. In *Gdańsk*, try the

Accommodation Bureau at Gdańsk Tourist Office, Ul. Elżbietańska 10-11.

If you have anything against private accommodation, here is a selection of reasonably-priced hotels. In *Warsaw*, I recommend Hotel Saski, Plac Feliksa Dzierżyńskiego 1; Dom Chłopa, Plac Powstańców Warszawy 2; Pensjonat Zgoda, Ul. Szpitalna 1, and if you are a teacher the House of Teachers (ZNP), Wybrzeże Kościuszkowskie 31-33. If these fail, you can try the Tourist Office in the Orbis Grand Hotel, Ul. Krucza 16, but they will inevitably propel you in the direction of the dearer hotels. Students willing to share two-four beds to a room in July-August can enquire at Almatur, Ul. Kopernika 15, for a directory of the current youth hostels throughout Poland, which vary every year, and for vouchers to pay for nights in these hostels. Cheapest of all is the youth hostel at Ul. Smolna, for which the I.Y.H. card is essential, with fifteen beds to a room.

In *Cracow*, good hotels are expensive, and cheap ones not very good, so again private accommodation is recommended. If you do need a hotel, try the Hotel Polski, Ul. Pijarska 17, for its location in the lovely Old City, near the Czartoryski Gallery with Leonardo da Vinci's 'Lady with an Ermine', and near the excellent Restauracja Paryska, in the Hotel Francuski, Ul. Pijarska 13. The hotel itself seems too expensive by comparison. Students can check with Almatur, Rynek Główny 7, between mid-July and late August only. Nearby, students have another accommodation bureau at Rynek Główny 15 from mid-July to mid-September.

In *Zakopane*, pension life in delightful chalets with three meals a day (if desired) can be enjoyed at Orion, Lipowy Dwór and any one of a dozen other inns. Of the hotels, the cost-conscious will like either Dom Turysty in Ul. Załuskiego or Hotel Morskie Oko in Ul. Krupówki. Almatur, for student accommodation, is located at Ul. Marusarzowny 15, open until 4 on Monday to Friday and until 1 on Saturdays.

In *Gdańsk*, you cannot believe your luck if you find a room free at Hotel Jantar, Ul. Długi Targ 19, for its urban view is magnificent. Prices vary significantly between high season (July through September) and the rest of the year. Adjoining *Sopot* and *Gdynia* are less crowded: private accommodation in Sopot can be arranged at the bureau at Ul. Dworcowa 4. Sopot's atmospheric Hotel Grand Orbis might be sampled; cheaper hotels include the Pensjonat Maryla, Ul. Sępia 22 and Hotel Bałtyk, Ul. Bieruta 83.

Restaurants

Polish cuisine is unadventurous. Most menus show dozens of dishes, but prices against only those few that are presently available. Unlike the accommodation, food is very cheap, and even the most expensive-looking restaurants are likely to offer extremely good value, like the excellent Cyganeria opposite Cracow's Słowacki Theatre, or the Restauracja Wierzynek at Cracow's Rynek Głowny 15. In Warsaw, try the Bazyliszek-Hortex at Rynek Starego Miasta 7-9, the nearby Pod Krokodylem (no. 19) or the Maryla in Hotel Forum, Ul. Nowogrodzka 24-26. In Zakopane, sample a meal at the Obrochtowka, Ul. Kraszewskiego 10a, or the Jędruś, Ul. Świerczewskiego 5. In Gdańsk, try the seafood at Pod Łososiem at Ul. Szeroka 54 or steak or duck at the Tawerna, Ul. Powrożnicza 19-20.

Passports and Visas

You need a valid passport to enter Poland, and a visa for which an application must be made at least two weeks in advance. Apply for a visa personally at the Polish Embassy nearest to you, by post, or through your travel agent, who will charge an extra fee. Your passport must be valid for a year beyond the date of submission and contain one empty page for a visa. You must complete a Visa Application form and attach two passport-size photographs, with money-vouchers corresponding to the number of days. Money-vouchers are evidence of prepayment in hard currency: currently US$15 or £10 daily for tourists and businessmen, except that a lower rate (currently $7 or £4.40 daily) is payable by those of Polish origin or spouse or children of Polish passport-holders, anyone under 21, and students (with a valid international student card). You exchange your dollars or pounds in vouchers for złotys in notes or coins on arrival. Add the current visa fee (by enquiring beforehand) and make sure that both applicants on a joint passport complete separate visa application forms and pay separate fees. The Polish Consulate in the U.K. is at 73 New Cavendish St., London W1N 7RB (Tel. 01-580-0476). In the U.S.A. apply to the Polish Embassy (Consulate, 2224 Wyoming Ave., N.W., Washington, D.C. 20008 (Tel. 202-234-3800), or to the Consulates at 233 Madison Avenue, New York, N.Y. 10016 (Tel. 212-889-8360) and 1530 North Lake Shore, Chicago, Illinois 60610 (Tel. 312-337-8166). In Canada, apply to the Consulates at 2603 Lakeshore Boulevard West, Toronto, Ont. M8V 1G5 (Tel. 252-5471) or 1500 Pine Avenue West, Montreal, Québec H3G 1B4.

Customs and Currency

You may not take złotys into or out of Poland, hence the money vouchers. The złoty devalues at about 20% a year at present, so this protects the foreigner at times when sterling, the dollar and the D-mark suffer lower inflation. Once in Poland, you can change money at an airport, bank or hotel, because (unlike the West) there is no difference between exchange rates. But you must *keep* your evidence of exchange when buying goods or services (like accommodation) in hard currency. At the Immigration desk you will have to show passport and visa, and at the Customs complete a form declaring your travellers' cheques, hard currency, leather goods (leather jackets are eagerly sought after) and gold, such as rings or watches. This form must be retained to show at departure, though during my departure from Cracow a crestfallen nun who had lost hers was gently given a blank to complete! Your cases will usually be examined minutely: I recommend composed and patient cooperation rather than the sardonic or irate manner adopted by a number of tactless Westerners. The law prevents your taking into Poland publications they may classify as pornographic or anti-socialist, narcotics, firearms, and penalises heavily anyone obviously bringing in goods for resale, such as three computers or ten calculators. Penal duty is charged on high-value goods not provenly bought for hard currency in duty-free stores, so you should keep all receipts banded round your passport for safe keeping. Credit cards are accepted in the major hotels, but most business is done in cash. Poles trying to obtain dollars or pounds or D-marks can be found outside major hotels and in recognised tourist areas, such as the Old Town Square in Gdańsk, Cracow and Warsaw. They offer an exchange rate ranging from two to four times the official rate; balance this theoretical advantage with the practical disadvantage of up to five years in a Polish prison for currency offences and with the fact that every facet of life except accommodation is already much cheaper than in any Western nation.

Embassies
The British Embassy in Warsaw is located at Aleja Róż 1 (Tel. 28-10-01). The United States Embassy is situated at Aleje Ujazdowskie 29 (Tel. 28-30-41), and U.S. Consulates exist at Cracow (Ul. Stolarska 9, Tel. 214-000) and at Poznań (Ul. Chopina 4, Tel. 595-86).

Health
British citizens who remember to take their National Health Medical Card can obtain reciprocal free treatment in Poland. Citizens of other Western countries could ask their hotel or host in an emergency, or contact their Embassy or nearest Consulate. Telephone numbers for emergencies are 999 for first aid, 997 for police, and 998 for fire: these numbers will however *not* be manned by English-speaking operators. Check with your own insurance company whether your policy covers you for illness or hospitalisation in Poland or for air conveyance back home in emergency. A pharmacy is signed *Apteka* and does not sell the wide range of goods you expect in an American drug-store or British chemist's.

Speaking the Language

Polish, like Russian, is a Slavonic language, but unlike Russian does not use the Cyrillic alphabet; indeed, its alphabet is close to ours, omitting q, v, x, adding three vowels, and adding also six consonants. Readers are referred to the summary Berlitz *Polish for Travellers,* or to the much more systematic and useful *Colloquial Polish* by B. W. Mazur (Routledge and Kegan Paul 1983) with self-marking exercises and an accompanying cassette. If you have a Polish teacher who can help with explanations in English, I recommend *Uczymy się polskiego* by Barbara Bartnicka and others (Wiedza Powszechna, Warsaw, 1984). Summer courses for foreign students are arranged at the Jagiellonian University in Cracow, but their textbook by Miodunka and others is painfully jocular and elementary, absurdly expensive and seemingly intended for a very juvenile audience. Better for the self-taught is the rather old-fashioned *Teach Yourself Polish* by M. Corbridge-Patkaniowska (English Universities Press, 1948). There is a great need for bilingual texts of major writers such as Słowacki, Mickiewicz, Miłosz, Zbigniew Herbert and Tadeusz Różewicz, a need which the Polish authorities seem unwilling to fill.

The older generation of Poles still have some grasp of German, but among the younger generation English and (to a lesser extent) French are spoken. Russian is taught in schools, but few Poles seem comfortable in it.

Words and Phrases

Do you speak English?	Czy pan (m.)/pani (f.) mówi po angielsku?
I do not understand	Nie rozumiem
Yes	Tak
No	Nie
Good morning!	Dzień dobry!
Good evening!	Dobry wieczór!
Goodnight!	Dobranoc!
Hello! How are things?	Cześć! Co słychać?
Just the same; fine	Po staremu; dobrze
I should like to buy...	Chciałbym kupić...
... a town plan	... plan miasta
... a ticket to Warsaw	... bilet do Warszawy
Excuse me; sorry	Przepraszam
Where is the tourist office?	Gdzie jest informacja turystyczna?
Entrance, Exit	Wejście; Wyście

English	Polish
How much is it?	Ile kosztuje?
Open	Czynny; Otwarty
Closed	Nieczynny; Zamknięty
Please	Proszę
Thank you (very much)	Dziękuję (bardzo)
Just a moment	Chwileczkę
Large, small	Duży, mały
On the left; on the right	Na lewo; na prawo
Straight on	Prosto
Here; there	Tu or tutaj; tam
Cheap, expensive	Tani, drogi
Free, occupied	Wolny, zajęty
New, old	Nowy, stary
Hot, cold	Gorący, zimny
Difficult, easy	Trudny, łatwy
Forbidden	Wzbroniony
Poland	Polska
Polish; a Pole	Polski; Polak (m.) Polka (f.)
American; an American	Amerykański; Amerykanin (m.), Amerikanka (f.)
English; an Englishman	Angielski; Anglik (m.), Angielka (f.)
Great Britain; British	Wielka Brytania; brytyjski
U.S.A.	Stany Zjednoczone
U.S.S.R.	Związek Socjalistycznych Republik Radzieckich (Z.S.R.R.)
Canada	Kanada
England, Scotland	Anglia, Szkocja
Ireland, Wales	Irlandia, Walia
Where is the toilet?	Gdzie jest toaleta?
Men's toilet	Męski, Dla Panow, or a triangle pointing downward
Women's toilet	Damski, Dla Pań, or a circle
What time is it?	Która (jest) godzina?
7 o'clock- 7.30	Siódma; wpół do osmej (compare *halb acht* in German)
Restaurant; hotel	Restauracja; hotel
Café	Kawiarnia
Grocery	Spożywczy
Butcher's	Mięso, Wędliny
Fruit, vegetables	Owoce, Warzywa
Breakfast; lunch	Śniadanie; obiad
Supper	Kolacje

Tea, coffee	Herbata, kawa		
Street, road	Ulica, droga		
Post, telephone	Poczta, telefon		

Numbers and Days of the Week

1 jeden 2 dwa 3 trzy 4 cztery 5 pięć 6 sześć 7 siedem 8 osiem 9 dziewięć 10 dziesięć 11 jedenaście 12 dwanaście 13 trzynaście 14 czternaście 15 piętnaście 16 szesnaście 17 siedemnaście 18 osiemnaście 19 dziewiętnaście 20 dwadzieścia 30 trzydzieści 40 czterdzieści 50 pięćdziesiąt 60 sześćdziesiąt 70 siedemdziesiąt 80 osiemdziesiąt 90 dziewięćdziesiąt 100 sto 200 dwieście 300 trzysta 400 czterysta 500 pięćset 600 sześćset 700 siedemset 800 osiemset 900 dziewięćset 1,000 tysiąc

Monday	poniedziałek	When...?	Kiedy?
Tuesday	wtorek	Today	Dzisiaj
Wednesday	środa	Tomorrow	Jutro
Thursday	czwartek	Yesterday	Wczoraj
Friday	piątek	Morning	Rano
Saturday	sobota	Afternoon	Popołudnie
Sunday	niedziela	Evening	Wieczór
		Night	Noc

Holidays and Festivals

1 January	New Year's Day
Good Friday, Easter Day and Easter Monday	
1 May	Labour Day
Corpus Christi (early June)	
22 July	Liberation Day (1944)
1 November	All Saints' Day
25 December	Christmas Day
26 December	S. Stephen's Day

Books

There is a large degree of state control on the publication and distribution of books in Poland, and many authors cannot be sold officially 'over the counter', including currently the Nobel Prizewinner Czesław Miłosz or that other great poet Zbigniew Herbert. Most emigrant writers are not on sale in Poland, and very few books published outside Poland are on sale in the country, except in special shops such as those devoted to Soviet authors, mainly in the Russian original. Furthermore, there is centralised dispatched of books to kiosks and bookshops, with the result that you cannot 'order' a book, but just hope that sooner or later it will turn up in official or underground editions, the latter obtainable of course only through illegal channels. So my advice is to buy books when you see them in Poland, because the chance may never recur. Such books would include Bogdan Suchodolski's *A History of Polish Culture* (1986), very cheap guidebooks to cities, museums, and palaces, and city plans and maps. Unfortunately for the highly-educated, literate and sophisticated Polish reading public, most of the best books on Poland or in Polish are not available inside the country – and you should not attempt to take them in. Among these are the works of Tadeusz Konwicki, author of the dark novel *A Minor Apocalypse* and the journal *Moonrise, moonset* (both translated by Richard Lourie but available only illicitly in Poland); Norman Davies' *Heart of Europe; a short history of Poland* (1984), for those who do not want to read the whole of his exhaustive *God's Playground: a history of Poland* (1981); a grammar such as B.W. Mazur's *Colloquial Polish* (1983); and literary classics such as the *Selected Poems* (1977) of Zbigniew Herbert, *The Issa Valley* (1981) by Czesław Miłosz, and the 1927 experimental novel by Stanisław Ignacy Witkiewicz translated as *Insatiability* (1985) by Louis Iribarne. The very name of *Solidarność* (the free trade union 'Solidarity') has been deleted from the press, and from the history books, so if you want to find out anything about this movement, and its wider implications for potential democracy in Poland, you should read any one of the major contributions published in the West, such as Alain Touraine's *Solidarity: Poland 1980-81* (1983) or subscribe to the important monthly 'Voice of Solidarity' from the 'Solidarność' Information Office, 215 Balham High Road, London SW17 7BN. We must all look forward fervently to the time when Polish history can be viewed equally clearly from all sides, without prejudice, and without hatred. This time seems as far off as ever.

I take this opportunity to acknowledge the assistance of previous writers on aspects of Polish topography, history, art and culture, and to recommend their books for further reading. The basic route guide for motorists is the latest edition of the *Przewodnik po Polsce* from Sport i Turystyka of Warsaw, updated every eight or ten years. Your local Polish National Tourist Office will provide maps and current information about fares and facilities. Books go out of print very quickly, but you might try second-hand bookshops for the following: J.Z. Łoziński and A. Miłobędzki, *Guide to Architecture in Poland* (1967), published like the others mentioned in Warsaw, and *The Polish Jewry: History and Culture* (1982), by Marian Fuks and others.

Walking the streets of Warsaw, keep at hand J.A. Chróścicki and A. Rottermund's pocket-size *Atlas of Warsaw's Architecture* (1978) and the handy booklets on aspects of Warsaw published between 1978 and 1981: Wojciech Fijałkowski's *Wilanów*, Marek Kwiatkowski's *Łazienki*,

Jerzy Lileyko's *Warsaw: the Royal Way*, and *Warsaw: the Old Town* by W. Głębocki and K. Mórawski. The best souvenir album is Edmund Kupiecki's *Warszawa* (1970), and the most useful *Book of Warsaw Palaces* is that by T.S. Jaroszewski (1985).

The most expert detailed guide to the Triune City is Lech Krzyżanowski's *Gdańsk-Sopot-Gdynia* (1974), almost impossible to find these days. There are albums by J. Stankiewicz and B. Szermer *(Gdańsk,* 1971) and by M. and A. Szypowscy *(Gdańsk,* 1978).

For Małopolska, look no further than the excellent *In Cracow* (1973) by Jan Adamczewski. A memorable album of diverse art treasures is a must. I recommend *Cracow: City of Museums* (1976), edited by Jerzy Banach.

INDEX

Flemish art and architecture, 73, 81, 84-5, 91, 93-4, 118. *See also* under the names of individual artists and architects, e.g. Opberghen
Florian, *S.*, 19, 41
Foksal, 145
folklore, 176-7. *See also* Ethnographic Museums
Fontana *family*, 33-4, 41, 136, 144
forests, 54-5, 177
France and the French, 36, 73, 105, 110
Franciscans, 24, 87
Franciszek *of Sieradz*, 31
Franco-Prussian War, 36, 73
Frank, *Governor-General* Hans, 62, 156
French art and architecture, 175. *See also* under the names of individual artists and architects, e.g. Champaigne
Friedländer, David, 171
Frombork, 180
Fugger wineshop, Warsaw, 126
Fuks, Marian, 190
Fumo, Francesco, 160

Gameren, Tylman van, 41, 84, 130, 133, 135, 138, 143-5, 150, 157, 178
Garbo, Raffaellino del, 11
Gdańsk, vii-viii, 8, 13, 69, 72-109, 146, 180-5
Gdynia, 65, 72, 75, 80, 100, 107-9, 183, 185
German art and architecture, 43, 69, 88, 93, 133. *See also* under the names of individual artists and architects, e.g. Kramer
Germany and the Germans, 5, 15, 49, 63, 75, 77, 80, 94, 99. *See also* under the names of individual Germans, e.g. Frank
Gerould, Daniel, 87
Gerson, Wojciech, 27, 88, 169, 174
Ghetto, Kazimierz, 44-8; Warsaw, 114, 170
Gianotti, Jacopo, 123
Gierek, Edward, 115
Gierymski, Aleksander, 28, 174; Maksymilian, 174
Giewont, 59
Giordano, Luca, 175
Giorgioli, Francesco Antonio, 157
gipsies, 50
Gładysz, Jan. 144

Glaize, François, 118
Głębocki, W., 191
Gletker, Matthäus, 92
Głodówka, 60
Glotau, 93
Gniezno, 4, 15, 19, 21, 122
Gniński family, 145
Gogol, Nikolai Vasilievich, 39
Gołoński, Andrzej, 142
Gombrowicz, Witold, 34, 98-9
Gomułka, Władysław, 49
Gonzaga. *See* Marie-Louise Gonzaga
Gotenhafen. *See* Gdynia
Gothic art and architecture, 5, 8, 12-13, 18, 26, 29, 31, 33-4, 54, 69, 81, 90, 93, 98, 122, 126, 132, 134
Goths, 4
Gottlieb, Maurycy, 28
Goyen, Jan van, 88
Grass, Günter, 91, 102
Great Northern War, 14
Grotowski, Jerzy, 169
Grunwald, 13, 68, 176
Grzywacz, Z., 105
Gucci, Matteo, 45; Santi, 19-20, 34

Haberschrack, Mikołaj, 43
Haffner, Jean-Georges, 105
handicrafts, 26, 40. *See also* under the names of individual crafts, e.g. woodcarving
Hankis, M., 144
Hansa and the Hanseatic League, 68, 73, 80, 93
Hapsburgs, 13
health, 186
Heda, W. Cl., 175
Hel, 72, 108-9
Hendel, Zygmunt, 45
Herbert, Zbigniew, vi, 98-9, 111, 114, 136, 187, 189-90
Herle, Simon, 94
Himmler, Heinrich, 62
Historical Museum, Cracow, 26, 34; Gdańsk, 94-5; Warsaw, 123, 182; Polish Revolutionary Movement, Warsaw, 134
Hoess, Rudolf, 49, 53
Hohenberg, Martin, 160
Hohenzollern, Albrecht, *Duke of Prussia*, 27
Hołdanowicz, Leszek, 165

palaces, e.g. Uruski
Palloni, Michelangelo, 160, 162
Palma *il Vecchio*, Jacopo, 36
Panini, Gian Paolo, 175
Pankiewicz, Józef, 28, 43
passports, 185
Paul *of Gdańsk*, 81
Paulines, 45, 130, 144-5
Pelplin, 89
Pencz, Georg, 20
Peter and Paul, Cracow, *SS.*, 24
Petrini, Giovanni, 34
PEWEX shops, 129
pharmacies, 186
Piarists, 36, 130
Piast and the Piast dynasty, 4, 15, 18, 37, 41, 44, 122
Pieskowa Skała, 54, 56
Piłsudski, *Marshal* Józef, 21, 156
Pinturicchio, 175
Piola, Giuseppe, 138
Piotrowin, 19
Pipan *family*, 33
Placidi, Francesco, 15, 48
Planty, Cracow, 21
Płaszów, 46
Plersch *family*, 139, 144, 150-6, 160
Płoszyński, Edward, 49
Plużański, Stefan, 80
Pod Blachą Palace, Warsaw, 120-1
Podczasyński, Boleslaus Paweł, 161
Podkowiński, Władysław, 28
Polanians, 4
Poles and proto-Poles, 4
Polish Army Museum, Warsaw, 175-6
Polish language, 187-9
'Polonia', 138
Pomerania and the Pomeranians, 68, 80, 103-5, 174
Poncino *family*, 177
Popiel, Karol, 114
Popiełuszko, Jerzy, 15
Poronin, 60
portraits, 11, 164-5
Post Office, Gdańsk, 91
posters, 165
Potocki *family*, 33, 35, 138-9, 142, 160-5, 172
Potsdam Treaty, 95
Pourbus *the Younger*, Frans, 151
Powązki, 35, 170, 177
Poznań, viii, 4, 8, 40, 144, 180, 182
Prabuty, 65
Praga, Warsaw, 129, 171

prehistory, 55, 80
proletariat cult, 145
Prus, Bolesław, 136
Prussia and the Prussians, 36, 68, 73, 88, 90, 111, 114, 152
Pryliński, Tomasz, 26
Przebendowski *family*, 172
Przemyśl, 8
Przybyszewska, Stanisława, 85-6
Przybyszweski, Stanisław, 28, 40, 85, 98
Puck, 109
Puławy, 36
Pusłowski *family*, 147, 165
Pyjas, Stanisław, 115

Qur'an, 99

Rabelais, François, 38
Racewicz, Ryszarda, 169
Raczyński *family*, 130, 151
Radunia, 73, 90
Radziekowski, Michał, *Archbishop of Gniezno*, 143-4, 178
Radziwiłł *family*, 35, 135, 138, 165, 172, 177-8
Rajecka, Anna, 164-5
Rakowski, A., vi
Rakowski, Mieczysław, 146
Ranisch, Bartholomäus, 84
Raptis, Paulos, 169
Rau, Wilhelm, 148
Rębiechowo, 74
Regional Museum, Łowicz, 177
Rejtan, Tadeusz, 118
religion, 134
Rembrandt Harmenszoon van Rijn, 36, 151, 163
Renaissance art and architecture, 8, 13-15, 18, 20, 24, 26, 33, 40, 44-6, 54, 94, 98, 121, 126, 138, 148
Rennen, Pieter van der, 19
restaurants, 58, 85, 125-6, 129, 145, 160, 184-5
Ribera, Jusepe de, 178
Rigaud, Hyacinthe, 162
Rococo art and architecture, 35, 81, 85, 98, 103, 133, 136, 139, 177
Romanesque art and architecture, 4-5, 12-13, 21, 24, 26, 29, 40, 54
Romania and the Romanians, 63, 68
Rorbach, Christina, 101, 169
Roslin, Alexander, 165
Rossellino, Antonio, 175

THE OLEANDER PRESS

COASTAL FEATURES OF
ENGLAND AND WALES
J.A. Steers

A DICTIONARY OF COMMON FALLACIES
Philip Ward

THE GERMAN LEFT SINCE 1945
W.D. Graf

INDONESIA: A BIBLIOGRAPHY OF
BIBLIOGRAPHIES
J.N.B. Tairas

JAN VAN RYMSDYK: MEDICAL BOOK
ILLUSTRATOR
J.L. Thornton

THE LIFE AND MURDER OF
HENRY MORSHEAD
Ian Morshead

MEDICAL BOOK ILLUSTRATION:
A SHORT HISTORY
J.L. Thornton & C. Reeves

THE SMALL PUBLISHER
Audrey & Philip Ward

OLEANDER LANGUAGE AND LITERATURE

THE ART & POETRY OF C.-F. RAMUZ
David Bevan

**BIOGRAPHICAL MEMOIRS OF
EXTRAORDINARY PAINTERS**
William Beckford

CELTIC: A COMPARATIVE STUDY
D.B. Gregor

FRENCH KEY WORDS
Xavier-Yves Escande

FRIULAN: LANGUAGE & LITERATURE
D.B. Gregor

**GREGUERÍAS: Wit and Wisdom of
R. Gómez de la Serna***

INDONESIAN TRADITIONAL POETRY
Philip Ward

A LIFETIME'S READING
Philip Ward

MARVELL'S ALLEGORICAL POETRY
Bruce King

ROMAGNOL: LANGUAGE & LITERATURE
D.B. Gregor

ROMONTSCH: LANGUAGE & LITERATURE
D.B. Gregor

OLEANDER GAMES AND PASTIMES

**CHRISTMAS GAMES FOR ADULTS
AND CHILDREN**
Crispin DeFoyer

DARTS: 50 WAYS TO PLAY THE GAME
Jabez Gotobed

DICE GAMES NEW AND OLD
W.E. Tredd

**ENLIGHTENMENT THROUGH THE ART
OF BASKETBALL**
Hirohide Ogawa

ENNEAGRAMS: NINE-LETTER WORD GAME
Ian D. Graves

PUB GAMES OF ENGLAND
Timothy Finn

**SUMMER GAMES FOR ADULTS
AND CHILDREN**
Hereward Zigo

OLEANDER MODERN POETS

LIBYA PAST AND PRESENT

APULEIUS ON TRIAL AT SABRATHA
Philip Ward

THE LIBYAN CIVIL CODE
I.M. Arif & M.O. Ansell

LIBYAN MAMMALS
Ernst Hufnagl

THE LIBYAN REVOLUTION
I.M. Arif & M.O. Ansell

MOTORING TO NALUT
Philip Ward

SABRATHA
Philip Ward

TRIPOLI
Philip Ward

ARABIA PAST AND PRESENT

OLEANDER TRAVEL BOOKS